LOCAL HISTORY
IN ATLANTIC CANADA

LOCAL HISTORY
IN ATLANTIC CANADA

William B. Hamilton

Macmillan of Canada

ISBN 0-7705-1181-3

The author and publishers gratefully
acknowledge the assistance of the Canada Council
in the publication of this book.

Cover: *Bluenose II*, Nova Scotia
Communications & Information
Centre Photo

Printed in Canada

This book is for Brian.

Preface

Local History in Atlantic Canada is designed to provide the focal point for a secondary school course in local history. It follows the basic view that all too often history has been presented the wrong way round. Traditionally, many high school courses have begun with the civilization of the stone age, the patterns of life in the Nile and Euphrates river valleys, and the glories of ancient Greece and Rome. Rather than concentrating on the remote past, a better beginning may be made in one's own community by studying topics closer to personal experience. Then the student will be ready to move out, concentrically, to a study of the region, the nation, and the world. Not only will this approach promote a better understanding of the local heritage, it will also equip students to tackle in a creative manner the problems presented by advanced courses in the subject. Admittedly, some of the topics covered in *Local History in Atlantic Canada* have already been met in the elementary grades; however, at that time it was not possible to study these in depth and detail. In learning at the secondary school level how his community has changed in the more recent past, the student will absorb something of the historian's craft and the way in which evidence is sifted. Equally important, student and teacher will share in the total experience and the sheer pleasure of historical discovery. By original inquiry, by gathering and analysing their own material, it is hoped that the history of the region will become more relevant and meaningful. *Local History in Atlantic Canada* permits the student to go beyond factual history and to become involved with the sources upon which its writing was based.

The organization of a course in local history consists of three elements. The first concerns the total history of the region. Through using the text and related materials the class will be exposed to that which has shaped the character of the people and the institutions of their community, province, and region. It is suggested that the students read each chapter using all available references and then attempt those suggestions for further research that seem most profitable and applicable. Throughout this first part of the course many of the approaches, sources, and techniques used in history will have been encountered, so that the next step, which requires an assessment of the various materials used in the reconstruction of the past, is clear. Students will have reached the position where they can start to "write history" on their own. Such can be done in differing ways, many of which will have been suggested by earlier research. This, then, leads logically to the final stage—the individual research project. It is the responsibility of the student, in consultation with his teacher, to select areas for intensive investigation. Utilizing techniques already learned, students are equipped to prepare a report, an audio-visual production, or whatever other type of presentation is best suited to the portraying of their findings.

This book can trace its origin to a decade of teaching history in the secondary schools of Nova Scotia. Motivation for local history was always keen, resources were everywhere, yet teaching aids and materials—then as now—were minimal. *Local History in Atlantic Canada* is one response to an expressed need.

To a greater or lesser extent every book is a product of many minds, and this one is no exception. I have relied heavily upon the many general and specialized studies relating to Atlantic Canada, the advice and counsel of fellow historians, archivists, and other specialists in the field, as well as the recommendations and comments of both former associates and present colleagues. To name all who contributed by way of constructive criticism and encouragement is impossible; nevertheless, a number of people merit particular notice: R. M. Anderson, Audrey Barss, Clifford Dunphy, Donald Gilliss, Anna Hamilton, Kenneth Homer, Spencer Inch, R. C. Langman, Helen Marsten, David Murdoch, Peter Neary, E. R. Procunier, J. D. Purdy, Evelyn Richardson, Malcolm Squires, and Manford Wasson.

I would also like to record a note of gratitude to my students in Education 418 at Memorial University. Their enthusiasm for the concept behind the book was of tangible assistance. Appreciation is also extended to Miss Phyllis Blakeley, Assistant Archivist, Public Archives of Nova Scotia, and Miss Agnes O'Dea of the Centre for Newfoundland Studies at Memorial University. Their extensive knowledge of local history helped solve many bibliographic and historical problems. For co-operation and assistance in all phases of the project, acknowledgment is given Mrs. W. E. Nicholls and Mrs. H. Vlasman, typists. To Mrs. Vlasman, who gave careful attention to preparation of the final manuscript, to Mrs. Vivian Holland and Mrs. Eleanor Sinclair for skilful editorial assistance, and to my wife Marian, for invaluable help along the way, my sincere thanks.
March 31, 1974

Contents

Preface / vii

How To Use the Book / xi

Section I   Introduction to Local History

1. Working Backwards into History / 1
2. Settlement and Political Development / 5

Section II   Sources of Local History

3. Place Names / 22
4. Legacy of the Sea / 35
5. Legacy of the Land and the People / 54
6. The Amerindian Heritage / 74
7. Archaeological Evidence / 93
8. Documentary Evidence and Literature / 116
9. Folk Songs and Folklore / 139
10. Art and Architecture / 157
11. Economic Development / 182
12. Biographical Studies / 203

Section III   Applications of Local History

13. Researching History Where It Is / 222

A Bibliographic Note / 232

Footnotes / 233

How To Use the Book

In order to utilize this book to the fullest extent it is important to know something of the author's intent. This may be made clear by stressing what *Local History in Atlantic Canada* is not.

It is not a traditional history textbook. Full responsibility is placed on teacher and student to select, to adapt, and to organize the material as may best suit their purpose. Portions not applicable to one part of the region may well be omitted, while others with local relevance will require greater stress. Everyone who uses this book is encouraged to develop an individual syllabus.

It is not a history of Atlantic Canada, although every attempt was made to give a broad overview of topics as they relate to the four provinces. From Cape Chidley to Grand Manan there are vast differences and these require notice. There are also common themes important in gaining a broader understanding of the region. To cover all such topics was impossible and many interesting subjects had to be omitted.

It is not arranged in the usual chronological fashion. The approach is deliberately thematic in keeping with the wide coverage and the necessity for selection and adaptation. Whenever general principles are presented, specific examples will follow. These are suggestive and are intended to encourage the reader to take a closer look at his own community.

It is not dependent on the printed word, though considerable emphasis on documentary material is necessary. The student is urged to range widely beyond the classroom walls, to interview people whose memory may reveal much of a bygone day, to search his home community for reminders of the past, and to develop an interest in material as diverse as folk songs, place names, Amerindian lore, and postage stamps.

Using this book is not easy and the author does not pretend to have found a magic formula that will apply in every instance. At the very least *Local History in Atlantic Canada* strives to utilize individual interests as a springboard to an understanding of the local environment. To do so with any degree of effectiveness one must use subject matter frequently considered as being outside history. This interdisciplinary approach will in turn develop techniques of inquiry not necessarily historical—although better calculated to answer some of the questions raised. An open and unstructured method provides maximum opportunity to enjoy learning and to learn how to learn.

LOCAL HISTORY
IN ATLANTIC CANADA

Section 1
INTRODUCTION TO LOCAL HISTORY

1. Working Backwards into History

Very often the mere mention of the word "history" creates the picture of a chronological or systematic age by age study from caveman to spaceman. If the field to be surveyed is Canadian the approach is often the same. The early explorers, Cartier, Champlain, and others, are followed in quick succession by the fur traders, the rise and fall of New France, the American Revolution, and the coming of the Loyalists, until finally the events of the recent past are reached. There is logic in this method of tackling the sweep of history; however, it does not follow that it is the only approach. Instead of starting with the very remote past, why not use more recent times as a vantage point? As an alternative to the history of distant lands, why not begin with what is familiar—one's own community? Why not work backward into history? While local studies can never replace national or world history, they will satisfy the emotional urge in all of us to know more about our origin. Along the way, history can be transformed from something that is remote and often uninteresting to that which is relevant and meaningful.

Perhaps the greatest attraction of local history is simply that it took place in one's own community or in the region of which one's community forms a part. This means that much of the source material is readily available and can be studied at first hand. In every locality, in every corner of Atlantic Canada, there are surviving links with the past—buildings, implements, clothing, memorials, cemeteries, the very place names themselves—all may help you in your study. Do not be deterred by the fact that some sources mentioned in this book are unavailable locally—observe, collect, and classify *all* available data and you may be

1

surprised at the amount of history uncovered. Interviews with older residents, a search of attics and storerooms, an examination of school registers and parish records are but a few suggestions; others will occur to you as you read on. Moreover, by working backward from the known to the unknown, from the familiar to the unfamiliar, you will develop a sense of historical time. When was your school built? Were there ever other school buildings on the same site? When, where, and by whom was the first school erected in your community? By searching for answers to questions such as these, past events will become recognizable milestones. Stephen Leacock once wrote,

> I find myself drawn more and more to the charm and meaning of the history of little places. Who lived here first? Who first set the stones that lie beneath the simple frame of that house? How did life feel for these first comers? Such queries and such reflections may arise in any last corner of our countryside and may fill the reflecting mind with wonder and interest.[1]

By far the most intriguing part of this course will be your own research. Exploring (on foot wherever possible) the geographical features that have moulded community life, map-reading and studying aerial photographs, examining old churches and lighthouses, barns and bridges, searching for letters and diaries, interpreting yellowed newspapers and faded photographs—all this and more can be great fun! It is also hard work, but the work is more than compensated by the satisfaction gained from tracking down the solution to some perplexing riddle. Once you have gained expertise in handling research projects at the local level, you will want to proceed farther afield to historic sites, libraries, and archives. These extended investigations will enable you to see how the history of your own community relates to that of the township, county, province, or region.

Still another claim may be made for local history. When approached in an organized and logical manner it provides one of the essential keys to an understanding of our national history. In recent years a new phrase, "regional disparity", has been coined to describe the economic ills of Atlantic Canada. What does it mean? By analysing economic development at the community level, by studying the rise and fall of certain industries, by making comparative studies with other areas, not only will you answer this question but you will touch upon important federal-provincial problems. Other examples abound. Who were the first settlers in your part of Atlantic Canada? Although settlement patterns are of local significance, they also form an important part of the provincial, regional, and national mosaic. Religion and politics are important considerations in the history of any town, village, or hamlet; however, they are but the initial steps leading to an understanding of national issues.

There is opportunity in area studies to utilize all kinds of historical techniques. To begin, you should never blindly accept an historical judgment without, as far as possible, checking all relevant facts. Deductions should never be drawn without supporting evidence. Thus, through personal research you will participate directly in the "finding-out process". This method has been aptly described as "Miss Marples history".[2] Readers of Agatha Christie's mysteries will recall that one of her most famous characters, Miss Marples, is able to uncover clues in the most unlikely places or solve seemingly unsolvable murders by paying attention to the smallest of details. So in history, and a comparison with the approach of the private investigator is appropriate. Read Robin W. Winks: *The Historian as Detective* (New York: Harper Colophon Books, 1970), for an interesting analysis of this point.

It is recognized that many students who read this page are not aspiring historians. Some are probably asking the question, "What is there in local history for me?" The answer may well come in some of the fascinating byways of the subject. We are now living in what is commonly referred to as the post-industrial society. Automation guarantees that the day is not far distant when abundant leisure will be the birthright of all. How will this time be spent? Perhaps in activities such as scuba diving and marine exploration, stamp and coin collecting, restoring antiques, investigating folklore, or researching costume and design—to give but a random sample of hobbies and interests that benefit from a knowledge of local history. The popularity of such places as the Kings Landing (N.B.) and Sherbrooke (N.S.) Historical Settlements or the vast sums invested in the restoration of Louisbourg prove that there is a reawakening of interest in things historical. The decision of the Prince Edward Island Centennial Commission to mark the anniversary of that province's entry into Confederation by the establishment of historic sites at Green Park, Orwell Corner, and Basin Head or the campaign of the Newfoundland Historical Trust to restore Quidi Vidi Village further underline the point.

Beyond the limits of general interest in history there is yet another consideration. Alvin Toffler in *Future Shock* has warned us: "No society racing through the turbulence of the next several decades will be able to do without specialized centers in which the rate of change is artificially depressed. To phrase it differently, we shall need enclaves of the past— whole communities in which turnover, novelty and choice are deliberately limited."[3] There *is* a future for those interested in history—a future conditioned by past events.

The poet and author, Alden Nowlan, has captured for us the essence and appeal of local history:

As a child I lived with my grandmother, an old peasant woman who played the autoharp and believed in witches. She used to tell me about the days when farmers in the Annapolis Valley produced everything that they used except tea, sugar, rum and tobacco. This fascinated me when I first heard about it as a child of eight; it fascinates me even more now that I'm a grown man. It's the kind of fascination that has kept *Robinson Crusoe* alive for 250 years: man's repressed desire to be utterly self-sufficient and, therefore, wholly free. My grandmother also told me about the days of the sailing ships, when the highest honour that could be attained by a Maritimer was to be a master of a three-masted schooner. From my grandmother I learned not only that such men lived, but that in some enigmatic yet indisputable way they were connected to me.[4]

Through your study and research of the topics presented in this book you will work backward in time to those things that "in some . . . indisputable way" are connected to you. Along the way you will learn of the diverse history of Atlantic Canada. For " . . . through it all the inheritance remains. It has always been of vast importance on the ground where it first flourished. What has not been fully realized, even by those who possess it, is the part [local history] plays in the continuing existence of Canada as a whole."[5]

2. Settlement and Political Development

Before turning to a discussion of the major sources which can be utilized in local history, the political development of the region will be traced in outline. While this section of the book is intended as a reference, it will be useful to read as background material before embarking on local studies. You will, in all probability, want to refer to it from time to time as you relate events in your own community to the total history of Atlantic Canada.

France was the first European power to assert control over much of what is today Atlantic Canada. The seventeenth century saw a gradual expansion of French settlement and influence, until modern Nova Scotia, Prince Edward Island, and New Brunswick along with portions of the state of Maine and the Gaspé peninsula were claimed as part of their colony of Acadia. The exact boundaries were never clearly defined and this later became a key factor in the struggle for control of the region. Centuries earlier the Norsemen had penetrated as far south as Newfoundland; however, their contact was temporary and of no lasting political significance. Gradually most of the original inhabitants, belonging to various branches of the Algonquin family of Amerindians, were pushed aside, as in the case of the Micmacs and Malecites; the Beothucks were simply exterminated.* More important, politically, was the presence of English, Spanish, Portuguese, and Basque fishing fleets. Lured by the

*The Micmacs inhabited Nova Scotia, Prince Edward Island, and eastern New Brunswick; the Malecites, western New Brunswick; the Naskapi, the interior of Labrador; the Beothucks, the island of Newfoundland. The Innuit or Eskimos inhabited the coast of Labrador. See Chapter 6.

potential of the Grand Banks fishery these nations, and particularly England, were by the sixteenth century making annual visits to the area. Study a modern atlas and note the abundance of place names of west European origin along the coast. Especially is this true of Newfoundland, for if the history of such ports as Placentia or Port-aux-Basques could be traced to their origin, they would undoubtedly rank among the oldest in the New World.

In the long run it became the lot of France and England to settle the ultimate fate of Atlantic Canada. Wars and rumours of wars dominated the region during the colonial period; however, it should not be forgotten that these were often extensions of larger European struggles for power. Thus, Spain and Portugal, although not without some continuing influence, were declining in significance and never became serious contenders in the North Atlantic. From the beginning it was England who challenged the territorial claims of France. While the exact landfall of John Cabot in 1497 is disputed (Newfoundland, Cape Breton, and Prince Edward Island all point with pride to his landing-place!), Sir Humphrey Gilbert in 1583 claimed possession of territory in the vicinity of St. John's for England*—a point not forgotten in later negotiations.

The first successful attempt by the French to found a colony occurred in 1604-5. In 1604 a settlement was established at Dochet's Island, in the Ste. Croix River. Conditions here were unsuitable and the following spring a move was made across the Bay of Fundy to Port Royal. Farther down the Atlantic seaboard, at Jamestown in Virginia, the English staked a claim by founding a settlement in 1607. Three years later, a group of Bristol merchants under the leadership of John Guy landed an expedition at Cuper's (modern Cupid's) Cove on Conception Bay. While this colony failed to prosper, it did demonstrate that Newfoundland was capable of permanent settlement. The battle lines between England and France were gradually being drawn and competition between the two was to dominate the history of Atlantic Canada for the next century. While for much of this period Acadia remained in the hands of the French, it was subject to frequent capture by the English, only to be restored by subsequent recapture or treaty negotiations. It is claimed that Port Royal has changed hands more frequently than any other portion of the North American continent. Check Volume I of the *Dictionary of Canadian Biography* for information on the men who laid siege to Port Royl. Names such as Samuel Argall, Sir David Kirke, Col. Robert Sedgwick, and Sir William Phips figure prominently, and a look at their careers will reveal something

*Space will not permit detailing the territorial claims and counterclaims of England and France or the voyages of the numerous explorers. The interested reader will find these outlined in any standard history textbook or encyclopedia.

of the international scene of the day. Can you determine the motivation for these attacks? Was it European or North American?

The name Nova Scotia, or New Scotland, dates from 1621 when a Scottish nobleman, Sir William Alexander, was granted all lands "between New England and Newfoundland" for the purpose of founding a colony. A coat of arms and a flag were officially granted and in 1625 the Knight Baronets of Nova Scotia were created. It was essentially a money-raising scheme. The prospective baronets on paying for their title were spared the inconvenience of crossing the Atlantic to claim their lands: a portion of the Edinburgh Castle esplanade was officially designated as "Nova Scotia". Standing on this plot of ground, marked today by a nearby plaque, the baronets took their oaths. Two attempts at colonization were made by Alexander—at Charlesfort near Port Royal and Rosemar at Baleine Cove in Cape Breton. The Scottish venture failed, succeeding only in creating the place name "Nova Scotia", which was to be revived by Britain in 1713.

In reality there were two Acadias—one the area settled and developed by the Acadians, the other a much larger portion claimed as French territory. Beginning with the area around Port Royal, the Acadians had by the end of the seventeenth century spread up the Annapolis River and through to the Cornwallis valley where they founded one of their largest and best known settlements at Grand Pré. Gradually, their villages ringed the Cobequid Bay from Windsor (Pisiquid) to Truro (Cobequid), and stretched on to the Tantramar Marshes and down the north shore of Nova Scotia to locations such as Wallace (Remsheg) and Tatamagouche. The explanation behind this settlement pattern was simply that the people favoured locations where, through the building of dykes, they might farm the fertile marshlands. The homeland of many Acadians was the west coast of France where the estuaries, marshes, and tidal waters were similar to those of Acadia.

Then, in 1710, the final blow came. Port Royal surrendered for the last time and France gave up her claim to Acadia by the Treaty of Utrecht signed in 1713. In the words of the treaty, "All Nova Scotia or Acadia with its ancient boundaries as also the city of Port Royal, and all other things in these parts which depend on the said lands and islands . . . are yielded and made over to the Queen of Great Britain and to her crown forever." It was clear that the phrase "ancient boundaries" would be given widely differing interpretations. The British reverted to Sir William Alexander's claim of the land "between New England and Newfoundland"; the French not surprisingly were unwilling to accept such a broad definition. For them, the surrender had been merely the southerly portion of the peninsula of Nova Scotia and they were able to make good their

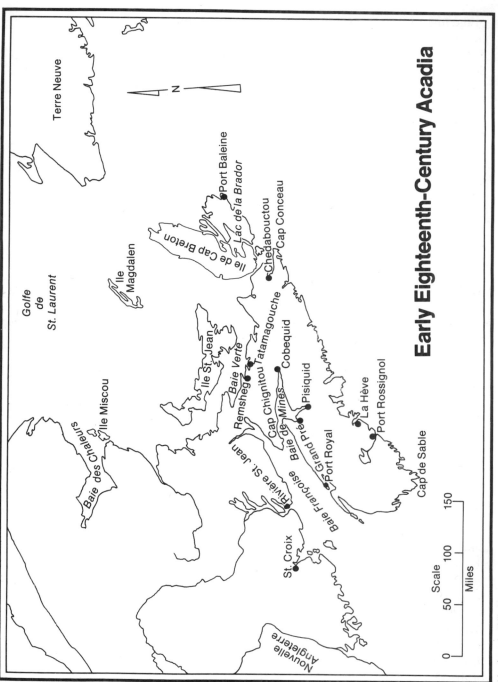

Early Eighteenth-Century Acadia

Map drawn by Philip Litrenta

claim to Cape Breton (hereafter known as Ile Royale) and Ile St. Jean (modern Prince Edward Island). Shortly thereafter, the French began the construction of Louisbourg on Ile Royale, from which base they hoped one day to recapture that which was lost in 1713.

For the next period of time little change took place beyond the substitution of flags. A weak British garrison at Port Royal (now Annapolis Royal) was the only outward sign of the new order. While they had little difficulty with the British troops, the position of the Acadians, who by 1750 numbered about 10,000, was becoming increasingly uncertain. Their only desire was to be left in peace and neutrality. They resisted French enticements to vacate their lands and move to Ile Royale, Ile St. Jean, or the neighbourhood of Fort Beauséjour (erected in 1750 to guard the Isthmus of Chignecto). A few heeded this call but the vast majority remained behind to eventually become another set of statistics in the long line of displaced people.

Meanwhile, the supposedly impregnable fortress of Louisbourg was captured in 1745 by a force of New Englanders, only to be returned by the Treaty of Aix-la-Chapelle in 1748. The middle of the eighteenth century witnessed a reawakening of interest in the area by Britain. In 1749 Halifax was founded as a counterbalance to Louisbourg and the capital moved there from Annapolis. Immediately on the heels of this action some 1,400 German- and French-speaking "Foreign Protestants" were encouraged to settle in Nova Scotia, and located eventually in and around Lunenburg. As a prelude to the Seven Years War (1756-63), the majority of the Acadians were, according to Governor Lawrence, expelled "in such manner as may best answer our design in preventing their reunion".[1] Probably more words have been written about this tragic event than about any other in the history of Atlantic Canada. In spite of research, reflection, and review it remains one of the most controversial events in history. It is a topic that defies summation and you are encouraged to read some of the books listed on page 20. Here is how one writer apportioned the blame:

> It was a Massachusetts government that devised the scheme. It was New England soldiers and officers who carried out the expulsion. It was New England vessels, chartered from New England merchants, officered and manned by New England captains and crews that carried the Acadians to exile. It was New England Planters who moved to Nova Scotia and occupied the Acadian lands. Why the excessive denouncing of British officials in London who did not know the expulsion had happened, who had practically forbidden such a proceeding? The extremists who always picture burly redcoats beating old women into

boats at the water's edge should examine the records. The truth is . . .
except at Annapolis . . . all were bluecoated New Englanders.[2]

Is his analysis fair? Who do you think was responsible?

Whatever opinions may be entertained on the subject, it is clear that
any intent of "preventing their reunion" was doomed to failure. Some
escaped deportation, while others lived to return in the 1760s and take
up land in eastern New Brunswick, southwestern Nova Scotia, and Cape
Breton. In the meantime, lands vacated by Acadians were occupied by
New Englanders. Two major groups were involved in this migration.
Planters or farmers were attracted by Acadian dyke-lands at Annapolis,
Minas, Cobequid, and Chignecto.* Another group, principally fishermen,
settled in the coves and harbours of the south shore of Nova Scotia,
mainly in Yarmouth, Barrington, Liverpool, and Chester. Later to be
called "His Majesty's Yankees", these settlers were to play an unenviable
role in the American Revolution.

The Treaty of Paris in 1763 restored a degree of stability to Atlantic
Canada. Ile Royale and Ile St. Jean became part of Nova Scotia, although
six years afterward the latter was designated a separate colony.† Between
1763 and 1783 three additional strains were added to the population.
Around 1770 there was a migration of Ulster Scots to the head of
Cobequid Bay and in 1772 a group of Yorkshiremen settled in the
Chignecto area. About the same time (September 15, 1773) the vanguard
of the Scottish emigration arrived at Pictou on board the ship *Hector*. By
the outbreak of the American Revolution, although New Englanders
predominated there was considerable variety in the racial background of
Nova Scotia. T. C. Haliburton's Sam Slick put it this way: "Now, if you
want to know all about us and the Bluenoses—a pretty considerable share
of Yankee blood in them too, I tell you; the old stock comes from New
England and the breed is tolerable pure yet . . . all except to the easterd
where there is a cross of the Scotch."[3]

Meanwhile Newfoundland was gradually being transformed from "an
island moored for the convenience of the fishery" to the status of a colony.
For years, historians have accounted for the slower pace of development
in Newfoundland (as compared with other British North American colonies) by suggesting that it was to the mutual advantage of the English
government and certain fishing interests to discourage settlement on the
island. In the early period the Newfoundland fishery was dominated by

---

*A small number settled in the Maugerville area of the Saint John River valley.

†Between 1769-98 the colony was known as St. John's Island. The name Prince Edward
Island (in honour of Prince Edward, Duke of Kent) was adopted February 1799.

the "West Country Adventurers", located in the English seaport towns of Dorset and Devon, Somerset and Cornwall. The traditional explanation for lack of progress has been that direct control of the fishery was necessary to help England maintain a favourable balance of trade. Aside from a profitable business in dried cod, the same industry would also provide a reservoir of naval manpower in time of war. To preserve these objectives, the discouragement, or better still the prohibition, of settlement was essential, for a resident population might well gain dominance over the lucrative fisheries. This theory was summarized by one writer as " . . . [changing] the course of nature, to keep the island of Newfoundland a barren waste, to exterminate the inhabitants, to annihilate property and to make sailors by preventing population."[4]

On the surface, this is a reasonable explanation of events and one that has been repeated many times. However, as so often happens in history, the obvious answer does not reveal the whole story, nor does it follow that we should accept an historical judgment solely because it has been affirmed many times. Certainly, in this case, present-day historians are seriously questioning "a once basic theory in the ancient historical mythology of Newfoundland".[5] In the past, considerable emphasis was placed on a number of anti-settlement acts passed by Parliament and which, it would appear, officially recognized West Country interests. Thus we find the Western Charter of 1634 decreeing that " . . . no squatter might cut down any wood or plant [settle] within six miles of the sea shore, or take up fishing stages [for drying or curing fish] before the arrival of fishermen from England."

Legislation was one thing; enforcement was another. Despite parliamentary acts settlement did take place and by 1653 it is estimated that there were some forty settlements around the coast. While the population was not large, the presence of these fishing stations seriously questioned the effectiveness of the legislation. Furthermore, there is little concrete evidence to support the proposition that West Country interests opposed settlement—" . . . although [they] would occasionally agree with government, that *too much* settlement was undesirable. Even then they would hastily point out that conditions in the fishery were such that the colony would never become of any great size. After 1713 no West Country petitions ever complained about the existence of settlement in Newfoundland."[6] Reasons for the development of a resident fishery are obvious. The mere fact that they were on location gave them an initial advantage over the migratory fishermen who annually had to cross the stormy North Atlantic. No mean feat at any time, this trek became virtually impossible during the long periods of warfare between France and England. It is the conclusion of one historian that " . . . by the time of the Napoleonic wars the migratory fishery had been severely weakened and this conflict brought it to an end."[7] The rapid expansion of the population tends to reinforce this conclusion. In the ten-year interval from 1805 to 1815 an increase from 21,975 to 40,568 was recorded.

The situation was further complicated by the presence of France. In the 1660s Plaisance (modern Placentia) was fortified to strengthen the French claim to a portion of the Newfoundland coastline and provide shelter for her fishing fleets. The English countered by erecting fortifications to protect the harbour at St. John's—by this time a well-established rendezvous for their fishermen. The wars of 1689-97 and 1702-13 saw a number of raids on rival settlements with the French occupying St. John's for a time in 1708. By the Treaty of Utrecht France ceded Newfoundland to Britain and notwithstanding a later attempt at capture during the Seven Years War, 1756-63, it was to remain in British hands.* This did not, however, mean the end of the French influence, for by the terms of the Treaty of Paris in 1763 France was guaranteed the right to land and cure fish on the coast between Cape St. John and Point Riche on the Gulf of St. Lawrence. Later the privilege was extended to Cape Ray on the southwest tip of Newfoundland. Nor was this all. For generations the fishing fleets of New England had participated in the Newfoundland fishery. One reason for the migration of New England fishermen to Nova Scotia in the 1760s was the opportunity to be some five hundred miles nearer the Banks. Following the Treaty of Paris in 1783 the Americans were given the privilege of landing and drying fish on the coast of Labrador, a right that was reaffirmed in 1818. Taken together, the French and American fishing rights were a serious handicap to development and remained unsettled until the twentieth century. In 1835 Archdeacon Edward Wix, after touring the coast of Newfoundland, wrote: "I observed much sad inconvenience which may be traced to this impolitic indulgence on the part of [the British government] ... it has meant a perpetual collision between the people of rival nations who are thus brought into competition upon the same field of endeavour".[8] The "perpetual collision" between French, American, British, and Newfoundland interests remained until the twentieth century. Check in the *Encyclopedia Canadiana* or other reference works and learn the outcome of the 1904 negotiations with France and the decision of the International Court in 1910 which regulated American fishing rights.

If for no other reason than geography, the outbreak of the American

---

*A French expedition held the coast from Ferryland to Trinity for a period in 1762. Thus it was at "Saint-Jean-de-Terreneuve" that the French flag was lowered for the last time in present-day Canada. See G. O. Rothney: *Newfoundland from International Fishery to Canadian Province* (Canadian Historical Association, Historical Booklet), 18.

Revolution was bound to have a profound effect on Atlantic Canada. Ties between New England and Nova Scotia were close; both formed part of a natural North Atlantic trading unit and over half the population of Nova Scotia was of New England stock. During 1775 an informant wrote Governor Francis Legge concerning the New Englanders of the Annapolis valley: "As nineteen out of twenty are natives of New England, what dependence or reliance could your Excellency have on such troops? To put confidence in such fellows would be acting like the man who cherished a snake in his bosom, till heated with the warmth of his blood it bit him to death."[9] The dilemma faced by "His Majesty's Yankees" has attracted widespread attention among historians and novelists and many theories have been advanced to explain why Nova Scotia did not become the fourteenth colony to rebel. The preoccupation of historical novelists with this theme is discussed in Chapter 8.

It is clear from a careful study of the record that a combination of factors prevailed to keep Nova Scotia apart from the other colonies. In the beginning, many New England-Nova Scotians wanted to remain neutral, or, as the residents of Yarmouth expressed it, "to live in a peaceable state". As yet a scattered and comparatively new population, they were deterred by the British presence in Halifax and more so by British naval superiority. The one serious outbreak, led by Jonathan Eddy (a onetime member of the Nova Scotia assembly) in the Cumberland area, ended in failure. The inability of the revolutionary forces to lend support, coupled with the return to the thirteen colonies of a number who might have assumed roles of leadership, were contributing factors to the non-alignment of "His Majesty's Yankees". Parallel with the revolutionary period Nova Scotia was swept by a religious revival known as the "Great Awakening". Many historians feel that this event had widespread social implications and literally succeeded in turning Yankees into Nova Scotians.[10] Lastly, few ports along the coast were spared raids by American privateers (see page 47), so that any lingering support for the revolutionary cause was swept away.

The American Revolution was destined to affect Atlantic Canada in yet another way. By reason of its close proximity to major ports such as Boston and New York, Nova Scotia was a natural haven for the Loyalists. Between 1776 and 1782 there was a small movement to Nova Scotia; however, in 1783 some 30,000 people flooded the colony, with the largest numbers settling in the Saint John River valley and at Shelburne. Unfortunately for the Loyalist cause, the settlement at Shelburne failed. Approximately 10,000 newcomers could not be maintained in an area lacking suitable natural resources as a basis for support. Some Loyalists were but temporary residents of Atlantic Canada: a number returned to the United States, others relocated in Upper Canada, while a few of the very wealthy retired to England.

The arrival of the Loyalists led to significant political changes. In 1784 that part of Nova Scotia beyond the Isthmus of Chignecto was designated as a separate colony—New Brunswick. So too was Cape Breton Island, but this latter arrangement was destined not to last and in 1820 Cape Breton was re-annexed to Nova Scotia. In the main, Loyalist settlements were concentrated in New Brunswick, Nova Scotia, and Cape Breton; the numbers settling in Prince Edward Island and Newfoundland were considerably smaller.

The Loyalists also influenced the development of Atlantic Canada in more intangible ways. For the new colony of New Brunswick they provided the nucleus of a ruling class and quickly assumed positions of leadership in church and state. Esther Clark Wright, the leading historian of the New Brunswick Loyalists, has summarized the Loyalist impact thus:

> ... loyalty to the British crown meant respect for law and order and for orderly procedure. It meant unwillingness to resort to violence, and willingness to wait for years rather than to jeopardize ultimate victory by depending on [revolutionary] methods. It has been part of the invisible barrier which separates all of Canada, and particularly New Brunswick from the neighbour to the south. . . . As the Loyalist developed into New Brunswicker this was the most valuable contribution he made to the new province and the nation of which it ultimately became a part.[11]

The early decades of the nineteenth century witnessed a dramatic rise in the population of all regions of Atlantic Canada. In Nova Scotia the population increased from approximately 40,000 in 1800 to 80,000 in 1817, to 120,000 in 1827, and to 200,000 in 1838, while that of Newfoundland jumped from 40,568 in 1815 to 96,296 in 1845. This expansion can be largely accounted for by emigration from the British Isles. Economic pressures, overpopulation, and the Highland Clearances forced thousands of Scottish settlers to come to Nova Scotia, ensuring for all time that the colony would be New Scotland in character as well as in name. Soldiers freed from service following the Napoleonic Wars constituted another important element in the population. In Newfoundland, prosperity from increased opportunity associated with the inshore fishery was attracting many settlers. However, comparative isolation, a harsher climate, and scarcity of land for farming meant that Newfoundland did not continue to attract large numbers.

In 1825 a compromise settlement was attempted in the long-standing difficulties over the Labrador boundary. For some time Labrador had been considered a dependency of Newfoundland; however, for a period of thirty-five years (1774-1809) it was annexed to Quebec—only to be returned in 1809. Attention was concentrated this time on the coastline, with the area north of the Strait of Belle Isle to be administered by Newfoundland and the north shore of the Gulf of St. Lawrence by Quebec. The vast interior remained a question mark until a 1927 decision of the British privy council confirmed the present boundary.

The development of Prince Edward Island was hampered for years by the "land question". As early as 1767 the colony had been divided into lots which were granted to absentee landlords in England. These proprietors were expected to attract settlers and improve their land, but few regarded this regulation seriously. Consequently, there were frequent demands for land reform, along with occasional riots and a general feeling of ill will between tenants and agents of the absentee landlords. On one occasion in 1819, Edward Abell, agent for Lord Townshend's estate near Rollo Bay in King's County, was attacked by a tenant and died as a result of wounds inflicted during the quarrel. The man responsible, Patrick Pearce, was never arrested for murder although a substantial reward was offered for his capture. Despite efforts on the part of the Island government to settle the land question, it remained a barrier to progress until 1875. Then, by the terms of a Land Purchase Act, the absentee proprietors were dispossessed of their land by compulsory arbitration. The properties in question were transferred to the provincial government which later resold them to the tenants.

The gradual infusion of new elements in the population meant a quickening of interest in political matters. Nova Scotia was granted representative government in 1758, with the legislature meeting for the first time on October 2 of that year. The typical pattern of colonial administration is outlined in the diagram on page 16.

For many years the struggle between the elected lower house and the appointed councils (often the same personnel comprised both executive and legislative councils) was an unequal one. The councils were close to the governor; they included men of privilege and no little ability and were particularly skilled in adapting legislation to their own advantage. Perhaps the best way to gain insight and understanding of this important period is to approach it through the careers of the men who led the movement for responsible government: Philip Little and Robert Parsons in Newfoundland, George Coles in Prince Edward Island, Joseph Howe in Nova Scotia, and Lemuel Allan Wilmot and Charles Fisher in New Brunswick. The books listed on page 21 will be helpful in tracing the careers of these men and their associates.

The Evolution of Responsible Government

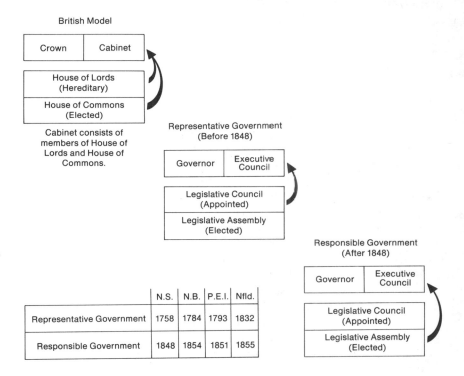

British Model

Crown	Cabinet

House of Lords (Hereditary)
House of Commons (Elected)

Cabinet consists of members of House of Lords and House of Commons.

Representative Government (Before 1848)

Governor	Executive Council

Legislative Council (Appointed)
Legislative Assembly (Elected)

Responsible Government (After 1848)

Governor	Executive Council

Legislative Council (Appointed)
Legislative Assembly (Elected)

	N.S.	N.B.	P.E.I.	Nfld.
Representative Government	1758	1784	1793	1832
Responsible Government	1848	1854	1851	1855

In Atlantic Canada, along with the achievement of responsible government the movement toward confederation must be regarded as the major political achievement of the nineteenth century. The idea of a local union on the Atlantic seaboard or of a larger union to include other British North American colonies was not new. A glance at a map was sufficient to convince many of the particular need for establishing one strong colony facing the Atlantic. In the end, it was two separate happenings that propelled events to a climax in 1867. During the early 1860s some form of union, especially of Nova Scotia, Prince Edward Island, and New Brunswick, was projected both locally and by the British government. The outcome was that a meeting to discuss Maritime federation was called for September 1, 1864, in Charlottetown. Coincident with these developments in the Atlantic colonies, the government of the United Province of the Canadas was at a standstill. Canada West (the former Upper Canada) felt under-represented in the Legislative Assembly, while Canada East (Lower Canada) was suspicious of representation by population. In 1864 the so-called "Great Coalition" was formed and pledged to seek, through a union with the other colonies, a way out of the political deadlock that gripped the government of the United Province. Accordingly, delegates from the Canadas came to Charlottetown to invite representatives from the Maritimes to meet in Quebec the following month to discuss a larger union. Thus it was to the surprise of many people that the Charlottetown Conference of 1864 produced in the end a federal union and Confederation. It has been stated that "the substitution of confederation for Maritime union was a brilliant stroke engineered by Canadians from the province of Canada who would not have dreamt of going to such a conference had it not been for their own political [needs]."[12]

Newfoundland, unrepresented at the first conference, sent delegates to the sessions that opened at Quebec on October 10, 1864. For two weeks the delegates hammered out seventy-two resolutions that eventually became the basis of Confederation. However, it must have been obvious to even the most dedicated supporter of a federal union that all would not be smooth sailing. Newfoundland rejected Confederation and although "tempted" and "courted" on several later occasions, most notably in 1869 and 1895, remained outside until 1949. In similar vein, Prince Edward Island refused to sanction the idea; however, financial difficulties incurred through railway expansion were largely responsible for a change of heart in 1873. It was in Nova Scotia and New Brunswick that the major obstacles to union were encountered and overcome. In 1865 the pro-confederation Tilley government of New Brunswick was defeated in an election wherein federal union was a dominant issue. Through some skilful political manoeuvring a pro-confederation government was returned to office in 1866 and New Brunswick reluctantly entered the new political arrangement. In Nova Scotia the anti-confederates found an articulate leader in the person of Joseph Howe. Launched first in a series of articles by Howe in the *Morning Chronicle* during the winter of 1865, the movement reached a peak in the first federal election of 1867, when eighteen anti-confederates and one supporter of confederation were elected. In retrospect, that solitary supporter, Charles Tupper, spelled the difference between victory and defeat for confederation. Arch rival of Howe, premier of the province prior to 1867, and staunch supporter of union, Tupper displayed coolness and political finesse in handling the tense situation during the years 1864-7. Later he was to play a prominent part in convincing Howe to enter the federal cabinet. With the change in attitude on the part of Howe, the anti-confederation movement subsided, although it did not disappear.

While much has been made of the opposition to confederation, one fact should not be lost. Forty per cent of Nova Scotians supported pro-

Modern Boundaries

Legend
⊕ Capital cities
● Cities, towns, villages
— —   International Boundary
----- Provincial Boundary

0   125   350
miles

Ungava Bay

Cape Chidley

Hebron

Nain

Hopedale

LABRADOR

Scheffdale

Rigolet

Cartwright

Churchill Falls

Goose Bay

Labrador City

Battle Harbour

Belle Isle

Str. of Belle Isle

St. Anthony

QUÉBEC

NEWFOUNDLAND

Sept-Iles

Fogo

Anticosti I.

Corner Brook

Grand Falls

Bonavista

Gaspé

Gulf of St. Lawrence

Cape Ray

Stephenville

Carbonear

Campbellton

Cape Ray

Burgeo

St. John's

QUÉBEC

Chaleur Bay

Magdalen I.

St. Paul I.

Cabot Str.

Port-aux-Basques

Burin

Bathurst

Edmundston

Chatham

P.E.I.

Cape North

Grand Bank

Cape Race

NEW BRUNSWICK

Summerside

Charlottetown

Woodstock

Moncton

Pictou

Sydney

Fredericton

Cape Breton I.

Atlantic Ocean

Saint John

Amherst

Truro

Bay of Fundy

Kentville

Canso

Grand Manan I.

Digby

NOVA SCOTIA

Halifax

Lunenburg

Liverpool

Yarmouth

Sable I.

Map drawn by Philip Litrenta

confederation candidates and the pattern of support and non-support was by no means universal across the province. Can you account for this divergence in voting patterns from county to county? Two books that will assist you in this research are Donald G. Creighton: *The Road to Confederation* (Toronto: Macmillan of Canada, 1964) and P. B. Waite: *The Life and Times of Confederation* (Toronto: University of Toronto Press, 1962). An analysis of the election of 1867 may be found in J. M. Beck: *Pendulum of Power* (Scarborough: Prentice-Hall, 1968).

In the years that followed 1867 the region suffered from a changing industrial technology. The financial successes and past glories were swept aside with the decline of the shipbuilding industry. While the Intercolonial Railway, completed in 1876, linked the region with central Canada, federal tariff policy did little to stimulate local economic growth. Dissatisfaction reached a peak in Nova Scotia in 1886 when a resolution recommending secession from Confederation actually passed the legislature. According to the resolution "Nova Scotia, previous to the union had the lowest tariff and was, notwithstanding, in the best financial condition of any of the provinces entering the union . . . now the commercial as well as the financial condition of Nova Scotia is in an unsatisfactory and depressed condition."[13] Despite the strong language no steps were taken to implement secession, even if it were economically feasible. This point will be discussed in more detail in Chapter 11, *Economic Development*.

Movements such as that of 1886 in Nova Scotia did serve as a reminder to successive federal governments that measures would have to be taken to remedy the financial burden of the smaller provinces. This problem assumed greater importance as provinces began to extend social services and educational facilities. Both were expensive fields that had been delegated to them by the British North America Act. A beginning was made in 1927, when, following a recommendation of the Duncan Royal Commission (on Maritime Rights), significant adjustments in freight rates were made. Later, the principle then enunciated was extended by successive federal governments in a continuing battle to offset regional disparity. Atlantic Canada in common with the rest of North America was hard hit by the economic depression of the 1930s. One immediate problem was the collapse of responsible government in Newfoundland, suspension of the constitution, and substitution of direct rule by a commission under the jurisdiction of the British government. This system continued in effect until 1949, when Newfoundland became the tenth province of Canada and the map of Atlantic Canada assumed its present proportions.

FOR READING AND REFERENCE

A. General

BECK, J. MURRAY: *The Government of Nova Scotia*. Toronto: University of Toronto Press, 1964.

BECK, J. MURRAY: *Pendulum of Power—Canada's Federal Elections*. Scarborough: Prentice-Hall, 1968.

COWAN, HELEN I.: *British Emigration to British North America*. Toronto: University of Toronto Press, 1961.

GARNER, JOHN: *The Franchise and Politics in British North America*. Toronto: University of Toronto Press, 1969.

GUNN, GERTRUDE: *The Political History of Newfoundland 1832-64*. Toronto: University of Toronto Press, 1966.

MACKINNON, FRANK: *The Government of Prince Edward Island*. Toronto: University of Toronto Press, 1951.

MACNUTT, W. S.: *The Atlantic Provinces: The Emergence of a Colonial Society*. Toronto: McClelland and Stewart, 1965.

NEARY, PETER: *The Political Economy of Newfoundland 1929-72*. Toronto: Copp Clark, 1973.

NOEL, S. J. R.: *Politics in Newfoundland*. Toronto: University of Toronto Press, 1971.

RAWLYK, G. A. (ed.): *Historical Essays on the Atlantic Provinces*. Toronto: McClelland and Stewart, 1968.

ROBIN, MARTIN: *Canadian Provincial Politics*. Toronto: Prentice-Hall, 1972.

THORBURN, HUGH G.: *Politics in New Brunswick*. Toronto: University of Toronto Press, 1961.

B. The Acadians

ARSENAULT, BONA: *Histoire et généalogie des Acadiens*, 2 vols. Québec: Université Laval, 1965.

BERNARD, ANTOINE: *Histoire de la survivance acadienne 1775-1935*. Montreal: les Clercs de St-Viteur, 1935.

BIRD, WILL R.: *Done at Grand Pré*. Toronto: Ryerson Press, 1955.

BLANCHARD, J. E.: *Acadiens de l'Ile du Prince-Edouard*. Moncton: 1927.

DOUGHTY, ARTHUR: *Canadian Exiles*. Toronto: Chronicles of Canada, 1920.

GRIFFITH, NAOMI: *The Acadian Deportation: Deliberate Perfidy or Cruel Necessity?* Toronto: Copp Clark, 1969.

GRIFFITH, NAOMI: *The Acadians: Creation of a People*. Toronto: McGraw-Hill Ryerson, 1973.

LEBLANC, EMERY: *Les Acadiens*. Montréal: Editions de l'homme, 1963.

MAILLET, ANTONINE: *La Sagouine*. Montréal: Leméac, 1971.

WINZERLING, OSCAR W.: *Acadian Odyssey*. Baton Rouge: University of Louisiana, 1955.

C. The American Revolution

AHLIN, J. H.: *Maine Rubicon: Down East Settlers During the American Revolution*. Calais: Advertiser Press, 1965.

BREBNER, J. B.: *Neutral Yankees of Nova Scotia*. Toronto: McClelland and Stewart, 1970.

BUMSTED, J. M.: *Henry Alline*. Toronto: University of Toronto Press, 1969.

MACKINNON, IAN: *Settlements and Churches in Nova Scotia*. Montreal: Walker Press, 1930.

POOLE, E. D.: *Annals of Barrington and Yarmouth in the Revolutionary War*. Yarmouth: Yarmouth Herald, 1899.

RAWLYK, G. A.: *Revolution Rejected 1775-1776*. Scarborough: Prentice-Hall, 1968. Also: *Nova Scotia's Massachusetts: A Study of Massachusetts-Nova Scotia Relations* (Montreal: McGill-Queen's University Press, 1973).

D. Confederation

BECK, J. MURRAY: *Joseph Howe: Voice of Nova Scotia*. Toronto: McClelland and Stewart, 1964.

BOLGER, F. W. P.: *Prince Edward Island and Confederation*. Charlottetown: St. Dunstan's University Press, 1964.

CREIGHTON, DONALD G.: *The Road to Confederation*. Toronto: Macmillan of Canada, 1964.

WAITE, PETER: *The Life and Times of Confederation*. Toronto: University of Toronto Press, 1962.

WHITELAW, W. M.: *The Maritimes and Canada Before Confederation*. Toronto: Oxford University Press, 1966.

UNDERHILL, FRANK H.: *The Image of Confederation*. Toronto: Canadian Broadcasting Corporation, 1965.

Section II
SOURCES OF LOCAL HISTORY

3. Place Names

How did your community receive its name? What was the origin of the word? Has it undergone change over the years? Wherever located, in Atlantic Canada or elsewhere, every place name is significant and forms an important part of local history. In discovering the source and development of place names you will find clues to troublesome historical riddles. Place names supply an excellent starting point for the detailed study of a particular community. Furthermore, they " ... form a permanent register or index of the course and events of a country's history; they are the fossils exposed in the cross-section of that history, marking its successive periods; and so lasting are they that records in stone or brass are not to be compared with them for endurance."[1]

A beginning can be made by examining the names that were first given to portions of the coast of Atlantic Canada: Labrador, Newfoundland, Cape Breton, and Acadia. The first three are in evidence on modern maps, while Acadia, the French name for much of the region, lives on in the Acadian people. Labrador was originally applied to a section of the coast of Greenland and is Portuguese in orgin. Derived from the word *lavrador*, or landowner, it was later transferred by early map-makers to the northeastern coast of the continent. The origin of Newfoundland, as the name implies, is straightforward. Originally *Terra Nova* on early Portuguese maps, the area soon began to be referred to by English sailors as the new-found land. By 1598 when Hakluyt's famous world chart was produced, Newfoundland as a place name was generally accepted. Cape Breton is also one of the oldest names on the Atlantic coast and is undoubtedly of Basque or Breton origin. Two theories exist concerning the evolution of Acadia as a place name. The most obvious is that the word is a contraction of Arcadia, the classical name applied to a land of rustic peace. Certainly this spelling appeared on early maps. Another theory traces Acadia to the Micmac *cadie*. More probable is the suggestion that the word is a combination of both. Early French explorers, upon hearing the Micmac word which meant a piece of land, and noting its similarity to Arcadia, gradually dropped the "r" to form Acadia.

Nova Scotia, Prince Edward Island, and New Brunswick are place names of later orgin. Although coined as early as 1621 when the charter of New Scotland was granted to Sir William Alexander, Nova Scotia was not a permanent fixture on the map until after the Treaty of Utrecht in 1713. New Brunswick was created in 1784, honouring the royal house of Brunswick, while Prince Edward Island (for the Duke of Kent, father of Queen Victoria) was designated in 1799. Already, in this discussion of regional place names, certain principles of naming or nomenclature emerge. Some place names evolved from another language, others are descriptive, and still others honour famous people. These, however, are merely a few of the categories. More will be described later. New Brunswick, Nova Scotia, and Prince Edward Island were subsequently divided into counties and a study of these will indicate additional categories. By far the more interesting names are those of Amerindian origin such as Antigonish or Madawaska. Several counties were named for places in the British Isles: Colchester, Westmorland, Inverness, and Gloucester are examples. The final classification illustrates a fondness for names with royal associations. All three provinces have a King's (or Kings) County, while the three divisions of Prince Edward Island are King's, Queen's, and Prince counties. Victoria (in both Nova Scotia and New Brunswick) and Annapolis are two other names with royal associations. Newfoundland escaped division into counties; hence its regions retained many of the more interesting names earlier applied to the coastline, such as Placentia Bay, Bonavista Bay, Trinity Bay. None the less, names such as Queen's River and Queen's Cove reflect the same preoccupation with royalty and regal traditions.

The study of place names is full of pitfalls and there is danger in accepting the most obvious sign of origin. A safer method is to amass all possible leads and then subject the evidence to close study. A few illustrations will suffice. The map of southern Nova Scotia reveals a town and a county named Lunenburg. Since it is well known that the area was settled in 1753 by the "Foreign Protestants" of French, Swiss, and German origin, we might conclude that the original settlement was named by these early colonists for the city of Lüneburg in Hanover. A similar conclusion was reached by historians, from T. C. Haliburton to W. S. MacNutt, and has been repeated many times. Yet it is wrong. There were few Hanoverians among the first settlers; the name was designated *before*

Royal Ontario Museum, Toronto

*Map of Acadia from Champlain's sketch of 1613.
How many modern place names can you find?*

their arrival, and in any event the naming of such areas was entrusted to the governor and council. It is apparent that Lunenburg was selected as a place name because of its royal associations. In 1714 the elector of Hanover, the Duke of Brunswick-Lüneburg, became king of England and consequently the district was designated in honour of the royal house.[2] Indeed, had the first settlers been of an entirely different racial origin, it is probable that the same place name would have been selected. Ferryland on the coast of the Avalon peninsula in Newfoundland would seem, at first glance, to be a place name of indisputable English origin. It might be a corruption of "Fairyland" or it could simply indicate the landing-place of a ferry. Not so. Those who study ancient maps have traced the spelling to: *Farilham* or *Port Farelhao* in 1529, *Forillon* in 1547, and *Ferriland* in 1627. The first word is Portuguese in origin, the second French, and it seems clear that the modern Ferryland is a distillation of the two. Place names of Amerindian origin can frequently pose problems in translation. Was Economy, Nova Scotia, so named by an enterprising Scot, or does it have associations with some local legend? Neither explanation is correct, for the word is much older and can be traced to the Micmac *Kenomee*, which means a long point jutting out into the sea. Penetanguishene is of undoubted Amerindian origin; however, its presence in Newfoundland lacks local significance for the name was borrowed from Ontario in the 1950s.

Fortunately, the vast majority of place names are not shrouded in mystery and are easier to trace. The above examples are cited as a warning to be wary of the obvious. Place-name exploration must be approached in an organized fashion, first through the study of maps of all kinds. Modern maps and charts will reveal physical features that might provide clues, old maps in historical atlases will show previous spellings, while directories, gazetteers, newspaper accounts, and local histories may well add additional information. Above all, do not neglect dictionaries of other languages, as they are a frequent source of leads. A teacher experienced in the study of languages would be a helpful consultant if you suspect a place name is of foreign origin. Watch dates very carefully and do not inadvertently attribute a strange-sounding place name to a European source. The books and gazetteers listed at the end of this chapter should be consulted whenever in doubt. Take one interesting example for a trial run. How did Signal Hill in St. John's receive its name? (It has nothing to do with Marconi's famous message and is of much earlier origin.)

Probably the easiest names to identify and among the most common are those associated with the landscape and prominent physical features such as the sea or coastline, rivers, lakes, or mountains. Prince Edward

Island has numerous headlands named Red Point or Red Head, all marking the distinctive red soil that is characteristic of the island. Names such as Bald Head Cove (Nfld.), Bald Rock (N.S.), Bald Mountain (N.B.), and Bald Point (P.E.I.) fit this category. Bridgetown (N.S., P.E.I., Nfld.) and Middleton (N.S., N.B., Nfld.) indicate obvious physical settings, while animals, birds, flowers, trees, and distinctive colours have all been utilized in designating physical locations. Not surprisingly, the sea and ships account for many place names in Atlantic Canada. Some tell their own story: Ship Harbour occurs in Nova Scotia, New Brunswick, and Newfoundland, while Prince Edward Island has a Shipwreck Point and a Shipyard River. Others have a more interesting origin. Cape Spear in Newfoundland is derived from the Portuguese, *Cauo de la spera*, "the cape of waiting" for fair winds to enter St. John's harbour. Tormentine, New Brunswick, comes from the French "Cap Tourment", a cape of storms, and Malignant Cove, Nova Scotia, was named because of the wreck near by of the British man-of-war *Malignant*. Nautical terms and navigational hazards have been another common source of names. Thus we have places such as Topsail, Pushthrough, and Little Tickle (a very narrow strait) in Newfoundland. Medea Rock, Shediac Bay, New Brunswick, marks the spot where on November 17, 1838, H.M.S. *Medea* ran aground.

Of near-equal popularity are place names that incorporate family names of first settlers. Thus Loyalist grantees have left their mark on the map of New Brunswick in Bull's and Ward's creeks, Bliss and Pendleton islands. Equally prolific were the earlier New England Planters in Nova Scotia: Billtown for Ebenezer Bill, Lockhartville for James Lockhart, Sheffield Mills for Amos Sheffield. and Starr's Point for Major Samuel Starr. However, not all family place names are as matter-of-fact as these and a study of the origin of other examples can lead the inquirer to much local history. Mount Stewart in Prince Edward Island was named for John Stewart (1758-1834) who emigrated to the colony from Scotland in 1778. He served as speaker of the House of Assembly for a number of years and published in 1806 *An Account of Prince Edward Island*. This book, containing items of geographical, historical. and political interest, is a valuable account of colonial life. The Uniacke family, deeply involved in the early political life of Nova Scotia, is remembered in Mount Uniacke near Halifax. Chaswood, Nova Scotia, perpetuates the memory of Lieutenant Charles Wood, a native of Halifax and the first Canadian soldier to fall in the South African war. He was the son of John Taylor Wood, one-time captain of the *Tallahassee* and a grandson of General Zachary Taylor, President of the United States. See page 128.

A group of eighteenth-century admirals have been immortalized on the coast of Newfoundland, e.g., Port Saunders, Hawke Bay, Keppel

Harbour, and Howe Harbour. Captain Samuel Holland, while mapping the coast of St. John's Island (Prince Edward Island) in 1765, succeeded in eradicating a number of pleasant-sounding Micmac place names in order to honour distinguished soldiers and sailors with whom he had served at Louisbourg and Quebec: Cape Wolfe, Monckton Cove, Colville Bay, and Murray River are examples. The map of Nova Scotia reveals that practically every early governor succeeded in enshrining his name. Cornwallis (River and Valley), Wentworth, Sherbrooke, Dalhousie, and Kempt are all illustrative of this preoccupation. The infamous as well as the famous have had their family names preserved. Kelly's Island in Newfoundland marks the name of a famous pirate in northern waters, while Turk's Cove and Turk's Gut have nothing to do with far-away Turkey but remind us that all pirates were once nicknamed "Turks". Some of the most interesting place names in Newfoundland came originally from the names of pirate ships. Black Joke Cove, Happy Adventure, and Heart's Desire are examples. Hall's Harbour, Nova Scotia, was a rendezvous for Captain Samuel Hall, whose acts of piracy became a legend in his time. Thus, one can find tremendous variety in "family" and associated place names.

It is obvious that place-name study derives much from other languages and peoples. Fortunately, for the sake of interest, not all of these associations are as straightforward as Portugal Cove (Nfld.), Portuguese Cove (N.S.), Spanish Ship Bay (N.S.), French Lake and Irish River (N.B.), or Scotchfort (P.E.I.). Newfoundland, understandably, is heavily endowed with names of Portuguese, Spanish, and Basque origin, all reminders of the west-European fishing fleets that for centuries crossed the Atlantic to fish the Grand Banks. Cape Freels is Portuguese and comes from *Ilha de freyluis* (the island of Brother Lewis). It is of particular interest because the early cartographers had mistaken a cape for an island. Catalina is traceable to the Spanish *Cataluña* or perhaps the French version, *Catalogne*. Place names of French origin abound in all four Atlantic provinces and may be subdivided into two groups: those resulting from early exploration (Baie des Chaleurs) and those associated with Acadian settlements (Grand Pré). Place names of the first type are encountered in coastal areas, but more predominantly in Newfoundland, while the second variety is concentrated in areas originally settled by the Acadians or repossessed by them after their return following the Expulsion.

By far the largest group of place names owes its origin to associations with the British Isles, a fact frequently overlooked in our preoccupation with the unusual. Examples of the direct links with England are Woodstock or St. George (N.B.), Bideford (P.E.I.), Sandringham (Nfld.), and Liverpool (N.S.). The abundance of Scottish place names in Nova

Scotia and Prince Edward Island, and New England names duplicated in New Brunswick are all indicative of early settlement patterns. In addition, the map of Atlantic Canada is heavily dotted with names of Amerindian origin. Such are found most frequently in New Brunswick and but seldom in Newfoundland. Rivers more than any other natural feature have tended to retain their original names. Miramichi and Restigouche in New Brunswick or the tongue twisters, Shubenacadie and Musquodoboit in Nova Scotia are typical. One interesting explanation has been advanced to account for this phenomenon. It is a fact of history that invading people tend to accept river names applied by those who occupied the land before them; consequently, the Clyde, Rhine, and Po rivers in Europe are traceable to Roman times.[3] It would seem that the pioneers of Atlantic Canada continued this process. Then, too, rivers provided the only transport for early settlers and their names quickly became household words.

Not infrequently a place name will commemorate a significant local event, often one with tragic overtones. After the fall of Louisbourg in 1758, a British naval force attempted to wipe out the scattered Acadian settlements fronting on the Gulf of St. Lawrence. This event gave rise to the name Burnt Church, a small community on Miramichi Bay. Mary March Brook in Newfoundland serves as a reminder of the extinction of the Beothuck Indians. The anglicized name Mary March was given to Demasduit, wife of the Beothuck chief Nonobawsut; she, like so many of her kind, died a victim of torture. Alexander Bay on the edge of Terra Nova National Park was once known as Bloody Bay because of the massacre of the Beothucks that took place here. Bloody Creek in Nova Scotia has a similar history, although on this occasion it was the blood of the white man that was spilled. On December 6, 1757, a detachment of British troops marched from Annapolis to search for several comrades who had been captured by the French and their Indian allies. For two days they scoured the countryside to no avail. On December 8 they began the return march when, in the words of the original account, they were "suddenly attacked with a dreadful shower of ball and buckshot seconded by as horrid a yell as ever heard". An ambush at René Foret Creek was responsible for the death, in a matter of minutes, of twenty-four men. Over two hundred years later this location is still known as Bloody Creek. Atlantic Canada has also its share of place names that serve as reminders of battles and historic events in other countries. Glenfinnan (P.E.I.) was settled in 1772 by immigrants from the area of the same name in Scotland and is forever associated with the tragic events of 1745.* Some indication

---

*Prince Charles Edward Stuart, the "Young Pretender", raised his standard at Glenfinnan, Scotland, on August 19, 1745, and the second Jacobite Rebellion was under way. It ended in disaster at Culloden the following spring.

of the impact of the Crimean War may be found in Alma (N.S., N.B., and P.E.I.), Inkerman (N.B.), and Kars (N.B.), all signifying battles; Port Williams (N.S.) commemorates Sir Fenwick Williams of Kars fame, although, to be precise, he was so honoured before his service in the Crimea. Florenceville (N.B.) is also said to have been named at this time in honour of Florence Nightingale.

The migration of people and changes in settlement patterns can also be traced in place names. The movement of Ulster Scots from Londonderry in Ireland to Londonderry in New Hampshire and thence to Londonderry, Nova Scotia, is an example. Rustico (P.E.I.) was named for an early settler, René Rassicot, who emigrated from Avanches, Normandy, and proves that there was some migration from France as late as 1724. The movement of the Acadians can be noted through the presence of familiar place names such as Gaspereau, Brule, and Barrachois in several parts of Atlantic Canada. The last name is particularly widespread. Designating a shallow bay or pond, usually enclosed by a sand bar, Barrachois has been utilized in more than eighty different locations. How many can you find? The use of this word underlines the point that many geographical terms adapted for use in place names have originated in the French language. Other examples are "anse" for cove or creek and "aboiteau" indicating a dam with a gate to control water. For more information on this topic see J. A. Rayburn: *English Geographical Names in Canada with Generic Terms of French Origin*, a publication that can be obtained from Information Canada.

An interesting sideline to note in the study of place names is the strenuous efforts that have sometimes been made to impose new names on particular localities. The success of Captain Samuel Holland in this connection has already been mentioned. In most instances the change is to be regretted—frequently the original forms were more interesting. Occasionally the older and more pleasing or euphonious names have survived. Coleraine, New Paisley, Alexandria, Donegal, Teignmouth, Southampton, and Walmsley were all tried in a vain attempt to eradicate the Micmac name Pictou. Port Mouton, the first name applied to a harbour on the south shore of Nova Scotia, has survived despite the imposition of Guysborough in honour of Sir Guy Carleton. The latter name, however, was simply transferred to the coast of Chedabucto Bay where it has remained. (Carleton has had his name perpetuated perhaps more often than anyone in Atlantic Canada, as witness the number of Carletons, Dorchesters, and variants thereof.) Some interesting place names have disappeared from modern maps. Skedaddle Ridge (near St. Stephen, N.B.) came by its name because it was a popular hideout for Americans who were not in sympathy with the northern cause in the Civil

War. Jack of Clubs Cove, Newfoundland, was changed to Aguathuna, and Famish Gut, Newfoundland, has become Fairhaven. Sometimes changes have taken place to end obvious duplication, as when Kingston (N.B.) was changed to Rexton. Can you find other examples of place-name changes?

A place name is never a mere arbitrary or meaningless sound; it embodies an important chapter in local history. To gain a deeper insight into the fascination of name lore, detailed studies of smaller regions are necessary. There is much to be learned and the time is now, for many small communities are disappearing. School consolidation, the closing of railways, the abolition of rural post offices, and the resettlement of many outport communities in Newfoundland have contributed to this development. An intensive place-name study of a local area—for example, a regional school district—can add immeasurably to a project in local history. (See H. M. MacDonald: *Memorable Years*, Antigonish, 1964, for a place-name survey of the school sections of Antigonish County.) In stagecoach days rest stops often inspired place names. Prince Edward Island provides some interesting examples. Hazelgrove marks the location of an inn once operated by the son of a Loyalist, Samuel Bagnall. Ten Mile House was originally the name of a tavern, so called because it was located this distance from Charlottetown. Traveller's Rest was also the name of a famous inn, while Summerside traces its name to the Summerside House, a hotel operated by a descendant of the original settler, Daniel Green.

A local industry is sometimes of sufficient importance to give rise to the name of a community. Argentia (Nfld.) was suggested by the opening of a silver mine, and although the enterprise failed, the name remained. Milltown (N.B.) and Goldboro and Imperoyal (N.S.) all belong in this category. In 1848 Donald MacLean MacDonald moved from New Glasgow to Inverness County in Cape Breton. Here he erected a mill for dyeing and fulling hand-made cloth. MacDonald became known as the "Dyer" to distinguish him from others with a similar name; his home was called "Dyer's Glen", later transposed to the attractive place name Glendyer.

A glance at a map or gazetteer seems to indicate that the early settlers of Atlantic Canada were a very religious people. Every county or township abounds in names of saints—although even here we have to exercise caution. St. Eleanor's (P.E.I.) lacks religious significance—it immortalizes one Eleanor Sanskey who emigrated to Prince Edward Island in 1804. New Brunswick on the other hand boasts numerous genuinely Biblical names. Study maps of Kings and Queens counties to see how many of these you can locate.

A consideration of interesting and significant place names would be incomplete without mention of the unusual and the bizarre. Newfoundland has a reputation in this category with Seldom Come By, Blow Me Down, and Come By Chance. However, the other provinces too may lay claim to the unorthodox. Consider Pull and Be Damned Rapids, Hell's Kitchen, and Left Hand Grindstone Brook in New Brunswick, or Anthony's Nose and The Devil's Burrow in Nova Scotia. Can you account for the origin of some of these unusual place names? Finally, the history of street names in towns and cities will reveal a vast amount of information about the evolution of the community. Many street names in Saint John and Fredericton are of Loyalist origin and towns and cities in all four provinces reflect the fondness for royal associations. Still other street names commemorate famous sons and early settlers. Make a street-name study of your home town, using the categories suggested in the diagram below.

Place-Name Check List

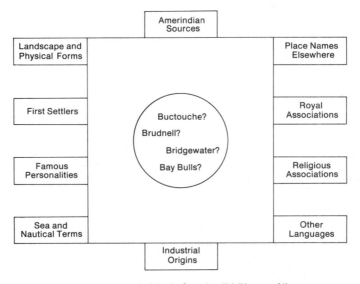

Most place names in Atlantic Canada will fall in one of these categories. Note also place names that have disappeared or changed over the years.

The place names of Atlantic Canada have not come about by accident; there is usually a reason, well rooted in history, as to why a location continues for years to be identified by a particular name. Almost invariably place names may be traced to some event in local or national history. It is fair to say that the history of this region, in broad strokes, may be found in its name lore. Place names are one of our oldest primary sources and "records in stone and brass are not to be compared with them for endurance". More than a half-century ago the New Brunswick historian and cartographer Dr. W. F. Ganong cited four major reasons for the study of place names. The justification is equally valid today. He suggested: (1) They facilitate the study of geography and history by providing a connecting link between the two subjects. (2) They contribute to the amassing of factual historical material. (3) They locate the site of historical events and "make the geography of old documents intelligible". (4) They provide an interesting study in their own right and make available to all concerned a valuable and inexpensive hobby.[4] Good place-name hunting!

FOR READING AND REFERENCE

ANDERSON, WILLIAM P.: *Micmac Place Names*. Ottawa: Geographic Board of Canada, 1919.

ARMSTRONG, G. H.: *The Origin and Meaning of Place Names in Canada*. Toronto: Macmillan of Canada, 1972. (A revised edition is to be issued in 1975.)

FERGUSSON, C. BRUCE: *Place Names and Places of Nova Scotia*. Halifax: Public Archives of Nova Scotia, 1967.

GANONG, W. F.: *Place-nomenclature in the Province of New Brunswick* (Reprinted). Toronto: Canadiana House, 1972.

KIRKCONNELL, WATSON: *Place Names in Kings County, Nova Scotia*. Wolfville: n.p., 1971.

RAYBURN, ALAN: *Geographical Names of Prince Edward Island*. Ottawa: Information Canada, 1973.

SEARY, E. R.: *Place Names of the Avalon Peninsula of the Island of Newfoundland*. Toronto: University of Toronto Press, 1971.

Principles and Procedures. Ottawa: Canadian Permanent Committee on Geographical Names, Information Canada, 1969.

All school libraries should have copies of the *Gazetteer of Canada*, published by authority of the Canadian Board on Geographical Names, Ottawa. There is a separate edition for each of the Atlantic provinces and these may be ordered from the nearest Information Canada Bookshop.

SUGGESTIONS FOR FURTHER RESEARCH

1. Can you account for these?
   (a)   The origin of the place names of the capital cities of the Atlantic provinces.
   (b)   Five place names associated with governors in provinces other than Nova Scotia.
   (c)   The use of the word "Thrum" or "Thrumcap" in place names in all four provinces.
   (d)   The absence of Amerindian place names in Newfoundland.
   (e)   The comparative scarcity of French place names in New Brunswick.
   (f)   The origin of the following:

New Brunswick	*Newfoundland*
(i) Kennebecasis	(i) Fogo
(ii) Baie Verte	(ii) Botwood
(iii) Maugerville	(iii) Trepassey
(iv) Sackville	(iv) Bauline
(v) Doaktown	(v) Jerseyman's Head
Nova Scotia	*Prince Edward Island*
(i) Meteghan	(i) Point Prim
(ii) Pereau	(ii) Bedeque
(iii) Earltown	(iii) Crapaud
(iv) Margaree	(iv) Borden
(v) Dunvegan	(v) Cape Traverse

2. Compile a list of place names that are to be found in more than one Atlantic province. Examples: Amherst, N.S., Amherst Cove, P.E.I., and Amherst Cove, Nfld.; or Caledonia, N.S., and Caledonia, P.E.I. Ascertain if the place-name origin is the same in each case.

3. Select an area in Atlantic Canada for an intensive study of place names. (This could be a regional school district, a county or township, or a specific area such as the Saint John River valley or the Burin peninsula). Using this chapter as a guide, develop a detailed place-name analysis of the area of your choice.

4. Legacy of
the Sea

On the edge of Louisbourg harbour looking eastward to the open sea stands a modern lighthouse, very near the location where the French erected the first such structure in Atlantic Canada. For over two centuries Louisbourg light has swept the horizon, alerting mariners to the dangers of the rockbound shore. Explorers and privateers, fishing craft and rumrunners, salt bankers and cargo schooners in infinite variety have for an even longer span of years plied this coast. Thus it is that the many lighthouses of Atlantic Canada symbolize a kinship with the sea. Most major settlements are found near the coast, while the shoreline is deeply indented with numerous harbours, wide estuaries, and penetrating rivers. Through war and peace, depression and prosperity, the sea has become deeply etched in community life from Grand Manan to Cape Race, and from Scatarie to the Labrador. Unlike other parts of Canada, the pioneers of this region were fishermen and sailors who preceded by many years the settlers on the land.

Because the sea comprises such an integral part of our understanding of the past, its total effect can best be understood at the local level. Should you live in a coastal town or community, much of what follows will have an individual application. If your home is inland, then a visit to a nearby seaport or marine museum may be arranged. Look for signs of the influence of the sea in years gone by, rather than for the more obvious wharves and fish plants that mark the economic importance of the sea today. Many of the best locations for in-depth study are found in out-of-the-way places and a casual visitor is apt to miss evidence of their former fame. Communities such as River John, Maitland, or Barrington in Nova Scotia, St. Martin's or Dorchester in New Brunswick, Bideford or Souris in Prince Edward Island, and Grand Bank or Carbonear in Newfoundland are examples of interesting locations for study.

In all such towns and villages large white clapboarded homes provide a first inkling of the historic effect of the sea. Before highways and railroads, the only outlook was seaward; consequently, the houses were usually built to face in that direction. A small verandah-like structure on the roof, the "captain's walk", is a reminder that the house probably dates from the heyday of wooden ships. In a number of communities some of these homes are open for public inspection. Try to visit one and note the finely detailed workmanship, wood carving, and sturdy construction, the handiwork of the carpenters and joiners who acquired their appreciation of line and form in shipbuilding. Look for exposed beams in attic or basement and you may detect tool marks of the carpenters who built these homes as strong and as true as their tall-masted ships. Should the home have remained in the same family for four or five generations, there will be evidence of voyages to all parts of the world. A conch-shell-lined walk, tropical curios, china tea sets, teakwood chests, oriental screens, satinwood and lacquer boxes are just a few of the things to watch for. Frequently you will find a captain's desk adorned with ship models or barometers, paintings of famous vessels, nautical scenes from around the world, and other reminders of seafaring life. The John Churchill home in Hantsport, Nova Scotia, is one example of many fine old houses to be found in all four Atlantic provinces. The Churchill shipyard was once the fifth largest in the world and the house, built around 1860, provides evidence of the prosperity of its owners. Spacious rooms, ceiling mouldings with designs from ships, wall paintings, and plaster that has survived for over a century, heavily embossed wallpaper in near-original condition, and crystal chandeliers imported from France are among the highlights of this house. Now a community centre, it contains a marine exhibition so that visitors may see something of the ships of John Churchill's day. It is not always necessary to visit the home of a wealthy shipbuilder or sea captain to gain an appreciation of the past influence of the sea. Many modest homes in coastal communities exhibit the same sense of proportion and simplicity of design as their larger counterparts. The men who followed the sea were great builders and this characteristic has, in many instances, been passed on to the present generation.

Visits to the homes of famous sea captains and shipbuilders lead us naturally to investigate the histories of these families and to note their contributions to local development. The careers of many nineteenth-century sea captains are fascinating studies, for in some instances these men literally decided the character of community life. Fortunes came easily; many were able to retire early and more often than not they embarked on a second career in politics or business or some form of community service. The McKenzie-Carmichael family of New Glasgow, the Troops of Saint John, or the Cunards of Halifax and the Miramichi all fit this category. At this time Atlantic Canada was one economic unit and shipbuilders frequently migrated across provincial boundaries as new yards opened and further opportunities were presented. Today, in many instances, a few rotting timbers or remnants of an old wharf or launchway are all that remain of a once thriving industry. Yet if we know where and how to look, we can catch glimpses of an exciting chapter in local history.

Fortunately, we are well served by marine museums and a visit to one of these can help round out an understanding of the legacy of the sea. The Marine Gallery of the New Brunswick Museum recreates the mystery and romance of the sea through displays depicting shipbuilding and the whaling industry. Equally impressive collections are to be found in the Maritime Museum, Halifax, or the Marine Room of the Arts and Culture Centre in St. John's. Not to be neglected are smaller institutions—for example, the Yarmouth County Museum with its fine collection of ship paintings and models, the Trinity Museum containing hundreds of exhibits illustrating seafaring days in Trinity Bay, or the unique floating fisheries complex at Lunenburg consisting of a salt banker, a rumrunner, and a modern trawler. The Port de Grave Fishermen's Museum at Hibb's Cove, Newfoundland, deserves special mention because it exemplifies what can be accomplished with initiative and imagination on the local level. Begun in 1968 with a single artifact, a small rusty cannon ball dating from the seventeenth century, it has grown until now it attracts over 12,000 visitors annually. Housed in a well-designed building, the museum depicts through a varied collection of fishing gear, implements, household items, and other artifacts the life of pioneer fishermen in the outports of Newfoundland. Shipbuilding is a dying art in most parts of Atlantic Canada. Can you locate in your community some of the hand tools once used in this industry? If so, perhaps you can use these to start a classroom "mini-museum" on the legacy of the sea.

If there is one thing commonly shared by all parts of Atlantic Canada, it must be the sea and the sound of surf and water.

... on a hundred beaches, from Bay Chaleur down the coast of New Brunswick and The Island, round the headlands of Cape North, down the eastern and southern shores and round the coast of Fundy to Passamaquoddy and the edge of Maine. The grumbling sigh of calm bays at night, the rush of millbrooks and the soft slap on the shores of lakes.

The sound of rivers that run to the beat of their names, Matepedia and
Kennebacasis, Medway and Margaree. . . . [1]

Historically, this has dictated that the outlook of the majority of the
people has ever been seaward. The meandering coastline, deeply indented
in many places—most notably the south shore of Nova Scotia and the
northeastern coast of Newfoundland—has for centuries provided ideal
opportunities for landing and drying fish and safe harbours for fishing
fleets. Exceptions are to be found along the coast of the Bay of Fundy,
the northern part of Cape Breton, and portions of the coastline of Prince
Edward Island. Eastern Newfoundland, in addition, is well endowed with
large peninsulas and open bays. Archdeacon Edward Wix, who toured
this coast in 1835, recorded the following observation in his journal:

> I was frequently, during my journey, struck with surprise at the very
> marked difference which might be observed between the people only
> separated by a few leagues from each other. The inhabitants of
> Conception Bay, although a neck of land of only a few miles separates
> them from Trinity Bay, differ as much from the latter as if they were
> a different nation; the same may be said of the difference between those
> who live in Placentia and those who live in Fortune Bay.[2]

Modern communication and transportation have reduced the geographical isolation characteristic of the nineteenth century; however, its
long-range effect may still be noted.

When considering the overall impact of the sea on the history of the
Atlantic provinces, the continental shelf to the southeast of Nova Scotia
and Newfoundland should not be overlooked, for it is geologically an
extension of the mainland. In fact, the Grand Bank south and east of
Cape Race is a submarine plateau greater in area than the island of
Newfoundland. The significance of the Banks arises from the fact that
here the cold Labrador Current meets the warmer waters of the Gulf
Stream. The continuous mixing that takes place, combined with the salti-
ness of the water and favourable temperatures, encourages the growth of
plankton, the food supply for vast quantities of fish—more particularly,
the cod. Discovered in pre-Columbian times, this rich endowment of
nature encouraged the first explorers, prompted nations to go to war, and
indelibly stamped the character of the region. In recent years, with
evidence of deposits of oil and natural gas in the vicinity of Sable Island,
this area has assumed added importance. Constitutional experts may
debate the political implications of jurisdiction; however, there can be no
doubt as to the role of the continental shelf in the shaping of the history
of the entire area. To the people who live in Atlantic Canada, George's
Bank, Banquereau, and Green Bank are as significant as place names on
the land.

For mariners at sea, Banks fishermen returning homeward, or coast-
guard crews in from a mercy mission, the familiar lighthouse beacons or
the sonorous bell buoys are welcome sights and sounds. Whether or not
this has been part of your experience, a visit to a lighthouse or an interview with a lightkeeper will provide yet another focal point for studying
the legacy of the sea. (A résumé developed from the outline on page 40
will be of assistance in this research project.) Variety and charm of architecture, tales of rescue and shipwreck, and numerous unheralded acts of
heroism will be revealed in the process. Remote locations and inacces-
sibility in rough weather, combined with difficulties in building and
maintenance, meant that few lighthouses were built until well into the
nineteenth century. In 1752 a proposal was made in the Nova Scotia
Legislative Council to erect a lighthouse at Sambro Island,* marking the
approach to Halifax harbour. This was to be accomplished by a sale of
lottery tickets, but no action was taken until 1758. At this time £1,000 was
allocated from liquor duties to cover the cost of erection. In addition, a
duty of two cents a ton was levied on vessels entering Halifax harbour—an
amount sufficient to cover maintenance. The first lighthouse in New
Brunswick was established on Partridge Island (near Saint John) in 1791.†
The same year a range light was set in place to mark the entrance to the
harbour of St. John's, Newfoundland. This was eventually replaced by a
lighthouse erected in 1813 at Fort Amherst and maintained for a time by
voluntary contributions. Cape Spear near St. John's presented particular
difficulties for mariners because of the prevalence of fog; consequently,
"a heavy piece of ordnance was discharged every hour during daylight
to assist vessels in making the harbour."[3] Later, in 1863, a lighthouse was
erected at Cape Spear where the original building still stands, although
a more modern tower now houses the light. The annual reports of lighthouse inspectors are filled with accounts of the difficulties surrounding
the construction of these essential structures. In 1859, for example, three
attempts were required before equipment could be landed at Cape St.
Mary's, Newfoundland, and a start made on building the lighthouse.

Acts of heroism associated with lighthouses are well known; upon
occasion lightkeepers were forced to cope with varied forms of distress.
Extreme isolation, lack of transportation and communication, shortage of
supplies, sudden illness, and the ever-present danger of fire made their
lives difficult. In his annual report for 1877 the lightkeeper on Pictou
Island reported:

*The lens of the Sambro Island Light is displayed in the foyer of the Nova Scotia Museum
in Halifax. The original tower completed in 1758 was in use until 1967, although the lens
on exhibit dates from 1906.

†In addition, the first steam whistle in the world was erected on Partridge Island in 1854.
It was invented by a Scot, Robert Foulis, who had earlier emigrated to Saint John.

On the night of the 10th of April I lit the lamp at the usual hour, immediately after sundown. At half past 10 o'clock I made my usual inspection of the lamps before going to bed. I found everything as usual. At 12 o'clock a few minutes before my time of visiting the lantern I was awakened by a large explosion followed by several others. Upon rushing outdoors, I found the lantern one sheet of flames. We succeeded in subduing the fire, although we had scarcely any hope of doing so when we commenced. All the lamps were destroyed, the window glass broken, the ventilator blown off and broken, the stand burned down and the woodwork charred. The copper metal on the floor was also destroyed. A piece of the lamp that exploded (weighing 3 pounds) was thrown through the window a distance of 40 yards.[4]

By the mid-nineteenth century the coastline of Atlantic Canada boasted nearly 100 lighthouses—evidence of an increase in navigation and the

Construction
Height
Type of structure
Special features
Reason for this location
Type of illumination
Sketch or description
of light room

History
Length of service
History of previous
lighthouses
Records of sea rescue,
shipwreck, and disaster
Role in
Second World War

Interpretation
Range of the light
Supplemented by
sound signals,
radio, or radar
Particular hazards
marked
Log of a
lightkeeper's day

rising importance of the shipping industry. As each province entered Confederation the lighthouses, buoys, and beacons formerly maintained by a tonnage duty on shipping were taken over by the federal Department of Marine and Fisheries. A search through local records, early newspapers, and the federal Sessional Papers (where annual reports of the inspectors and keepers were published) will reveal when the lighthouses nearest your home were established. You will find when you read these accounts that seldom was there a year without incidents of shipwreck and disaster around the coast of Atlantic Canada. Nor was all that is of interest limited to the early days. During the Second World War the Canadian Broadcasting Corporation carried daily code messages such as: "Attention, all lightkeepers in Areas 1, 2, and 3. Order A for apples is to be carried out," or "Carry out Order B for butter," or "C for Charlie". Can you discover what was meant by this code?

It is claimed that there has been at least one shipwreck for each of the 4,625 miles of Nova Scotian coastline. Equally grim statistics might be compiled for other areas—most notably the southern and eastern coasts of Newfoundland. The treacherous shoals that surround Sable Island, "graveyard of the Atlantic", are well known; however, five other locations—St. Paul's Island in the Gulf of St. Lawrence, Scatarie Island near Louisbourg, Seal Island off Cape Sable at the southwestern tip of Nova Scotia, Brier Island and Grand Manan, both in the Bay of Fundy—have in turn taken their toll. Proximity to major shipping lanes, treacherous ocean currents, and fog-shrouded shorelines have given these islands a grim reputation among mariners.

Today, one of the most peaceful areas in Atlantic Canada is the northern shoreline of Prince Edward Island. Yet few people realize that those pleasant dunes and sandbars accounted for many a shipwreck in the eighteenth and nineteenth centuries. Early in November 1775 the *Elizabeth*, bound for New London, Prince Edward Island, was " ... so near its desired port as to see the lights in the windows and the wind fair ... but there being a great sandbar before the harbour's mouth our captain thought it best to go in by daylight."[5] Fate intervened before dawn in the form of a violent storm that continued unabated for forty-eight hours. Then, after being buffeted about by wind and brutal tides, the *Elizabeth* was blown closer to land. Her masts were gone and the anchors had failed. The ship was driven over four sandbars and eventually ran aground. The passengers and crew managed to reach land (east of Cavendish Inlet) and sought refuge in the scrub bush, the only shelter in an uninhabited area. By this time they were more than ten miles away from their original destination. Borrow from your local library the full account of this shipwreck. You will find it in D. C. Harvey (ed.): *Journeys to the Island of St. John*

(Toronto: Macmillan of Canada, paperback edition 1972). If you are unable to locate this account, another equally interesting tale of shipwreck on the coast of Cape Breton is G. G. Campbell (ed.): *Ensign Prenties's Narrative: A Castaway on Cape Breton* (Toronto: Ryerson Press, 1968).

Over a century later, in August 1883, the same north-shore area of Prince Edward Island witnessed another marine tragedy. The famous *Marco Polo*, built in Saint John, New Brunswick, and called "the fastest ship in the world", was caught in a gale and grounded on Cavendish Beach. Happily her entire crew was rescued. Many items retrieved from this wreck, including the magnificent figurehead depicting Marco Polo, may be seen in the New Brunswick Museum in Saint John. For centuries, in all parts of Atlantic Canada, salvage from shipwrecks was literally part of the livelihood of many people. Many homes still contain furnishings and other curios obtained from shipwrecks up and down the coast. One

The Public Archives of Canada

On August 13, 1872, the S.S. New England, *en route from Saint John to Boston, struck a reef in Passamaquoddy Bay. Fortunately, the passengers suffered "nothing worse than a detention of fifteen hours". Look for other engravings or sketches of early disasters.*

of the most interesting is a "Wreckwood Chair" built by Gilbert Nickerson (1859-1945) from pieces of wood rescued from dozens of wrecks on the south shore of Nova Scotia. The chair was purchased by the Shelburne Historical Society and may be seen in the Marine Room of the Ross-Thompson House Museum in Shelburne.

Seafaring has always been a hard and hazardous occupation and the ever-present element of danger has been responsible for numerous acts of heroism. Unfortunately, many such incidents are unremembered and one objective for research in your community or province might be to reveal the facts surrounding these cases. More than once the hero or heroine was a teenager. On a stormy night in late November 1797, near the village of Herring Cove, Nova Scotia, a vessel lay in distress, grounded on the dangerous Thrumcap Shoals. The ship, H.M.S. *Tribune*, sank during the night and by morning only a portion of the rigging remained above water. Of the two hundred and fifty persons on board a mere ten survived the night by clinging to the wreckage. The sea was described as " ... a perfect witches' cauldron of breaking waves, recoil, eddy and countercurrent".[6] Would any of those watching from land risk their lives in a rescue attempt? The answer was provided by Joseph Shortt. Only thirteen years of age, he put off singlehanded in his skiff and managed to rescue two survivors. This example of courage and determination inspired a volunteer crew to save the remaining eight men. Today, few people know this story, unless by chance they have read the plaque placed on the nearby lighthouse or wonder why this particular place is called Tribune Head.

Another incident with a happier ending occurred on July 13, 1828, near Isle-aux-Morts, Newfoundland, when the brig *Dispatch* from Londonderry, bound for Quebec, was noticed a mile off shore and obviously breaking up on the reefs. The discovery was made by John Harvey, his daughter Ann, aged seventeen, and a son, John Jr., twelve. No one else was present, and over the next two days the Harveys (principally father and daughter) were able, with the aid of a small boat, to rescue 163 men, women, and children. No mean feat when one considers the dangers involved! Once on land, the Harvey family shared their meagre provisions with the wet, cold, and hungry passengers until H.M.S. *Tyne* arrived, took on the survivors, and sailed for Halifax. But for the heroism of the Harvey family it is probable that all on board the ill-fated *Dispatch* would have been lost.

Sometimes it is those attempting a rescue operation who lose their lives. In Lakeside cemetery, North Sydney, there is a memorial bearing the following inscription:

In Memory of
William B. Cann
Bethel Keenan
Jeremiah Downey
who lost their lives on the 18th day of December, 1874,
in an attempt to rescue the crew of the brigantine *G. J.
Troop* when wrecked on Cranberry Head. This monument is
erected by the people of North Sydney, in honour and
commemoration of their bravery and devotion

Except for the loss of the three would-be rescuers, what happened was similar to the two episodes already mentioned. The *G. J. Troop* had cleared North Sydney with a cargo of coal for the West Indies. A sudden storm caught the vessel and in an attempt to return to port she ran aground on the rocks off Cranberry Head. In the rescue attempt that followed three men were drowned, while three others managed to scramble on board the *G. J. Troop*. Later, when the weather abated, the *Virgo*, inbound for Sydney, rescued all on board. Can you find similar tales of marine rescue in other parts of Atlantic Canada?

To move from stories of shipwreck and misfortune at sea to the many legends of phantom ships is an easy transition. Such legends are interwoven in story and song and emerge at almost any point along the coast. The north shore of New Brunswick and Nova Scotia from Shippegan Island to Cape George is noted for the phantom ship of the Northumberland Strait. An "appearance" has also been seen at many points along the south shore of Prince Edward Island. This ghost ship, usually sighted in the autumn, is regarded as the forerunner of bad weather and appears before a northeast wind. Those who claim a "sighting" describe it as a ball of fire which eventually develops into a three-masted ship. For many it is a reappearance of the barque *Colbourn* that was lost in Chaleur Bay on October 15, 1838. Forty-five days out of London, the *Colbourn* was enveloped in fog when suddenly the lookout spotted a light. The captain, convinced that this was a lighthouse, set his course accordingly, only to have the ship founder on a reef. Of the fifty-five persons on board, thirty-eight were drowned and a valuable cargo was lost. What was this mysterious light? Cases have been recorded where unscrupulous people placed false lights near rocks and reefs to lure the unlucky to inevitable shipwreck. One such story is told of Margaretsville, Nova Scotia. However, the wreck of the *Colbourn* remains unsolved. Those who live on Shippegan Island where the fire ship has been seen call it the *John Craig* light, since a ship of that name was once lost off Shippegan Shoals. Farther down the coast in the Amet Sound area of Nova Scotia, residents are convinced that the phantom is the *Isabella* which set sail December 10,

1868, from Tatamagouche on a maiden voyage to South America. The
Isabella was never seen again; no wreckage of the ship was ever found
and no trace of the crew. Still others claim it to be a pirate ship captured
and sunk near Merigomish, Nova Scotia, by a British warship during the
Napoleonic Wars. Whatever the legend, too many people over a long
period of time have sighted something on the waters of Northumberland
Strait for the phenomenon to be lightly dismissed. A few have attempted
to explain it. For some it is St. Elmo's fire (the glow that accompanies
charges of atmospheric electricity), for others it is simply a bank of fog
obscuring the full moon, or perhaps ignited gas from submarine coal beds.
What is your interpretation? Mystery goes hand in hand with life at sea.
Research the story of the *Mary Celeste*, built at Spencer's Island, Nova
Scotia, and found midway between Portugal and the Azores on December
4, 1872; or the *Resolven*, also found abandoned, with no trace of crew,
off Trinity Bay on August 29, 1884. Develop a scenario to account for the
disappearance of all on board these vessels.*

Understandably, many nautical apparitions, such as the *Teazer* light of
Mahone Bay, are associated with privateering, for this was big business
along the Atlantic coast during the late-eighteenth and early-nineteenth
centuries. A subtle distinction must be drawn between piracy and privateering. Piracy was no more than robbery on the high seas, while privateering was authorized by the granting of a government commission to
attack and capture enemy ships during wartime. Atlantic Canada had its
share of both. Newfoundland, in the early days, was a favourite haven
for such notorious individuals as Sir Henry Mainwaring, a seventeenth-century pirate who later became an English admiral; Peter Easton,
who operated from Harbour Grace and whose fame was a byword from
Panama to the Strait of Belle Isle; and Eric Cobham, the most notorious
of all, who made his headquarters at Sandy Cove, St. George's Bay, on
the west coast of Newfoundland.

Of equal renown for their feats of daring and the high drama of their
careers were the many privateers who operated from ports on the Atlantic
coast during the Seven Years War, the American revolutionary war, and
the Napoleonic Wars. Although privateering was essentially a commercial
enterprise, to engage in it the owners and commanders had to post bonds
of from £1,500 to £3,000 with the court of vice-admiralty, which would
eventually rule on the legality of their captures. They were then issued
"letters of marque" empowering them "to set upon by force of arms and
subdue and take the men-of-war, ships and other vessels, also the goods,

*See Stanley T. Spicer: *Masters of Sail: The Era of the Square Rigged Vessels in the Maritime
Provinces* (Toronto: Ryerson Press, 1968). 237-43, and Thomas Raddall: *Footsteps on Old
Floors* (New York: Doubleday & Co., 1968), 157-94, for detail on this topic. Michael
Harrington, Rupert Furneaux, and Sir Arthur Conan Doyle have also written on the mystery
of the *Mary Celeste*.

monies and merchandise . . . of the enemy." Ships thus captured were to be taken, usually, to Halifax and there the court of vice-admiralty would rule on any legal points in question and give direction as to the division of spoils. Recruiting for service on privateers was brisk, as illustrated by the following advertisements of the period:

All Tight Lads
Who are willing to serve His Majesty in that fast
sailing, excellent sea boat the *Canso* of 12 guns,
commanded by Lieutenant Croke, now fitting out for
a short cruise, to protect the trade of the British
provinces and pick up a few straggling American Bordeaux-men,
will meet with an honest hearty welcome, from a
sailor's friend, by applying on board that vessel
at the Navy Yard.

What Should Sailors Do On Shore?
While King, Country and Fortune point to the ocean!
His Majesty's Schooner *Pictou* of 12 guns commanded
by Lieutenant Stephens, as fine a vessel of her size
as ever floated on salt water, wants a few jolly,
spirited fellows to complete her complement for a
short cruise. . . . Apply on board at the Navy Yard.
May 21, 1813.[7]

The financial outlay required in posting the original bond gives some idea of the money to be made in privateering. In a single fortnight during the War of 1812, Liverpool, Nova Scotia, witnessed the following arrivals:

> June 23—Privateer *Retaliation* brought in schooner *Armistice*, from Boston for Eastport, with a cargo worth £3000. Had also ordered a sloop in; and put a pilot aboard a jebacco boat, taken by the *Bulwark*. Arrived schooner *Friends*, prize to the [privateer] *Shannon*. A prize to the *Liverpool Packet*, with 450 barrels flour is cast away on Cape Forchu; cargo saved. Two prizes are put in at Barrington . . .[8]

Small wonder that this port was called the "privateering capital of North America". The *Liverpool Packet*, regarded as the most famous of all the privateers, was responsible for taking forty-four prizes during the War of 1812. One of her owners, Enos Collins, began his career as a cabin boy on an earlier privateer, rose to found the Halifax Banking Company, became a member of the Legislative Council, and died in 1871 one of the richest men in Canada with an estate worth approximately six million dollars. Equally famous was Simeon Perkins whose well-known diary abounds with references to privateering. His home in Liverpool (open to the public) was built in 1766-7 and contains reminders of his career as a successful ship owner, privateer, merchant, and politician. Many other ports, including Yarmouth, Annapolis Royal, Saint John, and St. Andrews, were active in a trade that blended patriotism and good luck with a keen sense of business.

It should not be imagined that all privateers were as successful as the *Liverpool Packet*. Many men were ruined through a succession of losses, countless lives were sacrificed, and in many instances American privateers gained the advantage over their arch rivals. Liverpool was once invaded by a force from Salem, Massachusetts, with the avowed aim of "burning the nest". Lunenburg was sacked on March 15, 1782. In a most daring occurrence on November 17, 1775, two American privateers—the *Hancock* and the *Franklin* from Marblehead, Massachusetts—raided Charlottetown, ransacking the town, carrying away as prisoners Phillip Callbeck, administrator of the province, and Thomas Wright, the Surveyor-General. Released later, Wright was able on another occasion to take legal revenge on the Americans (see page 94). Perhaps the one American privateer whose ventures most closely paralleled those of the *Liverpool Packet* was the *Young Teazer*. The favourite trick of this daring vessel was to lie in wait off Sambro Light. The captain of the *Young Teazer* went so far as to challenge the British fleet at Halifax to try to capture his ship. His luck eventually ran out. The *Young Teazer* was cornered in Mahone Bay, only to be scuttled before capture. According to local legend, a great ball of fire, "the *Teazer* light", periodically appears on the waters of Mahone Bay.

In 1856, by international agreement, privateering was officially abolished; however, this did not spell the end of marine activities on the fringe of the law. The early history of the twentieth century records other ventures that compare with those of privateering. In 1917 an amendment to the American Constitution, calling for the prohibition of the production and sale of alcoholic beverages, was adopted by Congress and sent to the states for ratification. It was eventually approved, and "prohibition" became the law of the United States. One of the major sources of supply for the immediate and illicit liquor trade was Atlantic Canada. Smuggling along the eastern seaboard was not new. It had flourished during the American Revolution, was prominent during the War of 1812, and continued unabated until modern times. In 1868 a schooner, the *Echo*, was seized in Ipswich Bay, Massachusetts, with a cargo of 1,300 gallons of liquor from Nova Scotia. A forerunner of what was to follow!

While rumrunners were active all along the American seaboard, the major point of entry centred around the cities of Boston and New York and included the coastline from Cape Ann to Cape May. It was in this area that the notorious "Rum Row" was established. The normal practice of the rumrunners was to load vessels with cargos of liquor from ports of supply in Nova Scotia, St. Pierre and Miquelon, or Newfoundland and then sail to "Rum Row" where they dropped anchor and waited. The larger rumrunners were usually fishing schooners able to carry up to 3,000 cases per trip. Manned by experienced Nova Scotian and Newfoundland crews who knew the seacoast well, they were seldom captured by the American Coast Guard, for outside the three-mile limit they were safe. Once they were in position, contact with shore was made and American craft came out, took on the cargo and paid for it. In the early twenties "Rum Row" was located just beyond the three-mile limit. However, its later activities were forced by American law beyond a twelve-mile limit. There was also a certain amount of smuggling overland across the border between New Brunswick and Maine, although this trade was eclipsed by the vast amount of liquor shipped more economically by sea.

The rumrunners tried ingenious methods to throw the American Coast Guard off their trail. Fake radio distress signals which Coast Guard cutters were obliged to answer, derelict ships as decoys, smoke screens, and intricate sailing manoeuvres were all part of the game. The reason for the widespread smuggling was twofold: a large proportion of the American people did not support the concept of prohibition and, further, it was impossible to police adequately the vast sea and land boundaries of the United States. The cynical attitude of many Americans was summarized in a popular jingle of the day:

> Prohibition is an awful flop, we like it.
> It can't stop what it's meant to stop, we like it.
> It's left a trail of graft and slime,
> It's filled our land with vice and crime,
> It can't prohibit worth a dime—
> Nevertheless we're for it![9]

Rightly or wrongly, prohibition remained the law of the United States until its repeal on December 5, 1933. In Atlantic Canada during the fifteen years of its existence, fortunes were made and lost, shipyards for the building of rumrunners became common, and vessels designed and equipped solely for rumrunning were built. It was quite in character with the whole era that some incident would eventually bring the governments of Canada and the United States into diplomatic confrontation. The sinking of the rumrunner *I'm Alone* more than two hundred miles off the American coast had all the elements of comic opera. The *I'm Alone* was a vessel built and registered in Nova Scotia, flying the Canadian flag, owned by Americans, manned by a crew that included a French citizen, and skippered by a Newfoundlander, Captain Jack Randell. Try to discover details of this incident and how it was eventually settled.*

On balance, rumrunning, while it added to the drama and excitement of the "roaring twenties", cannot be described as one of the most positive aspects of seafaring life. None the less, it is a part of the history of the region and as such ought not to be disregarded. Of more enduring value is the legacy of the sea exemplified through various artistic and literary media. Poets E. J. Pratt and Charles Bruce, novelists Thomas Raddall and Harold Horwood, or artists Joseph Purcell and David Blackwood are but a few outstanding practitioners. Not to be overlooked is the contribution of craftsmen still skilled in trades which follow the sea. It was a Lunenburg shipyard which was commissioned by MGM to build a replica of H.M.S. *Bounty*, and later the same firm constructed *Bluenose II* from original plans.

Painting the Sea, a book by W. E. de Garthe containing reproductions of some of the best works of this marine artist, captures the full measure of the legacy of the sea. He writes: " ... one has to *experience the sea* to paint a comprehensive seascape, authentic as to the movements around the rocks as well as the ongoing wave, the incoming tide or the outgoing tide ... all these and more one has to study, to familiarize oneself with the everchanging aspects of the ocean."[10] Another who caught the same concept in a different medium was the photographer W. R. MacAskill. At the time of his death in 1956, not only was he internationally recognized but one of his photographs of the *Bluenose* found a place on the Canadian 50-cent stamp issued January 6, 1929. For a generation a design from the same photograph has appeared on the reverse of the Canadian dime. MacAskill's book *The Lure of the Sea* provides a companion piece for *Painting the Sea* by de Garthe.†

Of the selected topics that have been used to exemplify the legacy of the sea in this chapter, impact on language remains to be covered. A prominent linguist has stated that "the figurative language of a community reflects the interests and occupations of its members."[11] Thus the everyday language of a region will be characterized by words and phrases not commonly found elsewhere. Unlike other aspects of the legacy this contribution is intangible and not easily measured. While much of the terminology of the sea did not originate in Atlantic Canada, it has

*See Jack Randell: *I'm Alone* (London: Jonathan Cape Ltd., 1930); *Historic Headlines*, The Canadian Illustrated Library (Toronto: McClelland and Stewart, 1967), 73-82; and Janice Patton, *The Sinking of the I'm Alone* (Toronto: McClelland and Stewart, 1973).

†Of equal interest is Farley Mowat and David Blackwood: *Wake of the Great Sealers* (Toronto: McClelland and Stewart, 1973).

lingered longer here than elsewhere. Many a Maritimer will unwittingly betray his birthplace, not by accent, but through the nautical flavour of his speech. "To stem the tide", "Show your true colours", "Have you lost your bearings?", and "Everything is smooth sailing" are but a few random samplings of sea terminology that have come ashore to enrich our language. How many more can you list?

Finally, the legacy of the sea contains a mystical element that goes beyond language, ships, and tides. It is best described by Dr. Leslie Harris, a son of Newfoundland:

> It is to the sea that I invariably turn. . . . I recall now a September day when it is incredible in the brilliance of its blueness and when it is flecked with white as far as one can see; a white not of foam, but of northern phalaropes; or a day in November when a westerly gale is, as we say, "taking up the water" and when clouds of bull birds are scudding before the wind, sometimes obscured by stinging snow squalls; or a flat calm morning in July when you wait for the dawn light and the splendor of the rising sun to illuminate the marks that will make it possible to begin the day's fishing; or a day during the caplin skull . . . To one brought up near the sea there is nothing more magnificent (and the magnificence does not pall), nothing more awesome, nothing more continuously interesting, nothing so magnetically attractive as the sea, whether at peace or torn in a fury; nothing more exhilarating than the feel of spray stinging the face . . . [12]

FOR READING AND REFERENCE

A. General

APPLETON, THOMAS E.: *Usque ad Mare: A History of the Canadian Coast Guard and Marine Services*. Ottawa: Department of Transport, 1968.

LOWNDS, M. RUSSELL: *The Sea, Ships and Sailors*. Halifax: Petheric Press, 1970.

PARKER, JOHN P.: *Sails of the Maritimes*. Halifax: Maritime Museum of Canada, 1960.

PULLEN, H. F.: *Atlantic Schooners*. Fredericton: Brunswick Press, 1967.

RICHARDSON, EVELYN: *We Keep a Light*. Toronto: Ryerson Press, 1945

(Reprinted in paperback, 1961). See also *Desired Haven* (Toronto: Ryerson Press, 1953); *No Small Tempest* (Toronto: Ryerson Press, 1957); and *My Other Islands* (Toronto: Ryerson Press, 1960).

RUSSELL, FRANKLIN: *The Atlantic Coast.* Toronto: McClelland and Stewart, 1970.

SCHULL, JOSEPH: *Salt-Water Men.* Toronto: Macmillan of Canada, 1960.

SHERWOOD, ROLAND H.: *Atlantic Harbours: People, Places and Events.* Windsor: Lancelot Press, 1972.

SPICER, STANLEY T.: *Masters of Sail: The Era of the Square Rigged Vessels in the Maritime Provinces.* Toronto: Ryerson Press, 1968.

STEPHENS, DAVID E.: *Lighthouses of Nova Scotia.* Windsor: Lancelot Press, 1973.

B. Special Studies

BATES, GEORGE T.: "Some Seal Island Shipwrecks", *Nova Scotia Historical Quarterly*, 1 (March 1971): 47-66.

BIRD, WILL R.: "Nova Scotia Has Many Lights", *Canadian Geographic Journal,* March 1937, 91-103.

CAMERON, J. M.: *Wreck of the Melmerby and Other Stories.* New Glasgow: Hector Publishing Co., 1963.

FRASER, D. G. L.: "The Origin and Function of the Court of Vice Admiralty", *Collections Nova Scotia Historical Society*, XXXIII (1961): 57-80.

HARRIS, REGINALD V.: *The Oak Island Mystery.* Toronto: Ryerson Press, 1958.

KOTTMAN, RICHARD N: "Volstead Violated: Prohibition As a Factor in Canadian American Relations", *Canadian Historical Review*, XLII, 2 (June 1962): 106-26.

MULLANE, GEORGE: "The Privateers of Nova Scotia", *Collections Nova Scotia Historical Society*, XX (1921): 17-42. See also: Nichols, George E.: *Notes on Nova Scotia Privateers.* Toronto: Canadiana House, 1969.

RADDALL, THOMAS H.: *The Rover: The Story of a Canadian Privateer.* Toronto: Macmillan of Canada, 1960.

RANDELL, JACK: *I'm Alone.* London: Jonathan Cape Ltd., 1930.

RICHARDSON, EVELYN: *The Wreckwood Chair.* For the Shelburne Historical Society, Shelburne, N.S. See also "A Voyage to Australia", *Nova Scotia Historical Quarterly*, 3 (September 1972): 229-41.

SNIDER, C. H. J.: *Under the Red Jack.* Toronto: Musson Co. Ltd., 1928.

STORM, ALEX: *Canada's Treasure Hunt.* Winnipeg: Greywood Publishing Co., 1967.

C. Regional Studies

BALCOM, E. JOAN: *Fundy Tales*. Kentville: G. R. Saunders, 1969.

BLAKELEY, P. R., AND STEVENS, J. R.: *Ships of the North Shore*. Halifax: Maritime Museum, 1963.

CROWE, JOHN C.: *In the Days of the Windjammers*. Toronto: Ryerson Press, 1969.

HARRINGTON, MICHAEL: *Sea Stories from Newfoundland*. Toronto: Ryerson Press, 1958. See also numerous sea stories by the same author in the *Atlantic Advocate*, the *Newfoundland Quarterly*, and the *St. John's Evening Telegram*.

HORWOOD, ANDREW: *Newfoundland Ships and Men*. St. John's Marine Researchers, 1971.

MANNY, LOUISE: *Ships of Miramichi*. Saint John: New Brunswick Museum, 1960. See also *Ships of Kent County* (Sackville: *Tribune Press*, 1949); *Shipbuilding in Bathurst* (Fredericton: Brunswick Press, 1965).

MOWAT, FARLEY, AND DE VISSER, JOHN: *This Rock Within the Sea: A Heritage Lost*. Toronto: McClelland and Stewart, 1968.

PARKER, J. P.: *Cape Breton Sails and Men*. Toronto: G. McLeod Ltd., 1967.

PRATSON, F. J.: *The Sea in Their Blood*. New York: Houghton Mifflin, 1972.

The Troop Fleet in the Days of Sail. Saint John: New Brunswick Museum, 1960.

SUGGESTIONS FOR FURTHER RESEARCH

1. All sections of Atlantic Canada became involved in the "Golden Age of Sail"; however, particular ships stand out because of their size, records achieved, or deeds performed. Compile a "ship biography" of one of the following: (a) *Marco Polo* of Saint John, (b) *W. D. Lawrence* of Maitland, Nova Scotia; (c) *Tasso* of St. John's; (d) *Bluenose I* or *I'm Alone* of Lunenburg. If you live in a coastal community where shipbuilding was once carried on, compile a directory of the most famous ships built in local shipyards.

2. Behind the name of every ship there lies a story. Use the list compiled in (1) above or develop a directory of ship names from a nearby port in your province. See if you can ascertain the origin of the names or the reason for the selection of a particular name. (For example, Captain George McKenzie of New Glasgow, a friend and colleague of Joseph Howe, called one of his ships *The Three Councillors* to mark the appointment of reformers Howe, Uniacke, and McNab to the Nova Scotia Executive Council on October 6, 1840.) Your task will be made

easier if you subdivide your directory into categories such as the following: (a) Family Names of Shipbuilders, (b) Royalty, (c) Historic Events, (d) Battles, (e) Famous Personalities, (f) Classical Allusions. Books by John P. Parker, Stanley Spicer, and Andrew Horwood listed in the bibliography will assist you in this project.

3. Consult your nearest marine museum or public library and attempt to locate a ship's log. Copy or photocopy portions of it and with the aid of maps and nautical charts plot a typical voyage of this ship. Should this material be impossible to obtain, chart the course of Joshua Slocum, a native of Nova Scotia who was the first man to sail alone around the world. (See his book *Sailing Alone Around the World*, New York: Dover Paperbacks, 1956. See also the articles on Slocum to be found in the *Atlantic Advocate*, December 1970 and January 1971.)

5. Legacy of the
Land and the People

Atlantic Canada is a region of intense variety, of widely dissimilar physical features, and of many diverse moods. Labrador, with its forest wealth and rich natural resources, contrasts sharply with the agricultural potential of Prince Edward Island. The misty grandeur of the Cape Breton Highlands seems thousands of miles distant from the rugged moonscapes of the isthmus of Avalon. While the sea remains the dominant physical characteristic of the region, the land and the people have played their part in shaping its history. Taken as a region Atlantic Canada is both a "different" and in many respects a "difficult" place to live. Hugh MacLennan has written of his native Nova Scotia:

> I was born and raised in a part of Canada where nobody is able to change the landscape. Along the Atlantic coast you grow up with the conviction that everything in nature is as it is forever, and that man, living with the shifting immutability of the granite rocks, can never dominate his fate, never play artist with nature, but must take life and the world as he finds them. . . . [1]

Thus it is that much of Atlantic Canada is literally a laboratory of glacial erosion and geological formations. In some areas, so bare are the rocks that little beyond scrub spruce will grow.

Yet this is not a complete picture. A century before MacLennan, Joseph Howe described a scene only thirty miles distant from the granite-strewn south shore.

> Never shall I forget the surprise with which I looked down from the Ardoise Hills upon the softer scenery and richer soil of Windsor. As I

descended from the Horton Mountains, over the highest elevations of which the post road at that time wound [roughly the route followed by modern Highway 101], the Gaspereau valley, basking in sunshine, lay beneath me. The rich marshes of Horton and Cornwallis were beyond, Blomidon rose in majestic proportions in the distance, and I involuntarily thanked God that had given me such a country.[2]

Widely differing landscapes such as these are not uncommon in Atlantic Canada. The Saint John River valley in New Brunswick is a different world from the north shore of the same province, while the Codroy valley in southwestern Newfoundland presents the greatest possible contrast with the nearby Cape Ray barrens. In these comparisons, then, we have the geographic setting for an uneven distribution of population, an overall scarcity of agricultural land (except in selected areas), and an unequal allocation of raw materials.

"Landscape", when used in the geographic sense, refers to all physical and man-made features that contribute to the appearance of a particular location. Historically, every place and every region of Atlantic Canada possesses not one landscape but a succession of past landscapes. With this in mind a host of interesting questions arise: What problems did the Acadians have to overcome in building dykes to stem the restless tides of Fundy? What was Shelburne like when the first Loyalists arrived in 1784? Why did so many leave immediately thereafter? Why did Prince Edward Island insist on a solution to its transportation problems as one price of entry into Confederation? Why did the railway come so late to Newfoundland? To answer questions such as these one must study old maps and charts, directories and census records, documents and government reports, letters and diaries, newspapers and travellers' accounts—in short, the raw material of history and historical geography.

Certain key factors should be kept in mind when piecing together the past landscapes of any community, large or small. Major physical features, climate, vegetation, rock formation, and types of soil all have had an influence on historical development. The place to begin such an analysis is with topographic maps.* Study the sheet that covers your home

---

*It has not been possible to encompass within this unit comment on *all* physical features that have had some bearing on the history of Atlantic Canada. The student is encouraged to supplement the material presented by reference to any standard geography textbook that deals with the Atlantic provinces. Topographical maps should be readily available from your geography teacher. If not, the nearest Information Canada Bookshop will be able to help you. Failing this, check with the Canada Map Office, 615 Booth Street, Ottawa, K1A 0E9, Ontario. See also L. M. Sebert: *Every Square Inch* (Ottawa: Department of Energy, Mines & Resources, 1970) for the full story on Canadian topographic mapping. This booklet will also provide you with necessary technical detail on the interpretation of these maps.

community and note physical features such as marshes, swamps, rivers, lakes, and the contour of the land. How have these affected the development of settlement? Look also for signs of man's activities—trails and portages, cemeteries, bridges, churches, and schools, all of which will have had some bearing on the evolution of the community. Carefully used, these maps will not only provide information about the general physical setting in which local history has taken place, they will also portray valuable archaeological and historical information. Once you have gained confidence and expertise in map interpretation, move outside the classroom. Examine the appearance of prominent physical features and note how these are identified on the maps. A profitable exercise is to develop a detailed street or road map for a portion of your neighbourhood. Using the symbols to be found on topographic maps, indicate the physical as well as the man-made features. To further add to the usefulness of this project you may wish to carry out a classification of the buildings, developing symbols to indicate (a) those erected since 1950, (b) 1950-1925, (c) 1925-1900, and (d) pre-1900. Such a classification will prove useful when you study Chapter 10 on architecture.

Due to the widespread use of aerial photography, modern maps tend to be more precise than those of an earlier day. For evidence, all one needs to do is compare a topographic map and an aerial photograph for any given area.* In the years since the Second World War aerial photography, or the science of photogrammetry, has made spectacular advances. All of Atlantic Canada has now been charted from the air, enabling us to have detailed maps of isolated areas that seldom if ever have been explored on land. Aerial photography has come to the aid of historical research in ways other than the provision of maps, a point that will be elaborated upon in Chapter 7. Another approach in local study is the use of stereoscopic photographs (two photographs of a certain area, taken at a specified distance apart). These, when studied together by means of a binocular-type instrument similar to the stereoscope of Victorian days, are combined by the eye into one view that reproduces three-dimensionally the contours of the land. If your community is studied in this way, a much greater appreciation of its physical characteristics may be obtained. Better still, you may, as some schools do, be able to arrange

---

*If aerial photographs are not readily available, consult G. S. Tomkins and T. L. Hills: *Canada: A Regional Geography* (Toronto: W. J. Gage Ltd., 1970), 66-7; or C. L. Blair and R. I. Simpson: *The Canadian Landscape: Map and Air Photo Interpretation* (Toronto, Copp Clark, 1970), 62-3. Both of these sources depict comparative maps and air photos of the Lunenburg district. Emile Chevrier and D. F. W. Aitkens: *Topographic Map and Air Photo Interpretation* (Toronto: Macmillan of Canada, 1970), 91-3, compares a map and air photos of the Wolfville district.

a flight over your home town and thereby gain a vivid impression of the landscape.

Additional information may be found in geological maps, soil survey charts, and land utilization studies. These depict the hidden history of a given area by revealing the rock formation, mineral wealth, and potential for farming. The close relationship between surface geology and soil should always be noted, for these features not only contribute to the character of the land, they determine the agricultural history of a community. Comparative studies of various regions in Atlantic Canada will go a long way toward explaining settlement patterns, the location of industries or the lack of them, and the general way of life. For example, when studying your locality, watch for evidence of abandoned mining operations. In the mid-nineteenth century iron ore was mined at Upper Woodstock in New Brunswick and a blast furnace was established on the Saint John River. By about 1880 the operation ceased production and today few traces of a once-thriving industry exist. Wentworth, Nova Scotia, at the turn of the century, possessed a copper mine and smelter, and Guysborough County has many traces of gold mining.

Nautical charts comprise still another category of maps. Prepared by the Canadian Hydrographic Service, these are of value in the study of coastal regions as they depict wharves and landing facilities, breakwaters and fish plants, approaches from the sea and dangerous shoals, buoys and lighthouses. In addition, the "Pilot Series", providing a detailed description of the coast (for example: *The Newfoundland Pilot* or *The Nova Scotia and Bay of Fundy Pilot*), can add a useful dimension to a study of both the sea and the landscape. Try to obtain a nautical chart for a section of the coast of Atlantic Canada. (Example: Chart #4325 covers dangerous Seal Island off the southwestern tip of Nova Scotia.) Study this chart along with the corresponding section of the *Nova Scotia Pilot*. Why has this area such a grim reputation among mariners? Can you determine why "Blonde Rock" was so named?

As we move farther backward in reconstructing past landscapes, maps generally classified as "historical" will be of considerable assistance. By the mid-nineteenth century many wall maps and county atlases were published in the Atlantic provinces. These were intended to show all the houses and land holdings as they were at the time of compilation and consequently are of great importance. One prolific map-maker, or cartographer, was Ambrose F. Church. During the period 1865-88 he produced a large-scale map of Canada along with detailed maps of the province and counties of Nova Scotia. One of these, a map of Colchester County produced in 1874, included, in addition to the county, plans of Upper and Lower Stewiacke, Acadian Iron Mines, Folleigh Village, Earltown,

Tatamagouche, Great Village, Brookfield, and Truro, as well as directories of settlements and an inset of the Atlantic provinces. This ambitious
project was repeated for all other counties. In 1879 Roe Brothers of Saint
John and Halifax produced a handsome atlas of the Maritimes. Using a
scale of seven miles to the inch, it contained county maps for all three
provinces, and street maps for larger towns and cities along with a
patrons' directory. This was supplemented by a geographical description
of the area plus a geological map of the Maritimes and Newfoundland.
Equally useful is Meacham's Atlas of Prince Edward Island. Originally
published in 1880, it was reissued in 1972. The New Brunswick Archives
has produced a valuable folio of ten maps covering the period 1742-1936
and these should be consulted by anyone researching the past landscapes
of that province.

When using early maps one must be cautious. While the work of
Church, Roe, and their contemporaries was usually accurate, they did
make mistakes. It is wise in cases of this kind to attempt to establish the
accuracy of the cartographer. The date of the map should always be
checked. Was it published immediately after the original survey or did
several years elapse? If this information is not readily available, a
comparison with printed directories or similar records will yield an
approximate date. Verification of other information on the map can be
made by consulting local records. The quality of draftsmanship and
general cartographical details will indicate something of the map-maker's
ability. While reliance cannot be based solely on the evidence of these
maps, they do provide a good starting-place for local historical studies.
Comparisons with modern maps will often reveal details of great interest,
e.g., location of bridges and ferries, inns and "halfway" houses, canals and
early waterways, place names and earlier spellings.

Maps, sometimes called the "geographer's shorthand", are not alone in
providing evidence upon which to construct past landscapes. Sketches and
engravings (see Chapter 10) and, from the more recent past, photographs
and post cards should all be sought in an effort to gain a better understanding of the land and of what life was once like in your community.
You may also find a traveller's account of early life in your province. In
the nineteenth century these tales were bestsellers and recently a number
have been republished, bringing them within easy access. (See Suggestions for Further Research at the end of this chapter.) Because of
geographic proximity Atlantic Canada has always attracted visitors from
New England. In 1859 an American, Frederic S. Cozzens, wrote:

It is pleasant to visit Nova Scotia in the month of June. Pack up your
flannels and fishing gear, leave behind your prejudices and your

summer clothing, take your trout pole in one hand and a copy of Haliburton in the other and step aboard a Cunarder at Boston. In thirty-six hours you are there . . . ! My word for it, you will not regret the trip.[3]

There follows a fascinating account of a month spent in the province: travelling from Halifax to Sydney with a side trip to Louisbourg—a magnet then as now; the Shubenacadie lakes; the road from Halifax to Windsor; Cape Blomidon and the Gaspereau valley—these are just a random sampling of the locations visited and described. Can you find an early traveller's description of your own community? Tourist guides and related accounts, important as they are from the historical standpoint, serve to focus attention on an acute contemporary problem in Atlantic Canada. The sparse population, lack of industry, comparative absence of pollution, and freedom of access have all worked to the advantage of the tourist industry. As more people are attracted the question of foreign ownership of land has arisen. The matter came to a head in 1972 when Grassy Island, near Canso, a training base in 1745 for New England troops en route to Louisbourg, was about to be sold to a New Englander. Mounting pressure has caused Prince Edward Island to enact legislation

"Actually, we're New England Planters — we missed the boat in 1763."

June 8th 1972: Sale of land to U.S. citizens come under fire.

Cartoon by Chambers courtesy Halifax *Chronicle-Herald*

regulating outside ownership of land. Where do you stand on this controversial issue?

Important as physical features are in the moulding of the character of a community, they must never be studied in isolation. Concerning the rivers of her native New Brunswick, Esther Clark Wright has written:

> A river is something more than a feature of the landscape. Interesting as it may be aesthetically, geographically, geologically, what matters is its relationship to the *people* who come upon it and who live beside it. Who they are, where they come from, what use they make of the river, what kind of communities they develop, what they do to the river, what it does to them—these are the considerations that give purpose and vitality to the study of the river.[4]

Thus, we proceed naturally from a study of the land and related physical features to the legacy of the people. Here we will be concerned, not with individuals (this topic is covered in Chapter 12) but rather with the total impact of such topics as settlement patterns, population trends, and the reasons for emigration from Atlantic Canada. The best source of information is the census record of the Dominion Bureau of Statistics, or, more recently, Statistics Canada. These reports, running to many volumes, are usually found only in larger libraries, yet within the pages of readily available publications such as the *Canada Yearbook*, valuable population data can be gleaned. For the pre-Confederation period, census reports were published as appendices to the Journals of the House of Assembly.

The mere compilation of statistics is not enough. To be meaningful, sufficient data must be collected to permit comparisons over a period of time. A valuable source is Volume IV of the *Census of Canada 1871*, which contains summaries of the census taken at different periods. Nova Scotia is represented by 16 listings covering the years 1671 to 1861; Newfoundland by 10 listings, 1687-1869; New Brunswick by 8 listings, 1695-1861; and Prince Edward Island by 5 listings, 1728-1861. Taking the last-named colony and year, we find tables to indicate the population by age and sex, a record of marriages, births, and deaths, land and cattle, field and domestic products, industries, machinery, carriages, churches, schools, and statistics relating to the fishery. The birthplace of the inhabitants is also given, permitting us to get a glimpse of the ethnic background of the people.

Study carefully the section "Birth Places of the People" taken from the Prince Edward Island census for 1861 (see page 61). On sketch maps of the province indicate the distribution of population by ethnic groups.

What conclusions regarding immigration and settlement can you draw from this information? Compile similar maps for your own section of Atlantic Canada. Another extract from a census return is that found on page 62. Compare the statistics given with data from the most recent New Brunswick census. What deductions can you make on the basis of these comparisons? Do you detect any noticeable differences? Can you account for these? There are, of course, other sources for population and demographic study besides the census. Reports of urban and municipal governments, church and parish records, and records of probate courts can often be utilized in a meaningful way. From the probate records of the last century, for example, one can ascertain the wealthiest people at the time of their death and thereby get some notion of the distribution of wealth in a community. Quite often because of changes in local boundaries it is difficult to obtain precise information, yet often the *exact* number does not matter. What is significant is to know that an area doubled its population in a given number of years or that another suffered a significant decline. Such data will send you scurrying in many directions to discover the reasons behind these statistics.

Beyond the evidence provided by a study of population trends, census reports also reveal information concerning the changing occupational pattern of the people. A study of the Nova Scotia census returns for 1861 provides an interesting glimpse of industrial development more than a century ago. As one might expect, shipbuilding was extremely important and all counties with the exception of Victoria were engaged in this enterprise. However, it comes as something of a surprise to find that Digby, with 24 vessels launched and 33 in the process of being built, led the province. Colchester County boasted 33 grist mills, 123 sawmills, 3 foundries, and 12 tanneries. (Today there are no foundries or tanneries, only a very few sawmills, and but one grist mill at Balmoral, which exists as a museum.) Similar data may be found for other industries. In the same context, nineteenth-century directories are also useful. Through listing the householder's occupation they show evidence of a lifestyle that no longer exists. The same idea was caught by the novelist Thomas Raddall in his word picture of a typical seaport, "somewhere in Atlantic Canada".

... the village once stood pretty much as it stands now, but alive with a smell of new sawed wood in the air, and the sound of hammer and adze, and the clack clack of caulking mallets. They built good ships then. The hulls grew by the waterside with their bowsprits reaching over the road. A blockmaker and three families of coopers carried on business in sheds behind their homes, and a busy sailmaker squatted amongst billows of canvas in the long sail loft. The village blacksmith

made ironwork for vessels three parts of the year and . . . the tall iron
stack of the sawmill poured blue smoke at the sky. . . . [5]

On page 65 you will find an extract from a directory for 1871 that might
well be for the village portrayed by Raddall. All place names and direct
geographic clues have been deleted. From the information presented, can
you locate this community? (One hint—look carefully at the family names
and relate this information to the descriptive note at the beginning.) Study
an early directory for your own district and compare it with one of the
present day. What changes in community life are revealed?

Over the years the land has played a major role in deter-
mining the growth and development of individual communities; in other
instances the same influences have dictated wholesale removal and
resettlement of the people. Newfoundland with its more than 6,000 miles
of coastline has always been characterized by large numbers of small
outport villages that sprang up in response to the developing fishing
industry. While the fishery remains an important element in the
Newfoundland economy, modern trends in the industry, comparative
isolation, and the impossibility of providing modern services prompted
the provincial government to launch in 1953 a major resettlement scheme.
The original plan was superseded in 1965 by a joint federal-provincial
program and to date it has met with reasonable success. However, the
problems are many. They go well beyond finding a new home or job, for
in numerous instances those who move "live in a radically different society. They move from a subsistence economy to an industrial market
economy."[6] To find out more about this plan, read the publications of the
Institute of Social and Economic Research of Memorial University.
Particularly helpful are Noel Iverson and D. R. Matthews: *Communities
in Decline—An Examination of Household Resettlement in Newfoundland*
and Cata Wadel: *Marginal Adaptations and Modernization in Newfoundland*. To what extent are conditions in the other Atlantic provinces similar
to those of Newfoundland?

There is also the question of the outward migration of people, principally to the United States and other parts of Canada. Maritimers are a
restless lot and the explanation for this characteristic has not *always* been
economic, though admittedly this has frequently been a factor. To illustrate: In 1851 Rev. Norman MacLeod sailed from St. Ann's on Cape
Breton Island with 135 emigrants bound for South Australia. Two years
later they settled, not in Australia, but at Waipu, New Zealand, where
their descendants may be found today. During the same period other
groups of Maritimers, attracted by the discovery of gold at Bendigo and

—A thriving village situated at the confluence of river and bay, township of , county of . This place does considerable ship building and exports largely to the United States and West Indies. Western Union Telegraph Co. has an office here. Distant from , 20 miles, fare $1 ; from , 50 miles, fare $2.50. Mail daily. Population about 400.

Allen Wentworth, carter
Armstrong Thomas, ship carpenter
Barr Brock, farmer
Barr Charles, farmer
Barr Henry, farmer
Blackadar Christopher, shoemaker
Boudreau Timothé, sea captain
Brooks Abraham, carpenter
Brooks Cornelius, farmer
Brooks Ephraim, farmer
Brooks Harding, farmer
Brooks James, farmer
Brooks Timothy, sea captain
Burns Albert, sailmaker
Burns Alfred, seaman
Burns Charles, sea captain
Campbell Colin, sen., registrar of deeds
Campbell Colin, storekeeper and ship-owner
Comeau Cerino, farmer
Comeau Cyril, farmer
Comeau Henri, farmer
Comeau Marc, farmer
Comeau Michel, farmer
Comeau Solomon, farmer
Conway Philip, farmer
Cotter Mrs., wid Thomas
Cunningham Seth, farmer
Delap James, farmer
Dexter Ezekiel, lumberman
Dowling Jackson, carpenter
Doty Bennett, farmer
Doty George, farmer
Doty John P., farmer
Doty Joseph, farmer
Doty Pinkney, seaman
Doty Roland, farmer
Doty Tobias, farmer
Falvey Mrs., wid Denis
Falvey Stephen, blacksmith
Filluel rev. P.J., ch of England
Gaudet Frank, farmer
Gaudet Maxime, farmer
Gaudet John, farmer
Gilliland Reuben, ship carpenter
Goodwin F. W., flour mills and merchant
Goodwin John, lumberman
Goodwin William, lumberman
Grant Abraham, sea captain
Grant Alonzo, farmer
Grant David, farmer
Grant George, sea captain
Grant Henry, carpenter
Grant Jeremiah, farmer
Grant John, farmer

Grant William, farmer
Grant William H., seaman
Gray James, farmer
Haney Patrick, farmer
Hankinson Daniel, farmer
Hankinson Elijah, sea captain
Hankinson George D., farmer
Hankinson Gilbert, seaman
Hankinson Joseph, carpenter
Hankinson John, farmer
Hankinson Martin, seaman
Hankinson Reuben, builder
Hankinson Thomas, farmer
Hankinson William, jun., ship owner
Hankinson Wm., sen., J.P., millwright
Healey Aaron, farmer
Healey Moses, farmer
Hogan Edward, J.P., farmer
Hogan Mrs., wid John
Hogan Mrs., wid John, jun.
Hood A. M.
Hood Richard, sea captain
Hoyt Alexander D., hotelkeeper
Hudson Harris, caulker
Jones Alpheus, surveyor
Jones C. Dwight, of C. P. Jones & Sons, postmaster and telegraph operator
Jones Charles
Jones Charles H.
Jones C. P., & Sons, storekeepers
Jones C. P., of C. P. Jones & Sons
Jones John S., surveyor
Jones Norman, storekeeper
Jones Richard W., farmer
Jones St Clair, shipowner and merchant
Jones Wm. W., of C. P. Jones & Sons
Journeay Edward, carpenter
Kinney Abraham, farmer
Kinney David S., jun, farmer
Kinney David S., sen., farmer
Kinney Jacob, farmer
Kinney John, farmer
Kinney Joseph, farmer
Kinney Thomas, farmer
Lent Gilbert, farmer
Lent William, blacksmith
Lewis Abner, sea captain
Lewis Abraham, farmer
Lewis Charles, sea captain
Lewis George, farmer
Lewis Thomas, farmer
McCrum James B., tailor
Marshall Anthony, farmer
Marshall Robert, farmer
Marshall Richard, sea captain
Marshall William, farmer
Melan John, farmer
Melan John, farmer
Melançon Cyril, farmer
Melançon Henry, jun., farmer
Melançon Henry, sen., farmer
Melançon Joseph, farmer
Melançon Stephen, farmer
Melançon Stephen, sen., farmer
Montague Michael, wheelwright
Moody Henry, seaman
Morse James, cabinetmaker
Mullen Charlton, blacksmith

Ballarat, undertook the long voyage to Australia. Samuel Napier from Bathurst, New Brunswick, together with his brother Charles, discovered the 145-pound "Napier Nugget". Lured by these and other discoveries, many emigrants settled permanently "down under". Joseph Doane of Barrington, Nova Scotia, became mayor of Ballarat and achieved fame as an architect of many churches in the area. Read Evelyn Richardson's "A Voyage to Australia" in *Nova Scotia Historical Quarterly*, II, 3 (September 1972): 3-15, for more information on Doane. Try to discover if people from your community participated in the Australian, Californian, or Klondike gold rushes. Did you know that a native of Merigomish, Nova Scotia, Robert Henderson, was one of the first to discover the Klondike gold fields?

Closer to home, for many years there were more Newfoundlanders in Boston than in the city of St. John's and the same could be said of other communities both large and small in all four provinces. Again, one has only to refer to the map to find an explanation for this migration. During much of the nineteenth century Boston was the metropolitan centre for Atlantic Canada and even today most Maritimers have relatives in New England. Recently, the outward migration has tended to concentrate on central Canada, a point illustrated in the movie *Goin' Down the Road* and in the works of Newfoundland-born playwright David French. For years this exodus has been a matter of concern and comment to editorial writers, politicians, and statisticians. People have become so preoccupied with the detrimental effect of emigration that all perspective has been lost. A distinguished émigré from Atlantic Canada, Charles Bruce—poet, author, and newspaper executive—once wrote:

> There is a school of thought that deplores this kind of movement, regrets the fact that these provinces have not been able to keep all their children home. Without doubt, within limits, this is a valid point. No doubt also there were gentlemen in England who viewed with alarm the colonizing voyages of Raleigh and Penn. It is chiefly a story of expansion, not exodus. There is a side to this migration that should not be forgotten. A while ago I found a school register for the year 1834, thirty years before Tupper brought in free schools in Nova Scotia. Twenty house-holders were listed, along with their children. What caught my eye was this: most of the families had sent offshoots to establish the family and name in other parts of Canada and the world. But, with one exception, every surname is still there, stencilled on the mail boxes of Rural Route One.[7]

An important "spin-off" from population study is the consideration of minority groups. New Brunswick has Canada's largest Danish community. Where is it located and what is its historical background? Newfoundland, often regarded as the private preserve of the Irish and the English, has a noticeable proportion of Scots in its racial background. Interestingly enough many of these (located in the Codroy valley) were immigrants, not from Scotland, but from Cape Breton. Prince Edward Island had a significant intake of immigrants from the West Country of England (Somerset, Devon, and Cornwall). This fact raises the question: why were they attracted to Prince Edward Island?

One minority group that has been consistently ignored is the black population of Nova Scotia and New Brunswick. Look through the textbooks now in use in your school. In all probability you will find few references to this important segment of our population. For this reason the heritage of the black people of Atlantic Canada has been selected as a case study. A similar investigatory approach may be taken with other racial groups. Where did the blacks come from? Over the years there have been five distinct migrations to Atlantic Canada. Although we have evidence of a few blacks before 1783, their history in this region dates from the American Revolution. At that time two groups left the United States for Nova Scotia. Many white Loyalists "owned" slaves and brought these with them as a matter of course. In addition, there were sizeable numbers of Free Blacks, or former slaves who escaped servitude during the war. One squad known as the "Black Pioneers" won praise for their conduct and bravery on the British side. A third group, and one of the most interesting, were the so-called Black Maroons who arrived in Halifax from the West Indies in 1796. However, they remained a mere four years, leaving in 1800 for Sierra Leone to join some 1,200 Nova Scotian blacks who had earlier, in 1792, migrated to form a new settlement on the west coast of Africa. Their leader and the man largely responsible for this migration was Thomas Peters. A former slave in Wilmington, North Carolina, Peters served with distinction in the Black Pioneers. Investigate the career of this remarkable man by referring to *A History of Sierra Leone* by Christopher Fyfe and you will learn why Peters is regarded as one of the founding fathers of that part of West Africa. Next in point of time were some 1,500 to 2,000 black refugees from the War of 1812. Mainly from the Chesapeake Bay region, they eventually located near Halifax.* Then, of course, there were the fugitive slaves who fled from the United States to British North America during the years preceding

---

*Check Bruce Fergusson: *A Documentary Study of the Establishment of Negroes in Nova Scotia* (Halifax: Public Archives of Nova Scotia, 1948) for details surrounding this particular segment of the black population of Nova Scotia. Also, John N. Grant: "The 1821 Emigration of Black Nova Scotians to Trinidad", *Nova Scotia Historical Quarterly* II, 3 (Sept. 1972): 283-92.

the Civil War. The majority of these settled in Upper Canada, although a few filtered through to the Maritimes. Lastly, there are the more recent immigrants from the West Indies and the various countries of Africa.

Prejudice knows no boundaries and the treatment of the black population of Atlantic Canada is not an inspiring story; yet it must not be ignored. It is important for those of black origin to discover something of their past. To learn, for example, that highly civilized black societies existed in Africa well before Atlantic Canada was even discovered; that blacks did not accept slavery and that thousands died for their freedom; that blacks have made a valuable contribution to the development of the region; that black men have been outstanding explorers, soldiers, authors, artists, sportsmen, musicians, and scientists. There is, however, a danger in this latter approach. The foremost historian of the black race in Canada, Robin Winks, has written:

> Anyone engaged in research into Negro history is always in danger of being submerged in either a catalogue of grievances or a litany of accomplishments. Congratulatory references to the first Negro V.C. in Canada, William Hall of Hantsport, N.S., or the first Negro lawyer in Canada, Delos Davis of Sydney; to the first Negro policewoman in Canada, Rosa Fortune of Annapolis Royal, or to New Brunswick's Negro hockey player, Willie O'Ree, and the jazz pianist Oscar Peterson, are comforting but irrelevant.[8]

More to the point is an in-depth study of the totality of black history and culture as an integral part of the local history of Atlantic Canada.*

A study of the black heritage is equally important for those who spring from other races. If one has never lived in their situation and faced the inevitable discrimination, attention to black history can lead, hopefully, to a heightened awareness of the problems of a minority. In this study, some time may profitably be devoted to an investigation of the nineteenth-century court battles over the question of slavery. See *The Blacks in New Brunswick* by W. A. Spray and *The Blacks in Canada: A History* by Robin Winks for details. There were significant efforts on the part of many to suppress slavery. When Dr. James MacGregor, a Presbyterian missionary, arrived in Pictou in 1788 he was astonished to find evidence

---

*In addition to books already mentioned consult Christopher Fyfe: *Sierra Leone Inheritance* (London: Oxford University Press, 1964); William Katz: *Eyewitness: The Negro in American History* (New York: Pitman Publishing Corporation, 1967); Basil Davidson: *The African Past* (Boston: Little, Brown, 1964); Donald H. Clairmont and Dennis W. Magill: *Nova Scotia Blacks: An Historical and Structural Overview* (Halifax: Dalhousie University, 1970. An abridged version may be found in *Social Studies Review*, III, 2 (February 1973): 2-34, published by Nova Scotia Teachers' Union, Halifax).

of slavery in the new colony. Not only that, but a fellow clergyman, Rev. Daniel Cock of Truro, owned slaves! MacGregor made public his views in an open letter *To a Clergyman urging him to set free a Black Girl he held in Slavery*. By this act he succeeded in focussing public attention both on slavery and on the rights of the black people. During the same period there was a settlement of Quakers at Beaver Harbour, Charlotte County, New Brunswick, that proclaimed "No Slave Masters Are Admitted". It is the opinion of Professor Spray that this settlement was probably the only one in British North America where, at this time, slavery was strictly prohibited. Lastly, it should be noted:

> The Negro runs through Maritime folklore and place names, from Bog, back of Charlottetown, to Negro Island off Port Clyde, from Bible Hill in Truro to Elm Hill near Queenstown. He has become part of the general Maritime story in the person of Maurice Ruddick, the "singing miner" of the Springhill disaster of 1958, in Thomas McCulloch's *Stepsure Letters*. . . . His imprint is present in the daily speech of white as well as black Nova Scotians, and it is deeply rooted in Nova Scotian folklore and folksongs.[9]

We can never fully understand how a community has developed historically unless we have a knowledge of the legacy imparted by both the land and the people. In broader terms, we cannot begin to comprehend the whole of Atlantic Canada without reference to the physical features that have so profoundly influenced its way of life. Of Newfoundland it has been written, "the island is a far more northern place than its location on the globe would suggest."[10] The comment holds true for the remainder of the region, and many sections have qualities in common with parts of Scotland and Scandinavia. This may be seen not only in the coastline, climate, and vegetation but in the stark reality of life on the fringe of the North Atlantic. The people, too, have played their part. Marks of speech and racial traits from such varied sources as Normancy and Brittany, Devon and Cornwall, County Cork and Sutherlandshire are deeply ingrained in the culture of the area. The land and the people have provided a colourful backdrop for local history in Atlantic Canada.

FOR READING AND REFERENCE

A. Atlases

Any standard school atlas, e.g., Pleva, E. G., and Inch, Spencer (eds.): *Canadian Oxford Desk Atlas*. Toronto: Oxford University Press, 1972.

Atlas and Gazetteer of Canada. Ottawa: Information Canada, 1969.

BURPEE, LAWRENCE J.: *An Historical Atlas of Canada*. Toronto: Thomas Nelson Ltd., 1927.

CHALMERS, J. W.; ECCLES, W. J.; AND FULLARD, H.: *Historical Atlas of Canada*. Toronto: Moyer Division, Vilas Industries, 1966.

DEACON, G. E. R. (ed.): *Oceans: An Atlas History of Man's Exploration of the Deep*. Toronto: Thomas Allen, 1962.

KERR, D. G. G.: *A Historical Atlas of Canada*. Toronto: Thomas Nelson Ltd., 1961.

PEARSON, R. E.: *Atlas of St. John's*. St. John's: Memorial University, 1969.

ROE, FREDERIC B.: *Atlas of the Maritime Provinces*. Halifax: Roe Brothers, 1879; and *Illustrated Historical Atlas of Prince Edward Island*, Belleville: Mika Publishing Co., 1972.

N.B. Topographic maps are available from: Canada Map Office, 615 Booth St., Ottawa, Ont.

Geological maps are available from: Geological Survey of Canada, 601 Booth St., Ottawa, Ont.

B. General

BLAIR, C. L., AND SIMPSON, R. I.: *The Canadian Landscape: Map and Air Photo Interpretation*. Toronto: Copp Clark, 1967.

CAMU, PIERRE, et al.: *Economic Geography of Canada*. Toronto: Macmillan of Canada, 1964.

CHEVRIER, EMILE, AND AITKENS, D. F. W.: *Topographic Map and Air Photo Interpretation*. Toronto: Macmillan of Canada, 1970.

GENTILCORE, R. L.: *Canada's Changing Geography*. Scarborough: Prentice-Hall, 1967.

HARVEY, E. ROY: *Sydney, Nova Scotia: An Urban Study*. Toronto: Clarke, Irwin, 1971.

INCH, R. S., AND STONE, W. G.: *The Physical Environment*. Toronto: McGraw-Hill Ryerson, 1972.

INNIS, DONALD Q.: *Canada: A Geographic Study*. Toronto: McGraw-Hill, 1966.

IRVING, R. M. (ed.): *Readings in Canadian Geography*. Toronto: Holt, Rinehart and Winston, 1968.

PACKER, ROBERT W., et al.: *Workbook in Introductory Physical Geography*.

Toronto: McGraw-Hill, 1966.

PUTNAM, DONALD F., AND PUTNAM, R. G.: *Canada: A Regional Analysis.* Toronto: J. M. Dent Ltd., 1970 (86-122 on Atlantic Canada).

SCARFE, N. V., et al.: *A New Geography of Canada.* Toronto: W. J. Gage Ltd., 1964.

WATSON, J. WREFORD: *Canada—Its Problems and Prospects.* Toronto: Longmans, 1968.

C. Historical Geography

CAMPBELL, D., AND MACLEAN, R. A.: *Beyond the Atlantic Roar.* Toronto: McClelland and Stewart, 1974 (Carleton Library).

CLARK, ANDREW HILL: *Three Centuries and the Island.* Toronto: University of Toronto Press, 1959.

———: *Acadia: The Geography of Early Nova Scotia to 1760.* Madison: University of Wisconsin Press, 1968.

EAST, W. GORDON: *The Geography Behind History.* New York: A. W. Norton and Co., 1965.

LANGMAN, R. C.: *Patterns of Settlement in Southern Ontario.* Toronto: McClelland and Stewart, 1971. (Useful for comparative studies.)

MACPHERSON, ALAN: *The Atlantic Provinces: Studies in Canadian Geography.* Toronto: University of Toronto Press, 1973.

MANNION, JOHN J.: *Irish Settlements in Eastern Canada.* Toronto: University of Toronto Press, 1974.

SEBERT, L. M.: *Every Square Inch: The Story of Canada's Topographical Mapping.* Ottawa: Information Canada, 1970.

THOMSON, D. W.: *Men and Meridians: The History of Mapping and Surveying in Canada.* Ottawa: Information Canada, 1969.

D. Demographic and Population Studies

CLARKE, JOHN I.: *Population Geography.* London: Pergamon Press, 1965.

GEORGE, M. V.: *Internal Migration in Canada: Demographic Analysis.* Ottawa: Information Canada, 1970.

GRIFFIN, PAUL (ed.): *Geography of Population.* Palo Alto: Fearon Publishers, 1969.

HOLLINGSWORTH, T. H.: *Historical Demography.* Ithaca: Cornell University Press, 1969.

MONKHOUSE, F. J., AND WILKINSON, H. R.: "Population Maps and Diagrams", *Maps and Diagrams.* London: Methuen, 1952.

THOMPSON WARREN S.: *Population Problems.* New York: McGraw-Hill, 1953.

ZELINSKY, WILBUR: *A Prologue to Population Geography.* Englewood Cliffs: Prentice-Hall, 1968.

Of particular importance are the studies of early census records currently being issued by the Provincial Archives of New Brunswick. See Robert F. Fellows: *The New Brunswick Census of 1851*. Fredericton: Public Archives New Brunswick (Albert and Carleton counties).

The New Brunswick Canada Studies Project, "The Americans in our Midst", developed and written by Audrey J. Barss, is useful in its own right and as a model for others to follow.

SUGGESTIONS FOR FURTHER RESEARCH

1. New Brunswick is a land of rivers—the Saint John, Kennebecasis, Petit-codiac, Restigouche, Miramichi, and many more. Select one of the rivers of this province (or your own province) and develop an historical case study showing the impact of the river on local development. For example, if you select the Miramichi, questions to consider might include: How did the river affect the growth of Chatham and surrounding area? Did the topography of the river have any bearing on the development of the town? How have the river and its tributaries influenced settlement in Northumberland County? (Books by Esther Clark Wright on the rivers of New Brunswick will prove helpful in this project.)

2. Foreign ownership of land (particularly in coastal areas) has become a major issue in Atlantic Canada. As a means of analysing both sides of this question, arrange a class debate on the pros and cons of the issue. Before embarking on such a debate you should read Howard T. Walden's *Anchorage Northeast* (New York: William Morrow and Co., 1971). Check also the report of the Prince Edward Island Royal Commission on Land Ownership and Land Use.

3. (a) Compile a table or graph showing the rise or fall in population (by county for Nova Scotia, New Brunswick, and Prince Edward Island; by electoral district for Newfoundland). Use the census data, e.g., 1971, 1961, 1951, 1941, etc., and go back as far as possible. Which counties or districts have experienced the greatest decline and the greatest rise in population density over the years? What reasons can you give for these changes?

   (b) Obtain the topographic map for your area and compile a list of physical characteristics that have had some bearing on its evolution. If possible, compare the topographic map with an earlier version from an historical atlas. What significant changes can you detect?

4. Travel books have always been popular and present-day reading tastes reflect this continuing trend. Make a comparative study of a particular section of Atlantic Canada "then" and "now" by matching a nineteenth-century traveller's account with a contemporary counterpart. Examples:

Newfoundland
(a) Addison Brown: *Newfoundland Journeys* (New York: Carlton Press, 1971). A résumé of journeys made by visitors to Newfoundland over the years.
(b) Harold Horwood: *Newfoundland* (Toronto: Macmillan of Canada, 1969).

Prince Edward Island
(a) D. C. Harvey, (ed.): *Journeys to the Island of St. John* (Toronto: Macmillan of Canada, paperback edition, 1972).
(b) Helen Champion: *Over on the Island* (Toronto: Ryerson Press, 1939).

New Brunswick and Nova Scotia
(a) F. S. Cozzens: *Acadia—A Month with the Bluenoses* (New York: Derby and Jackson, 1859).
(b) Joshua Marsden: *The Narrative of a Mission to Nova Scotia and New Brunswick* (Archon Reprint, 1966, originally published in 1816).
(c) A. L. Spedon: *Rambles Among the Bluenoses* (Montreal: Lovell and Co., 1863). A tour of New Brunswick and Nova Scotia.
(d) W. R. Bird: *Off Trail in Nova Scotia* (Toronto: Ryerson Press, 1956). *These Are the Maritimes* (Toronto: Ryerson Press, 1959).
(e) Michael Collie: *New Brunswick* (Toronto: Macmillan of Canada, 1974).
(f) M. G. Parks (ed.): *Western and Eastern Rambles: Travel Sketches of Nova Scotia* (Toronto: University of Toronto Press, 1973).

6. The Amerindian Heritage

The local history of many communities in Atlantic Canada might well begin with the heritage of the native people. An in-depth study of Amerindian culture is important in ways far beyond mere knowledge of their lifestyle and contribution to civilization, significant as these may be. To interpret their history in an honest and responsible way it becomes imperative to take a fresh look at the past. It will, in effect, mean coming to terms with the history of the region as it actually was, not as we may have imagined it to be. In the process, you will learn something of the attitudes and values that characterized a way of life far different from that of the white race. To explore the Amerindian heritage is to place the total history of Atlantic Canada in perspective.

For too long many writers have tended either to ignore the Amerindians, or, what is probably worse, to play up selected aspects of their culture at the expense of all that is positive. In part this attitude, which unfortunately still exists, is traceable to a group of late-nineteenth-century historians and authors who tended to portray Amerindians in an unfavourable light. Even their vocabulary was loaded. Words such as "savages", "scalp-hunters", and "the happy hunting ground" (a fictitious invention of the white man), and phrases like "Indian giver" and "Indian devil", succeeded in reinforcing the picture of a sub-human species. Authorities have suggested that if we could eliminate or minimize but five words: squaw, halfbreed, savage, massacre, and murder, it would reduce in large measure the incidence of bias in modern textbooks. This does not mean that we shut our eyes to the events of history—murders and massacres there were, but to apply these to the

Amerindian while neglecting the atrocities of the white race is to falsify the record. Hollywood westerns and certain television dramas have added insult to injury by portraying the Indian as the villain, the proverbial loser, or as a character introduced for comic relief. Search the textbooks currently in use in your school and look for examples of bias directed toward Indians and the Innuit or Eskimo people.*

It was the famous American historian Francis Parkman who reached the following conclusion:

It is obvious that the Indian mind never seriously occupied itself with any of the higher themes of thought. The beings of its belief are not impersonations of the forces of nature, the courses of human destiny, or the movements of human intellect, will and passion. In the midst of nature, the Indian knew nothing of her laws. . . . His intractable spirit of independence, and the pride which forbids him to be an imitator, reinforce but too strongly that savage lethargy of mind from which it is so hard to rouse him. No race, perhaps, ever offered greater difficulties to those laboring for its improvement.[1]

Since many later textbooks merely paraphrased Parkman, these extraordinary ideas, through repetition, became deeply implanted. Further, what has been omitted in the history of Atlantic Canada from the viewpoint of the native people is as much in need of correction as the typical textbook portrayal.

Recent archaeological research has revealed a span of at least 10,000 years so far as Amerindian culture in Atlantic Canada is concerned. (See Chapter 7 for details on this point.) Yet even here a note of warning must be struck. In years gone by "souvenir" hunters have casually disinterred Indian dead and destroyed camping sites in an endless search for relics. Equally at fault and far more destructive have been

. . . the road builders, the land levelers, the housing contractors, the dam builders, and the outright vandals. For every skeleton that has reached the security—if not the dignity [of a museum or anthropological storage room] easily ten thousand have been ground under bulldozers, floated away under reservoirs, or ended up with skulls grinning on mantelpieces as candleholders or bookends.[2]

Fortunately, serious archaeological research in Atlantic Canada is in safer hands today. Trained personnel from various universities and the National Museum in Ottawa are responsible for most excavations. These are undertaken only with the most scholarly intent and with full respect

*Note that "Innuit" is gradually replacing the word "Eskimo".

for the understandable sensitivity of the native people. None the less, it is easy to see how thoughtless actions in the past have provoked Professor Harvey McCue, an Ojibway on the faculty of Trent University, to cry out: "*Enough* indignities have been suffered by our ancestors in the name of research."[3] In fact, some Indian activist groups have suggested, half seriously, that they turn the tables on white archaeologists and anthropologists who have been studying them for years. Thus, a group of Mohawks have hinted that they might apply to the Canada Council for a grant to dig up one of the white pioneer cemeteries in their neighbourhood. Whether serious or not, they made their point. For reasons such as those mentioned above, most governments now regulate archaeological excavation. Should you discover a campsite or burial ground in your area, *never* undertake to explore it on your own.

As a starting-point in our assessment of the impact of the original inhabitants on local history, we shall examine in brief the major facets of Beothuck, Naskapi, Innuit (Eskimo), Micmac, and Malecite cultures. This will be followed by an estimate of their contribution to everyday life in Atlantic Canada and elsewhere.

There can be little doubt that one of the most unfortunate chapters in the history of Atlantic Canada concerns the Beothucks of Newfoundland. Because of their wholesale extermination we have little by way of folklore or legend with which to piece together their development. Dubbed the "Red Indians" by the first explorers because they smeared their bodies with red ochre or oxide of iron, they were responsible in part for the widespread use of this nickname. In actual fact, it is believed that the red ochre was applied for religious reasons or, in more practical vein, because it warded off insects. In many respects the Beothucks resembled their neighbours on the mainland; however, there were certain points of difference. Their birch-bark canoes marked a departure in that each gunwale was shaped like a crescent moon. They did not make pottery but cooked their food in birch-bark containers. The Beothucks led a nomadic life, coming to the coast in the spring to catch salmon and to pursue the seal fishery, and then, as winter approached, retreating to the wooded areas of the interior. By the late-eighteenth century the Beothucks were concentrated in the Exploits River area of central Newfoundland. This portion of the island was comparatively isolated and there was less danger of surprise attack by Europeans.

The number of Beothucks was never large and from the early days of the colony they were systematically shot by visiting fishermen. The reason, when it was given, was always the same. The Beothucks were casual in their approach to property and frequently used supplies and stores cached by fishermen and traders. This fact illustrates in dramatic fashion the clash of two cultures. Possessions, except for very personal items, were held in common by the Beothucks and they were simply unable to comprehend the European attitude toward property. As a result, they were hunted down and shot in reprisal. Further detail regarding the extermination of the Beothucks may be found in "The People Who Were Murdered for Fun" by Harold Horwood in *Maclean's Canada: Portrait of a Country* (Toronto: McClelland and Stewart, 1960), 137-40. For interesting contemporary accounts of Beothuck life see the following publications: (a) C. W. Townsend (ed.): *Captain Cartwright and his Labrador Journal* (Boston: Dana Estes and Co., 1911). During the late-eighteenth century Captain Cartwright made six expeditions to Labrador. In 1792 he wrote an account of his experiences which contain observations on Indian and Innuit life in Newfoundland-Labrador. (b) David Buchan, a British naval officer, made a trip to the Exploits River area in 1810. His account is in J. P. Howley: *The Beothucks or Red Indians* (Cambridge: At the University Press, 1915). (c) William Epps Cormack, a native Newfoundlander, was the first white man to travel across the island on foot. The account of the journey completed in 1822 contains much information on the last days of the Beothucks. See F. A. Bruton (ed.): *A Journey Across the Island of Newfoundland* (New York: Longmans Green, 1928).

In the final liquidation, Micmacs armed by white men played a part. Disease took its toll, for the Beothucks—like so many Indians—were particularly susceptible to tuberculosis. In 1829 the last survivor died in captivity and today the Provincial Museum in St. John's provides us with one of the few opportunities to study remnants of the Beothuck culture. A visitor to this museum has written:

A sick feeling comes over me as I walk through this place. There is so little left of a once proud people. A people that once owned the whole of Newfoundland. The land was rich in game and beauty. They were free to go as they pleased. I like to believe that they loved as we love; were proud and ambitious, as we, the white race, are. But yet, there was not enough room for both to live in harmony side by side. We came to this country and completely destroyed all there was of Beothuck culture. Now we console ourselves in the fact that we have done our best to bring all that was Beothuck, under this roof. We can never be proud of the fact that all we have left to remind us of these people are a few artifacts. All that is left of the Beothucks could be placed, with the exception of the display cases, on the rear seat of a small automobile. My feelings can best be expressed in the title of a popular song sung by Peggy Lee: *Is That All There Is?*[4]

The Naskapi Indians and the Labrador Innuit barely escaped the fate of the Beothucks. The Naskapi (close relatives of the Montagnais of north-central Quebec) roamed the Labrador peninsula west of a line drawn from the point where the Quebec-Labrador boundary veers westward (some fifty miles north of Blanc Sablon) to Ungava Bay. East of this approximate limit and hugging the indented coastline. the Innuit held sway. Although the latter have been traditionally pictured as both friendly and peaceful, Admiral Sir Hugh Palliser, governor of Newfoundland-Labrador, described them in 1788 as "the most savage people in the world". Certainly, from the viewpoint of the fishermen who frequented the area, both Naskapi and Innuit were a nuisance as they frequently "borrowed" supplies stored on land. Thus, it was not uncommon for white fishermen and traders to shoot them on sight. A further factor in reducing the number of original inhabitants was a long-time feud between Indian and Innuit. Professor Vaino Tanner, whose extensive field investigations in the late 1930s made him an authority on Labrador, has written: " . . . even in these deserted places where mankind is a rarity, racial enmity to the death prevailed for a long time."[5] Today, the total Indian and Innuit population of Labrador is estimated at approximately 1,000.

Probably the one factor that spelled survival for both of these groups was the arrival in the 1770s of the Moravian missionaries (or United Brethren—*Unitas Fratrum* as they are sometimes known). The Moravians, already established a half-century earlier in Greenland, were allocated land by the British government. This was an unusual procedure, as land-granting and settlement were strictly prohibited to protect the monopoly of English fishing interests. The Moravians " . . . saw their venture as an attempt to convert . . . the Eskimo; the British government saw it as a means of converting into loyal British subjects the natives so that they might be an asset rather than a hindrance to the trade and fishery there."[6] Steadily, the Moravian missions spread north and south from their first settlement at Nain in 1771; they established Okak in 1775, Hopedale in 1782, Hebron in 1830, Zoar in 1865, Ramah in 1871, Makkovik in 1900, and Killinek in 1904. Today, all but three have been closed and the mission work consolidated at Hopedale, Nain, and Makkovik. Can you locate these mission outposts on a map? Why was it necessary to close so many in recent years? At Hopedale some of the timber and stone structures erected in the eighteenth century still stand. In part of the mission complex an attempt is being made to establish a small museum to exhibit items illustrating early days on the Labrador.

The Moravian role in the development of Labrador has not been without its critics; however, most authorities agree with Professor Tanner that their work is "one of the most remarkable gains of civilization" on the coast and a "monument to Christian mission history".[7] Two major reasons may be cited for this success. The Moravians came with a wealth of experience gained in a similar situation in Greenland, and their first leader, Jens Haven, was able to communicate with the Innuit in their native tongue. From the beginning, great stress was placed on language development, and the annual mission reports are filled with tales of efforts to teach reading and writing to the Innuit people. Although today much of the social-service aspect of the Moravian work has been taken over by government, the missionaries remain. As in the eighteenth century there is still great stress on making certain that religious material is translated into the Innuit language. Dr. F. W. Peacock, a veteran of thirty-six years as a Moravian missionary on the Labrador and now a research fellow in the Department of Linguistics at Memorial University, is translating the Book of Psalms into Innuit. He has also completed a dictionary in the same language. In an encyclopedia or religious reference work, see if you can locate more information on the Moravians. Their annual reports from 1752 onward form a consecutive history of Labrador—many of these may be consulted in the Newfoundland Room of the Memorial University Library. Read E. E. Gray's *Wilderness Christians* (Ithaca: Cornell University Press, 1956) for an account of Moravian work in another part of Canada. Harold Horwood's novel *White Eskimo* (Toronto: Doubleday, 1972) deals critically with the impact of the missionaries.

The lifestyle of both the Naskapi Indians and the Labrador Innuit has been conditioned over the centuries by the harsh environment in which they live. Although probably the first inhabitants of North America to have contact with the white race, they have been less touched by outside influences than, for example, the Micmacs and Malecites of the Maritime provinces. The reason for this can be summarized in two words—isolation and survival. To exist in the sub-Arctic tundra requires a high degree of adaptability and inventiveness—qualities possessed by these people* and required of anyone who lives there. Both Naskapi and Innuit were and are nomadic and live almost exclusively by hunting and fishing. Few readers of this page have ever visited northern Labrador; a description by anthropologist Douglas Leechman (who spent an *Eskimo Summer* on the islands at the tip of the peninsula) will convey to you an impression of an area described by Jacques Cartier as "the land God gave Cain".

It's a new world, not only physically, but also mentally. Physically, because it's a world stripped to the bare essentials, rock and water.

---

*A comprehensive account of the Labrador native is to be found in Vaino Tanner: *Outlines of the Geography, Life and Customs of Newfoundland-Labrador*, vol. II (Cambridge: At the University Press, 1947), and Diamond Jenness: *Indians of Canada* (Ottawa: Information Canada, 1967).

There is little else. Vegetation, that decent covering of Mother Earth, which we take so for granted, is unimportant or, at least, inconspicuous, often invisible at any distance over a hundred yards. There is the land, harsh and bare, with its ponds and streams; there is the sea, with its rocks and islands; and there is nothing else, save ice on the sea, and snow and glaciers on the land. It's a new world mentally, too. Danger and courage are the key notes. Danger, because one lives close to the elemental forces of nature. Though it is seldom mentioned, there is danger in one's daily travels—danger from storms at sea, from rocks awash, from tide rips and swirling currents, from cranky boats and balky motors, from wounded bears. There is danger from winter blizzards, from the penetrating frost, from starvation, from accidents which, often trivial in themselves, may leave one, helpless, to die only a few miles from mankind and safety. And there is courage, courage none the less heroic because it is never spoken of by the men who live down North. Courage to face dangers known and unknown, courage which leads men to venture as a daily habit, as a matter of course, where we, used to the shields and safe-guards of civilization, would go only under the spur of the most desperate necessity.[8]

The Micmacs originally occupied a large portion of Atlantic Canada—present-day Nova Scotia, Prince Edward Island, and a portion of the north shore of New Brunswick. The Malecites lived principally along the Saint John River, although their territory stretched westward to include a portion of the state of Maine. Both Micmacs and Malecites, who resembled each other in many ways, were of the Algonquin family. The major point of difference between the two, aside from language, stems from the fact that the Malecites practised a form of agriculture. In cultivating the soil they used an implement made of hard wood, not unlike a spade, and their method of growing corn and pumpkins (as described by Champlain) was little different from that of the present day. According to Malecite legend "the proper time to plant corn is when the maple leaf is as big as a squirrel's foot."[9]

Like other native peoples neither Micmacs nor Malecites lived in permanent villages, but changed location with the seasons. During spring, summer, and early autumn they migrated to coastal regions where clams and fish abounded. Here an ingenious method, using torches and spears, was developed for capturing salmon and eels. In the words of one observer: "Two men go together in a canoe at night; the one sits in the stern and paddles and the other stands with a spear over a flambeau of birchbark placed in the head of the canoe. The fish attracted by the light come in numbers around the canoe and the spearman then takes the opportunity of striking them."[10] (It is of interest that certain tribes in British Columbia have employed similar methods, and that this form of night fishing became the subject of a famous painting by Paul Kane.) Micmac and Malecite encampments were usually located near sources of fresh water and favoured inland sites were often on rivers below waterfalls, or at tide head where fishing was best. Coastal sites called for a level place near the water, a good beach for canoes, and a source of spring water. The reconstruction of a sixteenth-century Micmac village (on an authentic site) at Rocky Point, Prince Edward Island, is well worth a visit as it exhibits many of these features. The early missionary Father Pierre Biard has left us the following description of a Malecite encampment:

> Arrived at a certain place, the first thing they do is to build a fire and arrange their camp, which they have finished in an hour or two; often in half an hour. The women go into the woods and bring back some poles which are stuck into the ground in a circle around the fire and at the top are interlaced, in a form of a pyramid, so that they come together directly over the fire. Upon the poles they throw some skins, matting or bark. At the foot of the poles, under the skins, they put their baggage. All the space around the fire is strewn with soft boughs of the fir tree so they will not feel the dampness of the ground; over these boughs are thrown some mats or sealskins as soft as velvet; upon these they stretch themselves around the fire with their heads resting upon their baggage and what no one would believe, they are very warm in there around that little fire, even in the greatest rigors of the winter. They do not camp except near some good water and in an attractive location.[11]

Two interesting accounts of Indian life in the seventeenth century were written by Nicolas Denys who came to the region in 1632 and by John Gyles who lived as a captive of the Malecites in 1689. Denys comments at length on the Micmac way of life, skill in handcrafts, and adaptation to their environment. The chief weapon of the hunt was the bow and arrow, although use was also made of traps and snares. Transportation was provided by the canoe in summer and toboggans and snowshoes in winter. They were fond of games and developed their own brand of football. A very popular "gentler pleasure" was *altestagen*, a form of gambling played with bowl, dice, and counting-sticks. Birch bark was put to many uses. In addition to providing cover for wigwams, containers of all kinds were developed from this material. Pots or troughs for boiling water were made from wood, the water being heated by red-hot stones placed inside. The skin and fur clothing noted by Denys was typical of the native people of this period.

Our knowledge of the Micmacs and Malecites has been greatly enhanced by recent archaeological discoveries. (See Chapter 7.) A burial
site of the seventeenth century, discovered near Pictou, Nova Scotia in
1955, revealed much information regarding trading habits, native crafts,
and burial customs. What makes this site (and another at Portland Point,
New Brunswick) significant is that the burial of an important person was
the occasion of a potlatch, or festival, when the Indians deposited in the
grave many of their important possessions. Numerous artifacts (e.g., birch
bark with stitching holes along the edge, pieces of bear and beaver skin,
samples of weaving, and implements of all kinds) survived in part because
of the protection afforded by copper kettles obtained from French traders.
These were of great importance in the life of the Micmacs and were
believed to be endowed with a spirit of their own. The New Brunswick
Museum in Saint John as well as a private museum at Pictou provide a
remarkable collection of artifacts from these excavations.

Much has been written about the cruelty of the Micmacs and Malecites
in warfare. This was particularly true after their alliance with the French
who gave them every encouragement to raid New England settlements.
What is forgotten is that the late-seventeenth and early-eighteenth
centuries were anything but "gentle ages". Both French and English were
known to practise public torture. As for scalping, it is doubtful if this was
practised by the Indians *before* the advent of the white man. A New
Brunswick historian, W. O. Raymond, has placed the question in more
accurate context:

> But while cruel to their enemies, and even at times cruel to their wives,
> the Indians were by no means without their redeeming features. They
> were a modest and virtuous race and it is quite remarkable that with
> all the blood-thirstiness in the New England wars there is no instance
> on record of the slightest rudeness to the person of any female captive.
> ... Nor were they without a certain sense of justice. ... The unfortunate
> conduct of some of the Governors of New England was largely respon-
> sible for [their] hostility to the English. Towards the French they were
> from the first disposed to be friendly, and when de Monts, Champlain
> and Poutrincourt arrived [in 1604], they found awaiting them the
> representatives of a race of unknown antiquity, of interesting language,
> traditions and customs who welcomed them with outward manifesta-
> tions of delight and formed with them an alliance that remained
> unbroken throughout the prolonged struggle between the rival powers
> for supremacy in Acadia.[12]

Many aspects of Amerindian culture have become so firmly engrained
and so much a part of our everyday life that we tend to disregard the

extent of this contribution. What follows is a quick survey of the major areas in which Amerindians generally have added to our culture. Not all of these contributions are peculiar to Atlantic Canada; however, where some aspect is notably regional, it is so indicated.

(1) LANGUAGE   In the first instance we must recognize that many Amerindian words and phrases enrich our language. The very name "Canada" is generally taken to be of native origin,* thus from the beginning there evolved a custom that has made a significant imprint on the map. In fact, one writer has classified this development as "the battle the Indians won"! (See Chapter 3 for more details regarding the Amerindian contribution to place names.) Unfortunately, some of the more pleasing place names, such as Abegweit, freely translated from the Micmac as "cradled in the waves", for Prince Edward Island, have been lost. The map of New Brunswick is living proof that Amerindian names rank as one of the attractive features of that province. The poet, James De Mille, conveyed the idea in the following lines:

Meduxnakeag's waters are bluer;
Nepisiquit's pools are more black;
More green is the bright Oromocto,
And browner the Petitcodiac;
But colours more radiant in autumn
I see when I'm casting my hook
In the waves of the Skoodowabskoosis
Or perhaps of the Skoodoowabskook.[13]

As well as place names, many other interesting words have entered our language through Amerindian usage. Some depict unique aspects of their life and culture: moccasin, potlatch, powwow, succotash, wampum, and the Micmac tobakun which has evolved as toboggan. Still other words continue as designations for native animals and plants: moose, opossum, skunk, squash, tamarack, and quahog are examples. For more information on the Amerindian contribution to the language check *A Dictionary of Canadianisms on Historical Principles* (Toronto: W. J. Gage Ltd., 1967). It was Dr. Silas Rand, a Nova Scotian clergyman, who must be credited with saving much of the Micmac language. He compiled a dictionary of more than 40,000 words, worked out the grammatical basis of the language, and translated the Bible into Micmac. Originally it was his ambition to become a missionary and convert the Micmacs from Catholicism to Protestantism. As time went on this motive receded and he became more immersed in linguistics, gaining a command of ancient and

*See Mark M. Orkin: *Speaking Canadian English* (Toronto: General Publishing Co., 1970), 160-1.

modern Greek, Hebrew, French, German, Italian, Spanish, Micmac, Malecite, and Mohawk. His missionary endeavour may be judged a failure, yet Rand's contribution was of more enduring value, for, singlehandedly, he was responsible for saving not only much of the Micmacs' language, but their folklore and legends as well. Read more about his life in *The Cross in Canada* (Toronto: Ryerson Press, 1966), 160-4. A detailed account of Rand's career, along with a collection of Micmac legends, may be found in his own book: *Legends of the Micmacs* (New York: Johnson Reprint Corp., 1971).

Rand's monumental achievement was the dedicated work of a lifetime. Recently, more modern ways have been found to speed up linguistic study. At Memorial University the computer has been put to work in reconstructing early Amerindian languages. Working on data obtained from four Algonquin tongues—Fox, Cree, Menomini, and Ojibway— linguists and computer scientists are compiling a dictionary of "reconstructed proto-Algonquin". The system searches for cognates (related words) and from them reconstructs the protoform, or original form from which the cognates evolved. In this manner it is hoped to build up reconstructed proto-Algonquin, a prehistoric language of which we have no written record but which is the common ancestor of Beothuck, Malecite, Micmac, and Naskapi. Although this research is still in its early stages it holds exciting promise for the future. Many people are inclined to think that because the Amerindians possessed no written alphabet somehow their languages were primitive. One authority has written: " ... the vocabulary of many Indian nations was as large as that of their French or English exploiters, and was often far more eloquent; compare the coldness of *friendship* with *the one who carries my sorrows on his back*."[14]

(2) LEGENDS   Of importance to the total heritage of Atlantic Canada are the legends and folk tales of Micmac and Malecite. Perhaps the greatest of these is the story of Glooscap, the hero god. This is a legend that can be ranked among the great epic tales of all time. Glooscap lived on Cape Blomidon and created man from an ash tree. He rode on the backs of whales, and loons carried his messages over land and sea. Immortal, he was never sick, and, so the tale goes, he controlled the forces of nature. The mysterious tides of Fundy and the famous Reversing Falls were both credited to his supernatural powers. In fact, some folklore specialists are convinced that the origin of the Paul Bunyan legend, familiar from New Brunswick to Minnesota, is traceable to the Glooscap story. Certainly, tales of Paul Bunyan's prowess were common among the woodsmen of New Brunswick and Maine; thus it is highly possible that they were spread westward by itinerant loggers. Check the article on Paul

Bunyan in the *Encyclopedia Canadiana* and make a comparative study with the Glooscap legend. What points of similarity and difference can you detect?

The best way to appreciate the fascination of Amerindian legends is to read widely in such books as Marion Robertson's *Red Earth—Tales of the Micmac* (Halifax: Nova Scotia Museum, 1969). To whet your appetite there follows an abridged version of "Glooscap, Kuhkw, and Coolpujot" as recorded in 1869 by Dr. Silas Rand. Compare this account with that to be found in *Red Earth,* pages 67-8.

The tradition respecting Glooscap is that he came to this country from the east—far across the great seas; that he was a divine being, though in the form of a man. When Glooscap went away, he went toward the west. There he is still tented; and two important personages are near him, who are called Kuhkw and Coolpujot—of whom more anon. Glooscap was the friend and teacher of the Indians; all they knew of the arts he taught them. He taught them the names of the constellations and stars; he taught them how to hunt and fish, and cure what they took; how to cultivate the ground, as far as they were trained in husbandry.

The Indians sometimes visit Glooscap at his present residence, so says tradition; this is in a beautiful land in the west. He taught them when he was with them that there was such a place, and led them to look forward to a residence there, and to call it their beautiful home in the far west—where, if good, they would go at death. The journey to that fair region far away is long, difficult, and dangerous; the way back is short and easy. Some years ago, seven stout-hearted young men attempted the journey, and succeeded. Upon arrival they found three wigwams—one for Glooscap, one for Coolpujot, and one for Kuhkw. These are all mighty personages, but Glooscap is supreme; the other two are subordinates. Coolpujot has no bones. He cannot move himself, but is rolled over each spring and fall by Glooscap's order, being turned with handspikes; hence the name Coolpujot (rolled over by handspikes). In the autumn he is turned towards the west, in the spring towards the east; and this is a figure of speech, denoting the revolving seasons of the year—his mighty breath and looks, by which he can sweep down whole armies and work wonders on a grand scale, indicating the weather: frost, snow, ice, and sunshine. Kuhkw means earthquake; this mighty personage can pass along under the surface of the ground, making all things shake and tremble by his power.

All these seven visitors had requests to make, and each received what he asked for; though the gift did not always correspond with the spirit of the request, it oftentimes agreed with the letter. For instance, one of these seven visitors was excited about a fine country, and expressed a desire to remain there, and to live long; whereupon, at Glooscap's direction, Earthquake took him and stood him up, and he became a cedar-tree. When the wind blew through its boughs, they were bent and broken with great noise—making a thunder-storm that rolled far and wide over the country, accompanied by strong winds, which scattered the cedar-boughs and seeds in all directions, producing all the cedar-groves that exist in New Brunswick, Nova Scotia, and elsewhere.[15]

The legends of Glooscap lend themselves to dramatic interpretation. Try your hand at writing a play that centres around a favourite Glooscap story. Material to be found in *Red Earth* and in Kay Hill: *Glooscap and His Magic* (Toronto: McClelland and Stewart, 1964), and *More Glooscap Stories* (Toronto: McClelland and Stewart, 1970), will be helpful.

(3) EXPLORATION   Mention has already been made of the friendly reception accorded Champlain in his encounter with the Malecites at the mouth of the Saint John River on June 24, 1604. From that point onward the birch-bark canoe, toboggan, and snowshoes (all of which survive to our own day) became the constant companions of the early traders, trappers, and explorers. The Amerindians of Atlantic Canada depended to a large extent on the waterways for transportation and their principal means of travel was by birch-bark canoe, once described as "the most perfect product of Amerindian genius". So skilled were the Micmac craftsmen that flotillas of canoes crossed the Northumberland Strait with ease and the Beothuck Indians were able to range as far from land as the Funk Islands. For an excellent discussion of the birch-bark canoe and its influence on Canadian history, see the article by Dr. George Frederick Clarke in *Collections, New Brunswick Historical Society*, XIV (1961): 48-60.* From the Micmacs and Malecites came valuable information about the habits of fur-bearing animals, and the making of clothing and footwear from furs, all of which aided in the adaptation of the European to a new environment.

(4) NATIVE PLANTS   From earliest times, all tribes of Amerindians shared their knowledge of native plants with the newcomers. It has been estimated that some fifty plants useful as food have found their way into

---

*You will find historical accounts of the construction of canoes in Nicolas Denys: *The Description and Natural History of the Coasts of North America*, ed. W. F. Ganong (Toronto: Champlain Society, 1908, 420-2). More detailed contemporary accounts may be found in W. D. Wallis and R. W. Wallis: *The Micmac Indians of Eastern Canada*, 42-51, and G. F. Clarke: *Someone Before Us*, 154-94.

our diets as a result of earlier cultivation by Indians. Corn, fiddleheads, potatoes, squash, and sunflowers are but five scattered examples. Local nuts, edible roots and berries, tobacco, dyes from vegetable sources, and maple syrup illustrate further contributions. There is some doubt as to whether the Micmacs and Malecites were able to refine maple syrup into sugar; however, one early observer (Le Clercq) speaks of the use of the maple as early as 1684:

> As to the water of the maple, which is the sap of the same tree, it is equally delicious to French and Indians, who take their fill of it in the spring . . . through a very little opening which is made with an axe in a maple, ten to a dozen half-gallons may run out. A thing which has seemed to me very remarkable in the maple water is this, that if, by virtue of boiling, it is reduced to a third, it becomes a real syrup, which hardens to something like sugar, and takes on a reddish colour.[16]

The methods used to produce maple syrup serve to illustrate the Indians' ingenuity. The sap was run from trees by means of reeds or pieces of bark. Birch bark containers, sealed with pine resin for waterproofing, were used to gather it. Since the Micmacs and Malecites had perfected a method of heating water by placing red-hot stones in wooden troughs, it is logical to assume that the same method was employed to refine maple syrup. It is of interest to note that the "modern" process of freeze-drying is not so new, since the Malecites converted sap to syrup by allowing it to freeze, then removing the ice and collecting the residue.

(5) MEDICINAL LORE   The so-called "medicine man" has often been held up to scorn and ridicule by those not familiar with Indian ways. To the uninitiated, his practices may seem strange; however, we should recall that he possessed intimate knowledge of many healing drugs and herbs. The bark and leaves of the witch hazel produced a lotion for cooling and soothing the skin, fir balsam was used as a poultice for sores, a syrup made from the wild onion healed sore throats, while the cure for scurvy (boiling the bark of the spruce to remedy dietary deficiencies) saved many European lives. When bones were broken they were carefully reset and large pads of moss held the fractured parts in place. While it is generally recognized that the sauna is primarily Scandinavian, we find that both the Micmacs and Beothucks were aware of its therapeutic value.

> The sweat-house is a kind of hot room, built in the form of a little wigwam covered with bark, or with skins of beaver and moose, and so arranged that it has no opening whatever. In the middle thereof the Indians place some hot stones, which heat those inside so much that the water soon starts from all parts of their bodies. They throw water

upon those hot stones, whence the steam rises to the top of the wigwam, then it falls upon their backs, much like a hot and burning rain. This continues until some of them, unable to endure this heat, are obliged to rush out as quickly as they can.

This proceeding, which serves to torment some of them, is nevertheless a matter of amusement to others, who take a particular pleasure in throwing water from time to time upon the stones, in order to see who will have most endurance. They even sing and joke among themselves. Then, rushing quickly from this wigwam, they throw themselves into the river in order to cool themselves.[17]

Nicolas Denys added his endorsement of the practice: " . . . our Frenchmen make themselves sweat like them, and throw themselves into the water and are never inconvenienced thereby."

(6) ART   We have become so accustomed to seeing "Indian souvenirs" made in Taiwan or Hong Kong that the reality of Indian art is often overlooked. As one critic has expressed it, "The Indian has reserve and dignity which endow him with a capacity for discipline and careful work; he has naturally a fine sense of line and rhythm; and he has evolved an art form peculiarly his own, and one which [white North Americans] have been slower to appreciate than Europeans. This may be a commentary on our art sense."[18] Scholars are in dispute as to whether much of the artwork of the Amerindian in the seventeenth and eighteenth centuries was completely original. It seems fairly safe to assume that geometrical figures, such as zigzags and triangles, are very old and pre-European. Denys, Le Clercq, and other early observers testify that Micmac wigwams were decorated "with a thousand different pictures of birds, moose, otters and beavers which the women sketch with paints". The wigwam itself was a work of art. "The Indian was a natural architect who developed his skill in conformity with his sense of the beauties of nature and the requirements of his mode of life. His work well justified the dictum that form follows function."[19] Certainly, there is no dispute as to the authenticity of the petroglyphs, the carvings and inscriptions on rocks in Kejimkujik National Park in Nova Scotia. This unusual art gallery, carved on smooth brownish slate with beaver teeth, contains sketches of hunting and war scenes, fish, birds, canoes, and human figures. The significance of these petroglyphs goes far beyond their artistic merit, for they confirm that the Micmac had his own system of pictorial writing before the arrival of the European. (See Chapter 7.)

In this survey of the Amerindian heritage we have ranged widely—from Cape Chidley at the tip of the Labrador to Passamoquoddy

Bay on the border between New Brunswick and Maine. In fact, the extent of the Amerindian contribution is eclipsed only by the vast geographic area that has been covered. The conclusion reached in Volume I of the *Dictionary of Canadian Biography* rings true: "Unknown contributors to today's culture, obscure heroes who fell in many battles, interpreters and canoemen, they helped literally to haul half a continent into the modern age. It is to this anonymous multitude that Canadian history owes some of its most striking pages."[20]

FOR READING AND REFERENCE

A. General

BAILEY, ALFRED G.: *The Conflict of European and Eastern Algonquin Cultures.* Toronto: University of Toronto Press, 1969.

CLARKE, GEORGE FREDERICK: *Someone Before Us: Our Maritime Indians.* Fredericton: Brunswick Press, 1968.

DENYS, NICOLAS: *The Description and Natural History of the Coasts of North America.* Edited by W. F. Ganong. Toronto: Champlain Society, 1908. (An abridged version, *Concerning the Ways of the Indians*, is available from the Nova Scotia Museum, Halifax, N.S.)

DRIVER, HAROLD: *Indians of North America.* Chicago: University of Chicago Press, 1961.

ERSKINE, J. S.: "Nova Scotia Pre-history", *Dalhousie Review*, XLIV, 1 (Spring 1964): 16-27.

JENNESS, DIAMOND: *Indians of Canada.* Ottawa: Information Canada, 1967.

LE CLERCQ, CHRESTIEN: *New Relations of Gaspesia.* Edited by W. F. Ganong. Toronto: Champlain Society, 1910.

LEECHMAN, DOUGLAS: *The Native Tribes of Canada.* Toronto: Gage and Co., 1956.

OSWALT, WENDELL H.: *This Land Was Theirs: A Study of the North American Indian.* New York: John Wiley, 1966.

ROUSSEAU, JACQUES, AND BROWN, GEORGE W.: "The Indians of Northeastern North America", *Dictionary of Canadian Biography*, vol. I. Toronto: University of Toronto Press, 1966.

SETON, JULIA M.: *American Indian Arts: A Way of Life.* New York: Ronald Press, 1962.

SYMINGTON, FRASER: *The Canadian Indian*. Toronto: McClelland and Stewart, 1969.

THWAITES, R. G.: *Jesuit Relations and Allied Documents*, vol. I. Cleveland: Burrows Bros., 1895.

WALKER, JAMES W.: "The Indian in Canadian Historical Writing", *Canadian Historical Association Report*, 1971, 21-5.

B. Beothuck Culture

FRASER, ALLAN M.: "The Beothucks of Newfoundland", *Canadian Geographic Journal*, LXV, 5 (November 1962): 156-9. Also "Shanawdithit, Last of the Beothucks", *Atlantic Advocate*, LVI, 3 (November 1965): 34-9.

KELLOWAY, WARWICK F.: "The Beothucks of Newfoundland", *Newfoundland Quarterly*, LXVIII, 2 (Summer 1971): 33-5.

THOMS, JAMES: "The First Newfoundlanders—The Beothucks", *Book of Newfoundland*, vol. III. St. John's: 1967, 225-37.

WHITBY, BARBARA: "The Beothucks and Other Primitive Peoples of Newfoundland", *Anthropological Journal of Canada*, V, 4 (1967): 2-19.

C. Innuit-Naskapi Culture

BEN-DOR, S.: *Eskimos and Settlers in a Labrador Community*. St. John's: Newfoundland Social and Economic Studies, Memorial University of Newfoundland.

DESBARATS, PETER (ed.): *What They Used To Tell About—Indian Legends From Labrador*. Toronto: McClelland and Stewart, 1969.

GRENFELL, WILFRED T.: *Labrador, the Country and Its People*. New York: Macmillan Co. Ltd., 1922.

LEECHMAN, DOUGLAS: *Eskimo Summer*. Toronto: Ryerson Press, 1945.

TANNER, VAINO: *Outlines of the Geography, Life and Customs of Newfoundland-Labrador*, 2 vols. Cambridge: At the University Press, 1947.

D. Micmac-Malecite Culture

ERSKINE, J. S.: "Their Crowded Hour: The Micmac Cycle", *Dalhousie Review*, XXXVIII, 4 (Winter 1959): 443-52. Also "Before Jacques Cartier", *Nova Scotia Journal of Education*, IX, 2 (June 1960): 65-70, and *Micmac Notes*, Occasional Papers, Archaeological Series No. 1. Halifax: Nova Scotia Museum, 1961.

RAYMOND, W. O.: *The River Saint John*. Sackville: Tribune Press, 1950.

ROBERTSON, MARION: *Red Earth: Tales of the Micmac*. Halifax: Nova Scotia Museum, 1969.

SQUIRES, AUSTIN: "The Great Sagamore of the Maliseets", *Atlantic Advocate*, LIX, 3 (November 1968): 49-52.

STODDARD, NATALIE: "Indian Tools of Nova Scotia", XV, 2 (December 1965): 24-31, and "Micmac Foods", *Nova Scotia Journal of Education*, XV, 3 (February 1966): 31-7.

TRUEMAN, STUART: *The Ordeal of John Gyles*. Toronto: McClelland and Stewart, 1966.

WALLIS, WILSON D., AND WALLIS, R. W.: *The Micmac Indians of Eastern Canada*. Minneapolis: University of Minnesota, 1955.

———: *The Malecite Indians of New Brunswick*. Ottawa: Information Canada, 1957; and *Historical Background of the Micmac Indians of Canada*. Ottawa: The National Museum, 1959.

SUGGESTIONS FOR FURTHER RESEARCH

1. One of the best approaches to an understanding of the Amerindian way of life is through the case study. Select the Beothucks, Micmacs, Malecites, or Naskapi and research their history in detail. Some guidelines to keep in mind: (a) What impact did the land and the climate have on their way of life? (b) Investigate: attitudes toward property and neighbouring societies; role of men, women, and children in the society; form of government; religious beliefs. (c) Where did they live? What instruments or tools did they use? What can you ascertain about their food and diet? Many more questions will occur to you as you utilize the resources listed in the bibliography.

2. At the Indian pavilion at Expo 67 in Montreal, a tableau depicted Indian history from the first encounter with "Jacques Cartier & Co." to the present day. Underneath were written these words: "When You First Came To Visit Us, We Offered You Our Goods and Love. ... " Investigate the current situation of the Amerindians in Atlantic Canada and prepare a class report. Your task will be easier if each member concentrates on one aspect of life. Some helpful sources: Harold Cardinal: *The Unjust Society* (Edmonton: Hurtig Ltd., 1969); J. S. Erskine: "The Indian Dilemma", *Dalhousie Review*, L, 1 (Spring 1970): 34-9; C. W. Hobart: "Non-Whites in Canada: Indians, Eskimos, Negroes", in *Social Problems: A Canadian Profile* (Toronto: Macmillan of Canada, 1964); Norman Sheffe (ed.): *Canadian Indians* (Toronto:

McGraw-Hill, 1970). Government reports and briefs prepared by local Indian organizations should also be consulted. Two films produced by the National Film Board, *You Are on Indian Land* and *Indian Dialogue*, although not dealing specifically with Atlantic Canada, will assist in this project.

3. The diet of the white race has been greatly enriched by foods first used by the Amerindian. Some examples are mentioned in this unit and more information can be obtained from Wallis and Wallis: *The Micmacs of Eastern Canada*, 57-67. See also Natalie B. Stoddard: "Micmac Foods", *Nova Scotia Journal of Education*, XV, 3 (February 1966): 31-7; and Bernard Assiniwi: *Indian Recipes* (Toronto: Copp Clark, 1972). Another helpful book is Berndt Berglund and Clare B. Bolsby: *The Edible Wild* (Toronto: Pagurian Press, 1971). This is a complete cookbook and guide to all edible wild plants. On the basis of your research in these and other sources, devise a dinner menu composed *entirely* of foods that were available to the Amerindians of your region of Atlantic Canada.

7. Archaeological Evidence

Imagine that it is the year 5075. A visitor from outer space lands on the North American continent somewhere north of the forty-ninth parallel. He begins to search the surface dust and rubble. Quite by accident he picks up a shiny metallic object that we would immediately recognize as a Canadian dime. But the visitor is puzzled and decides to take the object away for further study. From one such discovery, what deductions could he make regarding a lost civilization on this planet? At first this question may appear unusual, yet it is exactly the one faced again and again by archaeologists who try to understand the meaning of artifacts they find. Artifacts are simply objects (usually tools or ornaments) showing human workmanship that have been discovered in the course of excavation. Unfortunately, some people feel that to study archaeology one must travel to Greece, Italy, or perhaps some area in the Near East. While serious study of the subject owes a great deal to discoveries in other parts of the world, you will find that there is much of archaeological interest in Atlantic Canada. Furthermore, archaeological evidence together with some knowledge of the subject's basic techniques will aid in a fuller understanding of local history.

The term archaeology is derived from two Greek words: *archaios*—ancient, or of the past, and *logos*—discourse upon, or study of, the same. Thus we can arrive at a simple working definition—a study of past remains. Yet the field is not simple, for the archaeologist is concerned with much more than objects of stone, bone, or clay. He must gain some knowledge of the people who created these artifacts. It is clear that we are talking about great dimensions in both time and space. One dictionary has defined archaeology as "reconstructing the story of humanity before recorded history". No one will deny that this is an important function of the subject, yet it is by no means the entire story. Archaeology does not stop with the advent of written history. It can answer questions about life in a particular community fifty or a hundred years ago. It is an indispensable tool in the restoration of early fortifications, old houses, and other structures of historic interest. Sometimes archaeology can provide the clue to settle an international dispute or some long-standing historical riddle.

One early excavation in Atlantic Canada ended just such a controversy. For years following the American Revolution the boundary between New Brunswick and Maine had been in dispute. In 1797 the Americans put forward the claim that the Ste. Croix River, mapped first by Samuel de Champlain in 1604, was in reality the Magaguadavic, while the British insisted that the river then called the Schoodic constituted the boundary. The matter was settled when Thomas Wright, later to become surveyor-general of Prince Edward Island, was sent to the area in an attempt to locate an island visited by Champlain and upon which de Monts had erected some buildings. Although the settlement had been abandoned nearly two centuries earlier, the foundations remained and were excavated by Wright* on Dochet's Island (in the then Schoodic), thus verifying the British claim.

In recent years archaeological headlines have been made through excavations, field explorations, and underwater searches, for it is through such means that we obtain our relics of the past. So important has this field become that governments in all four Atlantic provinces have passed legislation to protect archaeological discoveries and to regulate the excavation, ownership, and preservation of historic sites. These strict regulations grew out of the belief that such discoveries ought to be held in trust for all people and accordingly governments have a duty to control archaeological exploration. This means that school groups cannot and should not attempt, for example, to excavate an Indian campsite—if such were discovered in your community. Archaeology in this sense is for the professional. A prominent English historian, V. H. Galbraith, has written: "The amateur historian, even if he does not do much good, does no harm to his materials. But the amateur archaeologist is the bane of his subject, and can easily ruin the sites he excavates."[1]

This restriction does not mean that the subject lacks scope and significance for the individual. While few may acquire the training to actually participate in an archaeological "dig", there are other rewarding

*Earlier, the same Thomas Wright had been taken prisoner by the Americans. See page 47.

approaches to the subject. How often we have visited museums and been overwhelmed by the impressive rows of display cabinets and the sheer number of artifacts on exhibition. To understand that these institutions are the archives and records of the archaeologist and to gain some knowledge of how he explores his subject is to make such a museum visit come alive. Equally important is studying the correct archaeological approach to the past. It has been suggested that "archaeology is a little like sex or Batman's ability to fly: how do you explain it without encouraging everyone to have a go on their own?"[2] One answer has been provided by a newly formed organization in Britain known as Young Rescue, offshoot of Rescue, a public trust that has been established in the interests of British archaeology. Largely an educational organization, Young Rescue seeks to create an awareness of archaeology among secondary school students by keeping them in touch with new developments in research, enabling them (where possible) to have some contact with archaeological fieldwork, and particularly by "teaching them to think about archaeological problems that will face them in the future".[3] After reading this chapter and trying some of the projects you might like to form an organization with similar objectives in your school.* To do so would not only further your knowledge of the subject but should help you develop an "archaeological eye", the better to appreciate the opportunities, complexities, and working principles of this fascinating study.

What are some of these general principles? Many are similar to the techniques of a detective as he goes about solving a crime, from the manner in which the first clues are studied to the final exposé. Although it must be admitted that in some situations the archaeologist has to overcome more than an ordinary share of handicaps. To gain an understanding of what has happened he must concentrate, in most cases, (a) on the things made by man that have survived for long periods of time, (b) on what people did rather than what they wrote about themselves or others, and (c) on articles which, by themselves, were never meant to convey historical information. If this is not enough he must then go on to locate the "clue" or artifact in terms of geographic space and time. Such simple questions as: "Where was this object found?", "How old is it?", or "What was its function?" can become very complex. To test your powers of observation and deduction, see if you can identify the artifact pictured on page 98. Two important clues: the item is of nautical origin and it is made of wood.

An archaeological investigation has its true beginning not in the field or trench or underwater, but in the library. All available documentary

*Membership in Young Rescue is on an individual rather than a group basis.

sources that may shed light on the proposed investigation must be examined. Once this preliminary step is completed, an accurate survey of the area is undertaken. Topographic maps, geological surveys, guides, gazetteers, and any related sources are analysed. Then, and only then, is the archaeologist in a position to proceed to an "on location" reconnaissance. For most people a walk across an ordinary field may not be historically revealing. But to the trained eye many clues can be detected—perhaps a variation in the vegetation, a tell-tale stain in the earth, or, occasionally, an artifact lying on the surface. Dr. George Clarke has written:

> Many times I've been asked how I manage to find Indian artifacts. A quite natural question. Henry David Thoreau was once asked the same question by his friend Emerson as they were walking over a newly ploughed and harrowed field. Thoreau replied: "By looking for them," and bending picked up a stone spearhead. . . . But the answer given by Thoreau is [only a partial answer] . . . as to how I find Indian relics. Certainly by looking for them, but it also calls into action other facilities than mere keenness of vision. It is a knowledge acquired by long and intensive detective work.[4]

Fortunately the modern archaeologist can call upon many scientific aids to assist in detection. Since the Second World War aerial photography has become an integral part of all preliminary archaeological exploration. By this means a large area may be surveyed with an accuracy previously impossible. Aerial photography reveals detail that is invisible, or nearly so, on the ground. Buried ruins and foundations of buildings, evidence of previous cultivation, and other hidden records of past land use can be detected in the patterns that show up in terrain, vegetation, or soil. Several years ago it was noted that the old Acadian dykes at Grand Pré, Nova Scotia, were clearly discernible in aerial photographs. Stereoscopic examination (see Chapter 5) revealed an elaborate system of dykes otherwise undetectable. This discovery led Professor H. L. Cameron of Acadia University to launch the project "History from the Air", in co-operation with the Nova Scotia Research Foundation and the Royal Canadian Air Force. Subsequently, many of the major historic sites in Atlantic Canada were photographed and in the case of Louisbourg the resulting information was put to use in the preliminary plans for restoration of the fortress. Study the aerial photograph of the Louisbourg site taken in 1961. Note the many features that are visible even to the naked eye.

Numerous other short cuts have been borrowed from different branches of science and technology. Of these, a few examples will suffice to show the ingenuity of the archaeologist. In 1967 the National Historic Sites

Dept. of Indian Affairs & Northern Development

Vertical aerial photograph of the Louisbourg site, 1961.

Service decided to begin underwater research in the Restigouche River near Campbellton. It was known that three French vessels had been sunk in the vicinity in 1760—the last British-French naval battle for possession of Canada.* Normally, in the Canadian winter archaeologists retreat to libraries, archives, and research laboratories. Not in this case. A magnetic survey of Chaleur Bay was undertaken by criss-crossing the ice in a snowmobile. A sensor, which picks up irregularities in the earth's magnetic field, was towed on an iron-free wooden toboggan behind the vehicle. Because there was sufficient magnetic material in the wrecks it was possible to pinpoint locations with amazing accuracy. The next step was the modification of a dump scow to serve as a base for underwater archaeology. The diagram on page 98 will give you a picture of this part of the operation. Three methods were employed in raising artifacts: by hand, airlift, and crane. Fragmented ceramic artifacts and similar materials were raised in laundry baskets by divers. Airlifts were the most

*See C. H. Little: *The Battle of the Restigouche* (Halifax: Maritime Museum of Canada, 1962).

An artifact found in Atlantic Canada.
Can you identify it?

National Historic Sites Service

The diagram shows the surface
support craft positioned over the
wreck. To the right is the smaller
barge on which all of the debris
dredged out of each operation square
is individually screened. Under the
barges divers can be seen working the
flexible ends of the airlifts.

National Historic Sites Service

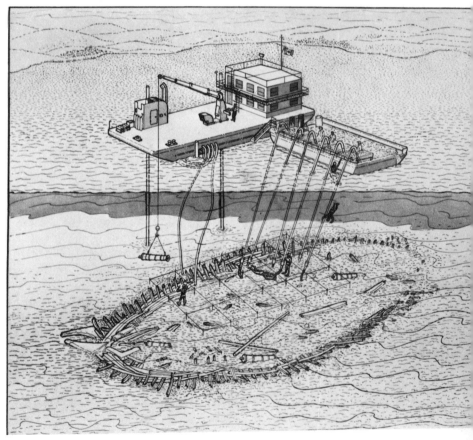

important excavation tools. On a smaller barge next to the renovated scow "six screens were positioned under the discharge ends of the airlifts to receive all material excavated from the wreck. An operator worked each screen to sift and sort the material brought up. Continuous use was made of the crane in raising heavy objects. As a safety precaution, divers left the water during the lifting operations."[5]*

Use of electronic detection devices to locate underground or underwater objects is fairly obvious; enlisting the aid of botany in archaeological research is not. The Arctic explorer Nicholas Polunin discovered, in southwest Greenland, living descendants of plants that evidently had been introduced from the North American continent by Norsemen, whose Greenland settlements died out centuries ago. Through botanical investigation it was found that some of these plants are native to restricted areas of the Labrador and Newfoundland coastline. Their presence in Greenland around known Norse campsites, although not conclusive evidence, is none the less a further link in the chain that helps prove the Norse discovery of North America.

Once a prospective site has been located and the excavation completed, the archaeological research has only begun. Identification and dating of objects that in many instances have lain buried for centuries must follow. Again science has come to the rescue. A major breakthrough in dating artifacts resulted from atomic research that followed the Second World War. This was the discovery of the Carbon 14 technique based on the measurement of the radioactive carbon content of organic materials. (Carbon 14 is an isotope, or variant, of common carbon with an atomic weight of 14 rather than the usual 12. It is formed in the atmosphere, and as soon as a plant or animal dies no further Carbon 14 is absorbed. From this point onward, what has already been absorbed will disintegrate at a predictable rate.) Suppose that an archaeologist has unearthed a piece of charcoal from an Indian campsite. Tests will determine how far the radioactive carbon has disintegrated since the tree was felled. This enables an approximate date to be struck. Other carbon-containing organisms such as peat, pollen, wood, and bone can also be classified in this fashion. The method is not entirely foolproof and errors in carbon dating can occur; nevertheless, it is a valuable archaeological tool.

Another technique that has attracted considerable attention is the study of the sequence of growth rings in trees, for even tree trunks can reveal secrets of the past. It is well known that a tree adds one ring of new wood each year and the age of a tree may be determined by counting growth

---

*The writer wishes to record his gratitude to Mr. Walter Zacharchuk (Head, Underwater Research, National Historic Sites Service, Ottawa), quoted above, for assistance in obtaining the photograph and diagram illustrating marine archaeology.

rings. It is almost as though the tree had kept a diary and recorded annual climatic conditions. Measuring the width of each ring will provide a picture of the variation in rainfall, drought, and other such factors during the life cycle of the tree. By starting with living trees and working backward over a period of time, a unique profile may be developed. Dates can then be obtained by comparing wood samples from excavations with a master chart that shows the ring pattern for many years. Obviously, this technique is only accurate in an area where there is reasonable consistency in climatic conditions. A few years ago it became necessary to remove a large elm tree from the campus of the University of New Brunswick in Fredericton. Upon examining the trunk workmen found that one hundred growth rings were clearly discernible. Perhaps you might be able to obtain a cross-section from a tree that grew in your community. By means of a chart or key, relate the growth rings to local historical events.* Radio carbon dating and tree-ring analysis, then, are but two techniques used by archaeologists to date their finds. If you are interested in obtaining more detail on this aspect of archaeology, check the references listed at the end of the unit.

Once an artifact has been located and dated, the important matter of analysis and explanation remains. All study of the past is based on inter-pretations of available sources and on the inferences and analogies that can be made from them. During an early survey on the Louisbourg site a curious wrought-iron chain was recovered from the harbour. After a variety of tests it was concluded:

1. From the rate of corrosion of wrought iron in salt water, the chain had been underwater for over one hundred years. (If it was part of a ship sunk during the siege of 1758 it had been underwater for 196 years before being recovered.)

2. The chain is a good grade of wrought iron and the links were hand welded.

3. Chemical analysis: Carbon .12 per cent, phosphorus .21 per cent, manganese .04 per cent. The high phosphorus content indicates a conti-nental European origin.

4. X-ray spectroscopic analysis revealed a very small trace of chromium and no titanium. This eliminates Canada as a source of the metal between 1750 and 1800. The absence of vanadium eliminates Scandinavia as a source.

*One tree that often survives to an advanced age is the white pine. In 1968 one such tree was discovered at Watson Settlement, New Brunswick, which forestry experts estimated was 210 years old. Measuring 13 feet, 6 inches, at the base, the tree had been a silent witness to the history of the province. Further, the tree itself was of historical significance, for white pine from New Brunswick was once in great demand for ship masts.

5. Comparison of slag inclusions with European wrought-iron slag makes it appear that the iron ore came from Lorraine or the Saar. The slag minerals under sensitive tint lighting appear more likely to have originated from ores in this region than from ores being worked in England, Germany, or France at the end of the eighteenth century.[6]

It is in this fashion that the archaeologist builds his case.

Since participation in an actual archaeological excavation is practically impossible, you may be interested in playing "Dig", a simulation game illustrating the archaeologists' work in reconstructing vanished civilizations. Failing this, you may wish to embark on a project such as the two neighbouring schools who " ... created their own cultures, made artifacts relating to them and buried them somewhere in the grounds of their schools. The students exchanged schools, located and dug up the artifacts planted by the other team, and tried to reconstruct the civilizations they were supposed to represent."[7] Experience in elementary archaeological techniques may also be gained through excavating a site that is of no special historical value. An old farm or industrial site or even the junk yards and refuse heaps of a bygone day are all possibilities—always, of course, with prior permission of the owner and under the supervision of your teacher. One such student excursion produced a hundred old bottles during a day's dig on an abandoned farmsite in Nova Scotia. A few were from the late-nineteenth century while the remainder were manufactured during the period 1900-20. See Azor Vienneau: *The Bottle Collector* (Halifax: Petheric Press, 1969).

Essential books for the above projects are listed under the heading "A. General" on page 113.

Most historians agree that the Norse were the first Europeans to visit North America. If this is true, the question arises: Can this claim be supported by hard archaeological evidence? Until the 1960s the proof put forward was, at best, flimsy. There were the Norse sagas telling of voyages westward and giving vague geographical details that might be interpreted as describing any of several portions of the Atlantic seaboard. A stone bearing a runic inscription (runes are a type of writing or ciphering) found near Kensington, Minnesota, in 1898 was hailed by many as proof of Norse penetration of the continent. Today, the majority of specialists are convinced that the inscription is not genuine. A similar find of relics near Beardmore, Ontario, although proven authentic were later found to have been brought to Canada from Norway and sold to someone who contrived to have them "discovered". An unusual tower at Newport, Rhode Island, has been claimed to be of Norse origin. While the structure displays mediaeval European features, it was quite probably built during the seventeenth century as a watch tower or windmill. Then there is the famous Yarmouth runic stone, discovered over a century ago on the south shore of Nova Scotia. Again, in spite of many supporters, there is no scientific evidence to prove that the inscription is Norse. In 1971 three stones bearing rune-like markings were discovered on Popham Beach, Maine. Their authenticity still remains to be proven.

Many interesting approaches have been taken in the quest for proof of the Norse explorations. A native of Norway. Reider T. Sherwin, has demonstrated a possible link between the old Norse and the Micmac and Malecite languages. This can be seen in certain similarities in pronunciation and meaning of prominent place names in Atlantic Canada. For example *Canso* (Micmac: Camsok, opposite bluff; Norse: Kambsak, ridge land); *Chebucto* (Micmac: Chebookt, large harbour or bay; Norse: Sjoe bugt, bay by the sea); *Shippegan* (Micmac: Chipigan, passage between island and mainland; Norse: Skipagang, course for ships' passage). You may read more about this theory in Reider T. Sherwin: *The Viking and the Red Man: The Old Norse Origin of the Algonquin Language* (New York: Funk and Wagnall, 1940). As with Dr. Polunin's botanical evidence cited earlier, the theory is interesting but not conclusive, since many language patterns possess elements of similarity.

It fell to another Norwegian, author and explorer Helge Ingstad, to provide the first archaeological proof of not only Norse exploration, but more important, an actual campsite. In 1961 Ingstad, after a systematic search from Rhode Island to Labrador, found some house ruins at L'Anse-aux-Meadows on the northern tip of Newfoundland. Subsequent excavations and the discovery of artifacts, supplemented by Carbon 14 dating, provided final evidence of the presence in Newfoundland of a Norse settlement around the year 1000. Once the preliminary excavation was done the site revealed a typical Norse house site with the remains of a long fireplace in the middle of a central hall. Beside a brook a smithy with anvil and charcoal was uncovered. When later submitted to Carbon 14 testing two readings were obtained. One was A.D. 860 plus or minus 90 years and the other A.D. 1060 plus or minus 70 years. In the smithy pit was slag from melted iron, while the discovery of a soapstone whorl (part of a spindle) indicates that the settlement probably included women. Having completed work on the major site the Ingstad team found traces of several other buildings. One location facing the brook aroused curiosity because a small room, containing a fireplace and a number of brittle burnt stones, had been dug out of the terraced ground. Although the facts are too few for a definite conclusion there is every indication that the settlement boasted a sauna or bathhouse. While archaeological investigation and research of the L'Anse-aux-Meadows site will continue, there is now no doubt of the Norse presence in Atlantic Canada. Those who may wish more detail on the project are urged to read Helge Ingstad: *Westward to Vinland* (Toronto: Macmillan of Canada, 1969).

When we turn to archaeological records of the Amerindians we have considerably more evidence than is the case with the Norsemen. Recent research has turned back the clock 8,000 years, although even here the questions outnumber the answers. First traces of prehistoric artifacts at Debert, Nova Scotia, were uncovered during the Second World War by a bulldozer clearing land for a large army base. In the summer of 1963 archaeologists from the National Museum in Ottawa began digging and soon uncovered hundreds of items indicating the location of a major campsite. Later research has shown that this location is one of the oldest in Canada and dates back over 10,000 years, or roughly to 8600 B.C. These Indians, however, were not related to the Micmacs who inhabited the area at the time of the European conquest. Instead, they were in all likelihood descendants of the Paleolithic people of Siberia who crossed the land bridge of what is now the Bering Strait and gradually worked their way across the continent. Archaeological digs at other locations—Canning, Nova Scotia, Souris, Prince Edward Island, and Quaco Head, New Brunswick—have revealed tools dating from the same period.[8] Since 1967, Indian campsites in the Passamaquoddy Bay and Ste. Croix regions have also been the scenes of extensive searches. These locations have revealed occupancy for upwards of 6,000 years. In 1971 Dr. William Fitzhugh of the Smithsonian Institution began work on an interesting site at Rattler's Bight on the Labrador coast. Here was once located a prehistoric Indian campsite and among a quantity of chipped stone stools a slate-bladed knife was uncovered. The intriguing factor is that this item is remarkably like slate knives used by Norsemen about 4,000 years ago. While there is always a chance of an historical accident (two separate cultures evolving similar tools), the possibility remains that Norse contact with North America began at a very early date. Much more archaeological research, however, is necessary before this point can be proven. In any event, since the discovery of the Paleoindian site at Debert, it has become customary to divide the prehistoric period of Amerindian culture into the following stages:

Prehistoric Period of Amerindian Culture

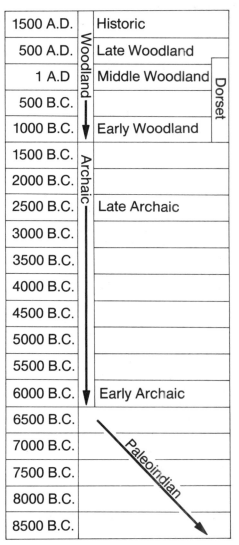

1500 A.D.		Historic
500 A.D.	Woodland	Late Woodland
1 A.D		Middle Woodland
500 B.C.		
1000 B.C.		Early Woodland
1500 B.C.	Archaic	
2000 B.C.		
2500 B.C.		Late Archaic
3000 B.C.		
3500 B.C.		
4000 B.C.		
4500 B.C.		
5000 B.C.		
5500 B.C.		
6000 B.C.		Early Archaic
6500 B.C.		
7000 B.C.		Paleoindian
7500 B.C.		
8000 B.C.		
8500 B.C.		

As we move along in time, the amount of archaeological evidence increases. Amerindian campsites dating from the late Archaic Period have been found from Maine to Labrador, with perhaps the most important discovery being made at Port-au-Choix, Newfoundland, by an archaeological team from Memorial University. Here a large burial ground with preserved human skeletons, along with articles made of bone and antler, was revealed. On the basis of discoveries made Dr. James A. Tuck has described the migratory habits of these people:

> A seasonal round was doubtless followed by small bands of hunters and their families who knew well where to move in order to take advantage of various plants, birds, fish and mammals as they became available. In the late fall and winter, caribou herds were intercepted during their annual migrations and the hunting of these animals probably continued until spring. When the Arctic ice began to drift southward, bringing with it herds of seal and probably walrus, the Archaic hunters were at the shore to make their kills. They probably spent the summer months at the shore as well, where moulting and nesting sea birds, fish, especially the Atlantic salmon, and several types of berries provided a stable summer subsistence. In the fall the first snow signalled the herding of the caribou and these early hunters returned to the interior.[9]

Today, a small but interesting museum at Port-au-Choix houses artifacts from these and related excavations in the area. Since, in the majority of cases, only Newfoundland students will be able to visit this museum, arrange to see the 16-mm. film *Port-au-Choix III* produced by Memorial University.

Another important achaeological find also dating from the late Archaic Period was discovered in 1970 at Cow Point, between Maquapit and Grand lakes in central New Brunswick. To the archaeologist few discoveries are more important than graves, and here the investigators were doubly fortunate for they uncovered a "red-paint" burial ground. The discovery is so described because these Indians buried their dead in red-ochre-lined pits. In fact, it was a trace of red stain on the surface of an eroded gravel ridge that led archaeologists to the spot. The presence of such locations in Atlantic Canada and in Maine have been known for some time. In 1955 seventeenth-century red-paint burial grounds were located at Pictou, Nova Scotia, and Portland Point New Brunswick. The most recent find is important because of its size—a total of fifty-four red-stained grave areas were excavated.

The Port-au-Choix area in Newfoundland is significant for more than discoveries dating from the late Archaic Period. The site was occupied for many centuries by the "Dorset People". The Dorsets were neither true Indian nor true Eskimo but take their name from artifacts first collected on southwestern Baffin Island in 1925. This culture is usually divided into two periods: an early Dorset era that lasted from about 1000 to 500 B.C. and was limited to the Labrador coast north of Nain, and a second, late

Dorset culture that continued until about A.D. 700. A five-year excavation program at Port-au-Choix under the direction of Dr. Elmer Harp of Dartmouth College had added greatly to a hitherto unwritten and unknown chapter in the archaeology of Atlantic Canada. The Dorset culture has been described as "one of the most beautiful and skilful in the ancient world".[10] Certainly, the carvings of stone and bone may be classified as masterpieces and are the earliest examples of true art so far discovered in Atlantic Canada. One unsettled question regarding the Dorsets is the reason for their dramatic disappearance. Most authorities agree that their culture was lost by about A.D. 700, hence they were probably not, as it is sometimes claimed, the mysterious "Skraelings" mentioned in the Norse sagas.

When we study the late Woodland and Historic periods of Amerindian culture in Atlantic Canada, the shell heaps, camping sites, and burial locations become more recognizable. Nevertheless, the forces of man and nature have conspired to erase much of this evidence. In 1846 Abraham Gesner, who had just completed a geological survey of Prince Edward Island, wrote concerning a discovery made near Miminegash Harbour in the western part of the island:

> By the encroachment of the sea a number of Indian skeletons have been exposed and washed from the bank. These skeletons were lying together in different positions, as if the bodies had been thrown together in a common pit, the top of which was one foot beneath the soil. . . . The site of this pit on the extremity of a small point of land supports the opinion that the natives had been surprised and cut off, or killed in battle, and as no relics or warlike instruments were found at the place, except those of the natives, it is probable that the event took place before the advent of the Europeans.[11]

One site that has largely withstood the forces of time is to be found in the Kejimkujik National Park in Nova Scotia. One may still see, spread over the rocks surrounding Fairy Lake, a fascinating series of petroglyphs, or rock carvings, created by the early Micmacs. Animals, people, fish, birds, canoes, hunting scenes, and war scenes are among the examples of pictograph art. Although many of the oldest carvings on the Kejimkujik rocks have been defaced or lost, rubbings or impressions of many were made in the 1880s. Fortunately, these are on file in the Nova Scotia Archives and Nova Scotia Museum. Their importance lies in proving that the Micmacs had a system of pictorial writing *before* the arrival of the Europeans. Further, it is now concluded that the system of hieroglyphic writing devised by Dr. Silas Rand (see Chapter 6) was not purely a white man's invention, but an adaptation of an earlier Micmac system of pictographic art. Reproductions of some of these pictographs may be found in Marion Robertson: *Red Earth: Tales of the Micmacs* (Halifax, 1969), and in *Rock Drawings of the Micmac Indians* (Halifax, 1973), by the same author.

One sign of increased interest in archaeological studies is the co-operation that exists between archaeologists and historians in the verification and restoration of historic sites. To command respect, historical restoration must be accurate, and this is achieved only after painstaking research. Such was the case with the rebuilding of the Habitation at Port Royal in 1938-9. Fortunately, in this instance, there was considerable documentary evidence on which to plan reconstruction. The basic information, obtained from Champlain's writings and his engraving, or picture plan, of the Habitation, was supplemented by contemporary accounts in Lescarbot's *Histoire de la Nouvelle-France* and the *Jesuit Relations*. Originally it was thought that the Habitation was of log construction,* and visitors are sometimes surprised to find an elaborate series of buildings framed with heavy timbers, squared, mortised and tenoned, floored with sawn boards and planks, and housing large fireplaces and chimneys built of brick. Archaeological evidence at Port Royal and information from the later English colonies to the south indicated that European building methods were followed. This led to a study of the style of construction popular in seventeenth-century Normandy and Brittany, home of the artisans who built the first Habitation. Then, when all of the evidence was sifted, a decision was reached to use the "colombage" type of construction, similar to "half-timber" in its structural features with an outside covering of weather-boarding and clay. Archaeologists unearthed most of the foundations at a depth of 21 inches below the surface. These consisted of piles of stones in positions that indicated where the piers, supports, hearthstones, chimney foundations, and runway platforms for cannon should be located. The well was found in the centre of the courtyard and the only cellar in the Habitation, when excavated, was noted to have measurements corresponding to those given by Champlain. Because of the minute attention to detail, the twentieth-century visitor to the Habitation can " . . . take a step backward in history and become part of a moment suspended in time."

---

*It is so shown in Charles W. Jefferys' sketch, drawn before the reconstruction of the Habitation. See *Canada's Past in Pictures* (Toronto: Ryerson Press, 1934), 17.

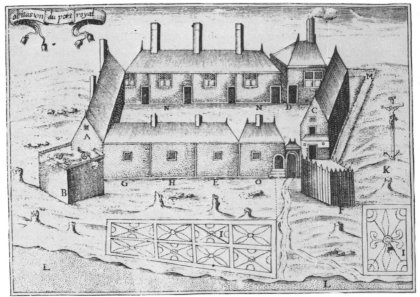

Royal Ontario Museum, Toronto

The Habitation at Port Royal as sketched in Champlain's Voyages, *published in 1613; and a re-enactment of "The Order of Good Cheer", initiated in 1606, the second winter at Port Royal.*

Nova Scotia Communications & Information Centre

Nova Scotia Communications & Information Centre

Symbolizing the French and English cultures and the traditions of Atlantic Canada, Louisbourg's grandeur can be glimpsed in these photographs of the restored exterior and interior of the Château St-Louis.

Nova Scotia Communications & Information Centre

By far the most significant restoration project in Atlantic Canada is the one under way at Louisbourg. Although a good deal was known about the ruins of the fortress from earlier excavations and aerial photography, it was not until 1961 that planning for reconstruction began in earnest. Again, as with the Habitation, it was necessary (on a much larger scale) to search archival collections in France, Britain, the United States, and Canada to obtain the required background information. One of the early decisions was to settle on 1745 as a "theme" date for the restoration. At this time Louisbourg had a population of over 5,000 and covered some 57 acres, giving an indication of the vast amount of archaeological and historical investigation needed.* Château St. Louis, the first major building to be restored, is 360 feet long and three storeys high, and in its original state was one of the most magnificent structures on the continent. Those who have had an opportunity to visit the restored château will agree that it is, even by today's standards, an impressive building. The artifacts uncovered during the early excavations numbered more than 50,000 and ranged from toys to kitchen implements to chamber pots. These domestic items, combined with a wide variety of military objects, provided an excellent base not only for the immediate task of restoration but for the general study of French culture in the eighteenth century.

The massive Louisbourg project, which will doubtless continue for many years, illustrates on a grand scale and in dramatic fashion all the problems associated with historical restoration. Research, excavation, and analysis must be combined in a meaningful way for any such project to succeed. It is not sufficient for the archaeologist to record what was *found*—he must go beyond and be able to project plans on the basis of historical and archaeological evidence. As one member of the Louisbourg restoration team has expressed it: "I must be able to offer positive suggestions as to how the structure originally looked, the type of roof, size and shape of windows and doors, internal decoration and heating arrangements ... the reconstruction problems posed by historical archaeology toughen up one's thinking and force the archaeologist to test his hypotheses."[12]

Total restoration of all historic sites is obviously not feasible because of the cost involved; however, even partial reconstruction and preservation, such as Fort Beauséjour, New Brunswick, or the Roma settlement at Brudnell Point, Prince Edward Island, add much to our appreciation of past historic events. In some cases—for example, Castle Hill, Placentia,

---

*Some idea of the scope of these studies can be obtained from Edward McM. Larrabee: *Archaeological Research at the Fortress of Louisbourg*, Occasional Papers in Archaeology and History No. 2 (National Museum of Canada, 1971).

Newfoundland—the fortifications are not being rebuilt to their original height, for this is not known in exact detail. Nevertheless, both at Castle Hill and at Beauséjour one can detect from the remaining pattern of the fortification how well their respective guns commanded the surrounding countryside.

Another form of historical restoration is the erection of buildings for twentieth-century purposes, yet in exterior design duplicating the architecture of a bygone age. On the Lequille River near Annapolis Royal, Nova Scotia, one may find a replica of a seventeenth-century mill. It stands on the site where Poutrincourt's grist mill (the first in North America) was erected in 1607. Five years of careful research lay behind this building, completed for the Nova Scotia Light and Power Company in 1969. Although the exterior corresponds in detail to the French architecture of 1607, inside it houses modern hydro-electric equipment.

We cannot think of historical restoration solely in terms of a museum complex open to public view. Many historically minded firms interested in preserving our heritage are adapting older buildings for modern purposes. It is not always necessary to "begin at the beginning". In these cases archaeologist, architect, and builder link forces to preserve the historic style of the exterior of the buildings, while at the same time providing modern services (often cleverly disguised) within. Halifax, in common with many other towns and cities in Atlantic Canada, affords examples of this type of development: the Black-Binney House, 1472 Hollis Street (1819), serves as headquarters for the Nova Scotia Division, Canadian Corps of Commissionaires; the Merchants Bank of Halifax, 1802 Bedford Row (1825), is now the district office for a banking company; Keith Hall, 1475 Hollis Street (1863), serves as the executive offices for a large company; Henry House, 1222 Barrington Street (1870), originally the home of William Henry, a Father of Confederation, is now a first-class restaurant.[13] Look over the communities nearest you and try to locate similar nineteenth-century buildings that have been adapted for modern purposes. Check Chapter 10 for information on the "living" museums of Atlantic Canada.

In the autumn of 1965 an event took place off the rocky coast of Cape Breton that was destined to capture the headlines and the imagination of people all over the world. The wreck of the French pay-ship *Le Chameau*, which sank in a southeast gale on August 26, 1725, was discovered. Since it was known that *Le Chameau* carried money for the garrison at Quebec amounting to 289,696 livres (over one million dollars in present value), most of the attention centred around the monetary worth of the discovery. Equally important was the fact that this operation served to emphasize the possibilities of marine archaeology in Atlantic Canada. (You may read about this story of a successful quest for treasure in Alex Storm and Brian Shaw: *Canada's Treasure Hunt*, Winnipeg: Greywood Publishing Ltd., 1967). Underwater exploration is as old as the art of diving; it has, however, gained prominence in recent years because of the refinement of techniques and the popularity of scuba diving. In the summer of 1962, off Cavendish Beach, Prince Edward Island, the wreck of the famous *Marco Polo* was discovered in thirty-five feet of water.* An ingenious method was devised to raise the two main anchors, each of which weighed over 1,000 pounds. They were brought to the surface by filling oil drums with water, sinking the drums, and fastening them to the anchors. When the water in the drums was displaced by air they could be raised. The Grand Manan area in New Brunswick, which during the heyday of sail witnessed two shipwrecks a year, has also been the scene of considerable underwater archaeological investigation. Among the shipwrecks discovered was the barque *Wallace* which foundered and was lost off Grand Manan on May 23, 1841. To date, the most detailed searches have been conducted by the National Museum in the Restigouche River area and at Louisbourg. Marine archaeologists have brought to the surface numerous artifacts from the sunken frigate *Le Machault*, largest of the three French vessels sunk in the Battle of Restigouche in 1760. Many of these were in unexpectedly good condition and included porcelain, stemware, cutlery, crockery, ceramics, an unused pair of boots resembling modern desert boots, cannon, and numerous military effects. One of the guns of *Le Machault*, a ten-foot cannon weighing several tons, is on display at a park in Campbellton, New Brunswick. So important are the possibilities for marine archaeology at Louisbourg that it is out of bounds to all divers except those authorized by the officials on the restoration project. Archaeologists and historians estimate that fourteen vessels sank in this harbour between 1713 and 1758, most of them during the second and last siege of the fortress. Over the centuries, the rugged coast of Newfoundland has claimed hundreds of ships; accordingly, in September 1972 a marine archaeological society was formed to gather data on the "underwater museum" of that province.

It can readily be seen that for the archaeologist underwater exploration presents a number of advantages. A shipwreck in good condition can be more satisfactory than a dig on land, since under the waves time and history literally stand still. All the material on board was in use the day the ship was lost and, if undisturbed, has remained as dated artifacts. Since it is estimated that there are over 4,000 wrecks around the coast of

*See page 42.

Nova Scotia alone, the opportunities for research are endless. Obviously, then, Atlantic Canada has many opportunities for marine archaeologists. An interesting project for those of you who live in a coastal region would be the compilation of a chart or map illustrating the approximate location of ships wrecked in the vicinity of your home. For a model, see the chart published by the New Brunswick Museum in Saint John depicting the shipwrecks around Grand Manan.

Of archaeological evidence it has been written that as the "handmaiden of history" it provides "some of the facts we want to know which were not written down, or which belonged to the prehistoric past before writing existed."[14] In local and regional history archaeology supplies an important link in the chain of understanding, for here, too, much of what we wish to know about the past was never recorded in an accessible form. To give but one example, the Amerindian heritage of Atlantic Canada is completely unintelligible without reference to archaeology and archaeological techniques. The study of artifacts uncovered from land or sea provides the means, as can no other, for translating abstract theory into concrete reality. The unravelling of such evidence possesses all the elements of a good mystery story and it is this that explains the widespread appeal of archaeology.

FOR READING AND REFERENCE

A. General

ALEXANDER, JOHN: *The Directing of Archaeological Excavations*. New York: Humanities Press, 1970.

BRAIDWOOD, ROBERT J.: *Archaeologists and What They Do*. New York: Franklin Watts, 1960.

HAMMOND, PHILIP C.: *Archaeological Techniques for Amateurs*. Toronto: Van Nostrand, 1963.

HEIZEN, ROBERT F., AND GRAHAM, JOHN A.: *A Guide to Field Methods in Archaeology*. Palo Alto: National Press, 1967.

ROBBINS, MAURICE, WITH IRVING, MARY B.: *The Amateur Archaeologist's Handbook*. New York: Thomas Crowell, 1965.

B. Amerindian Archaeology

CLARKE, GEORGE FREDERICK: *Someone Before Us: Our Maritime Indians*. Fredericton: Brunswick Press, 1968.

ERSKINE, J. S.: "Nova Scotia Pre-History", *Dalhousie Review*, XLIV, 1 (Spring 1964): 16-27. See also "Early Cultures of Nova Scotia", *Journal of Education*, May-June 1969 to June 1970.

HARPER, J. RUSSELL: "Four Thousand Years of History: The Story of Archaeological Excavation at Portland Point", *Atlantic Advocate*, XLVII, 6 (February 1957): 31-5. See also 7 (April 1957): 69, for comments by G. F. Clarke.

MACDONALD, GEORGE: *Debert: A Paleoindian Site in Central Nova Scotia.* Ottawa: Information Canada, 1968.

PEARSON, RICHARD J.: "Some Recent Archaeological Discoveries From Prince Edward Island", *Anthropologica*, VIII, 1 (1966): 101-9.

SANDERS, THOMAS E.: "The Museum of Manitou", *Indian Historian*, V, 3 (Fall 1972): 7-12, 22. This issue of the *Indian Historian* has several articles on the controversy that surrounds archaeological investigation of the Amerindian culture. See Chapter 1 for more details.

C. Norse Archaeology

JONES, GWYN: *The Western Voyages of the Norsemen.* London: Oxford University Press, 1964.

NICKERSON, M. H.: "A Short Note on the Yarmouth Runic Stone", *Collections Nova Scotia Historical Society*, vol. XVII, 51-6.

OLESON, TRYGGVI: *Early Voyages and Northern Approaches.* Toronto: McClelland and Stewart, 1963.

TORNOE, J.: *Early American History: Norsemen Before Columbus.* Oslo: Universitetsforlaget, 1964.

WAHLGREN, ERIK: *The Kensington Stone: A Mystery Solved.* Madison: University of Wisconsin Press, 1958.

Check also the references on page 115.

D. Marine Archaeology

BASS, G. F.: *Archaeology Underwater.* New York: Praeger Press, 1966.

BLAIR, CLAY: *Diving for Pleasure and Treasure.* New York: World Publishing Co., 1960.

BURGESS, ROBERT F.: *Sinkings, Salvages and Shipwrecks.* Toronto: Fitzhenry and Whiteside, 1970.

COFFMAN, F. L.: *1001 Lost, Buried or Sunken Treasures: Facts for Treasure Hunters.* Toronto: Nelson, 1957.

HANSEN, ERIK S., AND BLEAKNEY, J. S.: *Underwater Survey of Louisbourg Harbour.* Wolfville: Acadia University Institute, 1962.

PETERSON, MENDEL: *History Under the Sea.* Washington: Smithsonian Institution, 1965.

SUGGESTIONS FOR FURTHER RESEARCH

1. For years historians have quibbled over the location of "Vinland the Good", mentioned in the Norse Sagas. Three distinct areas have been put forward as possible sites: (a) Massachusetts, in Frederick J. Pohl: *The Lost Discovery* (New York: W. W. Norton, 1952) and *Atlantic Crossings Before Columbus* (New York: W. W. Norton, 1961); (b) Trinity Bay, Newfoundland, in Farley Mowat: *Westviking* (Toronto: McClelland and Stewart, 1965); (c) the northern tip of Newfoundland in Helge Ingstad: *Westward to Vinland* (Toronto: Macmillan of Canada, 1969). Another book of general interest is J. R. L. Anderson: *Vinland Voyage* (London: Eyre and Spottiswoode, 1967). Which theory, in your view, is the most plausible? Arrange a class debate on the question.

2. As we have seen, archaeology, although dealing with artifacts often thousands of years old, frequently enlists modern research techniques. Recently, the computer has been put to work deciphering ancient scripts and astronomical data. Check the books on computer study in your school library and learn how this is accomplished. Information on page 84 will provide one example of this technique. Can you find some additional applications of the computer in the history of Atlantic Canada?

3. Archaeology and the work of archaeologists often figure prominently in fiction. You will find Thomas Raddall's "The Amulet" (which deals with Amerindian archaeology) of particular interest. Read it in *Tambour and Other Stories* (Toronto: McClelland and Stewart, 1945), 253-68.

4. Because of the popularity of scuba diving, experienced divers may be found in almost every community. Invite such a person to your class to answer questions on diving techniques. If there is a swimming pool near by you may be able to arrange a demonstration. Additional information can be gained from pamphlets on diving issued by the Nova Scotia Department of Tourism and in the *Nova Scotia Magazine*, particularly the Spring 1972 issue, which features articles on marine archaeology and diving for historical treasure. There are also a number of excellent films on the subject, such as *Dive Nova Scotia*, which, while it highlights the diving potential of that province, is applicable to other parts of Atlantic Canada.

8. Documentary Evidence and Literature

Since archaeological evidence accounts for a mere fraction of our knowledge about the past, we are forever dependent upon one of man's greatest achievements—the written and the printed word. Existing in various forms, such sources are usually classified as either primary or secondary. A clear distinction must be drawn between the two. Primary materials are those that exist in original form—the text of a treaty, an act of Parliament, or perhaps the letters and diaries of a famous statesman. Those sources classified as secondary supplement first-hand accounts by detailed comment and explanation. Based in whole or in part on primary sources, they portray an author's opinion and ideas as he interprets the past for the present. Most standard history textbooks are examples. In this chapter we will first consider primary, archival resources—documents, newspapers, and similar materials—the foundation of historical writing. Later the literary heritage of Atlantic Canada will be taken into account.

Sir Arthur Doughty, for over thirty years Canada's national archivist, once wrote, "Of all national assets, archives are the most precious; they are the gift of one generation to another and the extent of our care of them marks the extent of our civilization."[1] As one might expect in an area so rich in history, Atlantic Canada is well served by such institutions. The advice given by Joseph Howe that a wise nation must preserve its records and gather up its documents has been taken to heart. In addition to the four provincial archives, which are responsible for maintaining the records of their respective governments and regions, we have other locations where both manuscript and printed records may be found. University libraries, local historical societies, religious organizations, and most museums—from those long established such as the New Brunswick Museum in Saint John to smaller institutions such as that of Trinity, Newfoundland—possess invaluable historical resources. If possible, arrange a visit to your provincial archives, for only in this way will you appreciate the extent of the records kept there and the possible uses of such materials.

Most of the research projects in this book depend on original sources, but may need to be completed without direct access to museums or archives What can be done in such cases? To begin, there are many collections of printed documents and microfilmed material that may be borrowed by your local library or school resource centre. Beyond this, there is much interesting information that can be obtained on your own doorstep Did your community suffer, as so many others did in the nineteenth century, from disastrous fires? Look for eyewitness accounts of such events, often to be found in newspaper clippings tucked away in an old scrapbook in someone's attic. You may be able to locate an old print or engraving (similar to the one on page 42). Persons who experienced an event can often add a touch of realism obtainable in no other way. Later events were probably captured in photographs—again, valuable additions to on-the-spot reporting.

Correspondence of all kinds, both business and personal, diaries, and contemporary accounts are also assets. The Loyalists were responsible for much of this type of material and many accounts are available. The narrative of James Moody, originally pubished in New York in 1783, was reprinted in *Acadiensis* I, 2 (Spring 1972): 72-90. Moody, once described as an "impenitent Loyalist", founded Weymouth, Nova Scotia, served as a member of the legislature, and may be considered a typical representative of his class. A valuable collection of Loyalist correspondence is to be found in the *Winslow Papers*, published in Saint John in 1901. *The Loyalists* by G. N. D. Evans (Toronto: Copp Clark, 1968) analyses through all kinds of documentary evidence the Loyalist impact on British North America.*

Sometimes even the most ordinary reference will add to our information about an event of importance. Before me as I write is a letter uncovered by chance when an old home was being demolished. For over a century and a half it lay between two inner walls, safe and secure, waiting to be discovered. The dateline is February 23, 1790, and it was written in Armagh, Ireland, by a relative of a family of Ulster Scots who had emigrated to Nova Scotia twenty years earlier. After two pages of local news the writer concludes: "I have nothing more to inform you, only

*For still another viewpoint on the Loyalists read Michael Pearson *Those Damned Rebels: The American Revolution as seen through British Eyes* (New York: G. P. Putnam, 1972).

that there has been some disturbance in this country for three years past between the Protestants and Catholics. Every means has been taken to settle the difference but I cannot say that it has come to an end yet." Sometimes today's news is not so new! The discovery of this letter was a happy accident; correspondence of much more recent vintage can be equally revealing and significant. Letters from relatives in New England, to and from Maritimers who went west on harvest excursions in the early part of the century, or from servicemen of two world wars, may be found in all sorts of places. Have a search! Various types of miscellaneous documents may also be uncovered. Business accounts and notebooks (see page 190), church and school registers, railway timetables, even old mail-order catalogues, are examples of items that may be used to describe life as it once was in your community.

Published diaries and memoirs are another valuable primary source as they often provide an indication of past living conditions. One of the most prominent journalists in Nova Scotia during the mid-nineteenth century was Peter Stevens Hamilton. For some eight years (1853-61) he was editor of the *Acadian Recorder* and became well known as an outspoken advocate of Confederation. Before turning to newspaper work he practised law, and for a brief period of time was an itinerant schoolteacher in Colchester County. During his lifetime, he kept a yearly journal of reminiscences and memoirs. This portion describes the trials of a rural schoolteacher in 1846.

My teaching was carried on under most distressing difficulties. The winter was usually severe, noted for its heavy snowfall and keen and continuous frosty weather. The school-house was a new one, merely a partly finished shell, and almost as cold as the open street. To "heat" it, there was a little, old, cracked, iron stove, with almost no draught, and the only fuel provided was sappy green wood, imperfectly prepared. Under the most favourable circumstances, the day was far spent before the school-room was fit to work in—some days it never was; and on a few occasions I felt bound to dismiss the school, lest the children should perish in the room. In severe weather, I could not in mercy forbid the shivering children from closing in around the wretched old stove, whilst I remained on my rostrum, and it is a positive fact that my feet were pretty severely frost-bitten that winter, whilst sitting in the school-room.

As for "boarding 'round", I could not complain for lack of variety. There were about a dozen houses in all of which I sojourned during some part of that three months—in about two or three of these I was quite comfortable. As the poor people, with a few exceptions, really tried to make me comfortable, I could utter no word of complaint. Often times I turned into bed with my outdoor clothing on (except hat and boots), and yet shivered almost sleeplessly until morning.[2]

Politicians as a group have more often than others had their diaries and memoirs published. Often, as in the case of Sir Robert Borden (see *Robert Laird Borden:His Memoirs*, Toronto: McClelland and Stewart, 1969), they act as their own editors. In other instances someone with access to their private papers is responsible (see W. S. Wallace, ed.: *The Memoirs of Rt. Hon. Sir George Foster*, Toronto: Macmillan of Canada, 1933). A lesser-known figure, Hon. E. M. MacDonald, who served as minister of national defence in the early Mackenzie King administration, has given in his *Recollections Political and Personal*, (Toronto: Ryerson Press, n.d.) an interesting account of early-twentieth-century politics. Did the political figures native to your area publish their memoirs?

Next in the list of primary source materials are government documents. Most of these will be found only within large libraries; however, current items are often still in print and readily available. If you must have certain material, such as data from early census records, this may be photocopied at nominal cost. Your most valuable reference for this type of material is *Publications of the Governments of Nova Scotia, Prince Edward Island and New Brunswick 1758-1952*, Olga Bishop, ed. (Ottawa: National Library of Canada, 1957). Using the definition of a government document as "any paper, map, pamphlet or book—manuscript or printed—originating in, or printed with the imprint of, or at the expense, or by the authority of any office of a legally organized government", it lists the vast array of government publications and should be consulted if your local research involves some aspect of governmental activity. Perhaps the most useful of such publications are the journals and debates of the legislatures.

While summaries of the debates were usually printed in the newspaper (not all legislatures recorded debates), the sessional papers and printed appendices to the journals are a mine of information for the local historian. To illustrate: the *Journal of the Prince Edward Island House of Assembly* (1857), Appendix "J", contains a report of a legislative committee called to look into the improving of communications between Charlottetown and Halifax by placing a steamship on a run between the island and the mainland. The committee engaged the steamer *Rosebud* and embarked upon an investigation of three possible ports of call on the Nova Scotian coast—Pugwash, Tatamagouche, and Brule. Subsequently, a biweekly service (operating in the summer months) was established between Charlottetown and Brule. This continued for over a decade and it was the *Heather Belle*, from Brule, that carried the Nova Scotian delegation to the Charlottetown Conference on August 31, 1864. Patient digging in house journals and sessional papers will reveal many interesting sidelights to local history.

Although postage stamps may be regarded by some as technically outside the scope of primary source material, they are, none the less, of considerable historic interest. The fulfilment of the dream behind the Charlottetown Conference mentioned above did not come about until December 11, 1948. On this date a sense of history was displayed, as pens were dipped in the very inkwell used eighty-four years earlier, and terms of union between Newfoundland and Canada were signed. Formal proclamation came on March 31, 1949, and Confederation was complete. The event was officially marked by the issuing of a four-cent postage stamp depicting John Cabot's ship the *Matthew*; appropriate enough since Newfoundlanders maintain that Cabot's landfall in 1497 was Cape Bonavista. Moreover, one of the last stamps to be issued by Newfoundland prior to Confederation also commemorated the 450th anniversary of Cabot's arrival.

The world's first postage stamps were issued by Great Britain in 1840 and shortly thereafter the idea spread to the colonies. New Brunswick began the practice in 1851, followed by Nova Scotia in 1853, Newfoundland in 1857, and Prince Edward Island in 1861.* Lack of space prevents anything approaching a detailed postal history of the region; however, two examples will illustrate the fascination of the topic. Perhaps the most famous stamp issue was that of New Brunswick in 1860. The story begins with Charles Connell, general merchant from Woodstock and Member of the Legislative Assembly for Carleton County, who was named postmaster general in 1859. Shortly thereafter the colony switched from pounds, shillings, and pence to decimal currency and Connell was instructed to arrange for a new set of stamps. No one at the time thought that such a routine matter would precipitate a political crisis; yet this is exactly what happened. Five stamps in all were designed: a wood-burning locomotive was chosen as an illustration on the 1¢, a ship on the 12½¢, a portrait of the Prince of Wales on the 17¢, that of the Queen on the 10¢ . . . and that of Charles Connell on the 5¢ stamp.

When Connell's colleagues discovered what had taken place they were aghast. Some regarded it as an affront to Queen Victoria, while others maintained the action exemplified extreme vanity on the part of the postmaster general. Charges of "creeping republicanism" and "imitation of the United States" (since that country depicted ordinary mortals on its postage stamps) were hurled at Connell. Steps were taken to prevent the

*See Victor Seary: *A Postage Stamp History of Canada* (Toronto: McGraw-Hill Ryerson, 1972).

5¢ stamp from reaching the public; it was quickly replaced by another bearing the Queen's portrait. Only a few of the Connell stamps survived and as a result they are extremely valuable. (Check the current value in a standard stamp catalogue.) In the midst of the great stamp debate Connell resigned from the Executive Council, although the episode had little lasting effect on his political career. Later in 1867, he was elected to the House of Commons for Carleton and served until his death in 1873.

Newfoundland, with a longer philatelic history than other parts of Atlantic Canada, has many stamps with engrossing stories. In January 1866 a new 5¢ issue bearing the picture of a seal on an ice floe was placed on sale. Errors in printing are eagerly sought by collectors and it was long felt that this stamp (depicting a seal with forefeet) resulted from an artist's ignorance of zoology. Eventually the design was vindicated, for the great grey seal common to parts of Newfoundland has forefeet. Because of their detail, map stamps are prone to error. In 1928 a 1¢ stamp bearing the map of Newfoundland was issued, with Cape Bauld and Cape Norman (on the northeast tip of the island) reversed. The following year the error was corrected and a potentially valuable stamp (to collectors) was removed from the market. The greatest interest in stamp-collecting from the standpoint of regional history centres around commemorative issues. Study a stamp catalogue and compile a list of those stamps that mark events in the history of Atlantic Canada. If there are stamp collectors in the class an exhibit of some of these may be arranged.

What newspapers were your great-grandparents reading a century ago? The Saint John *Morning Freeman*? The St. John's *Newfoundland Express*? The Charlottetown *Patriot*? The Halifax *British Colonist*? Newspapers remain one of the most valuable resources for the study of local history. They " . . . reported and informed; they commented and they criticized; and in the broadest sense they revealed the diversity not only of men and politics but of life itself."[3] Atlantic Canada's journalistic heritage goes back to the eighteenth century and Halifax can lay claim to publication of the first newspaper. Shortly after the founding of the city a printing press was shipped from Boston and on March 23, 1752, copies of the *Halifax Gazette* went on sale. The pioneer newspaper in present-day New Brunswick, the *Royal Gazette and Nova Scotia Intelligencer*, was established as early as 1783, a year before the creation of the province. The name was later changed to the *Royal Saint John Gazette*. Loyalist influence pervaded many of these early journalistic efforts and James Robertson, after an unsuccessful attempt to launch a newspaper in Shelburne, later began Prince Edward Island's first newspaper, the *Royal American Gazette and Weekly Intelligencer*. A similar outgrowth may be noted when another Loyalist, John Ryan, was lured from Saint John to St. John's and founded the *Royal Gazette and Newfoundland Advertiser* in 1807.

By modern standards these early newspapers were modest efforts. Frequently one individual was both publisher and editor—and sometimes typesetter. Certainly a paper such as the *Novascotian* is inevitably associated with the name of Joseph Howe; however, not to be neglected are some of the other journalistic giants of Atlantic Canada: Jotham Blanchard of the Pictou *Colonial Patriot*; Edward Whelan of the Charlottetown *Examiner*; James A. Pierce of the Chatham *Gleaner*; Timothy Anglin of the Saint John *Morning Freeman*; Henry David Winton of the St. John's *Public Ledger*. All were noted for their sense of political commitment, their support of public causes, and their sometimes acid prose. It is no coincidence that two of these crusading editors, Pierce and Whelan, served their apprenticeship under Howe. Typical of the group was Winton, once described as "the war horse of Newfoundland journalism". Unfortunately, he had the unhappy knack of annoying enemies to the point of reprisal. During the 1830s Winton, a Protestant, indulged in a journalistic tirade against the Catholic members of the House of Assembly. His strong view provoked a riot in December 1833, when a mob attacked his house, only to be repelled by troops from the St. John's garrison. On May 15, 1835, he was "set upon by a gang of ruffians" at Saddle Hill, or "the Saddle", near Carbonear. In the struggle that followed Winton lost both ears—yet he lived for another twenty years to, in his words, "unflinchingly advocate the glorious principles of civil and religious liberty".[4]

What sort of material is one likely to find in a typical nineteenth-century newspaper? Let us take the Chatham *Gleaner* for Saturday, September 21, 1867, as a fairly representative sample. Page one, unlike contemporary newspapers, did not cover headline news; rather, most of the space was taken up with a "continued" story—the Victorian version of the soap opera. Under the heading "Select Literature" the *Gleaner* carried "Aunt Martha's Love Story", a gushing romance set somewhere in rural England. The second page was more important for it contained the editorials and letters to the editor. Shipping news noted arrivals and departures from the port of Chatham, giving indication of great activity. The lead editorial discussed the merits of a north-shore route for the proposed Intercolonial Railway. Some returns from the first federal election (then in progress) were noted and satisfaction was expressed over the election of Timothy Anglin in neighbouring Gloucester County. "On Thursday evening last, friends of Mr. Anglin ... lit a bonfire in his honour." The next page contained a digest of news highlights, short summaries of European events taken from recent English papers, more detailed accounts of provincial happenings such as a serious fire in Woodstock, and lists of marriages, births, and deaths. A page and a half of advertisements rounded out the issue.

Journalistic research need not be limited to matters of strict historical interest. Early newspapers have a fascination all their own. The purple prose and news stories often bordering on the libellous attract our attention, but these were often eclipsed by the exorbitant claims of the advertisers. The *New Brunswick Reporter* for March 25, 1859, contained a full page of medicinal advertising ranging from Ayer's Pills and Cherry Pectoral to Youatt's "Celebrated Gargling Oil"—an item recommended "For Man or Beast"—it was "Better than any pain killer, linament or gargling oil ever invented". Before we become overly critical of these advertisements we would do well to examine the exaggeration apparent in modern television commercials. Many of these are not unlike the examples quoted. More restrained were the notices of shipping companies and of professional men, and the announcements concerning forthcoming events. Study the advertisement section of a nineteenth-century newspaper. On the basis of the information presented, what conclusions can you make regarding the lifestyle of people in Atlantic Canada during that particular time?

Humour may also be found in abundance. Classic examples such as the early works of T. C. Haliburton and Thomas McCulloch first reached the public through newspapers. The *Novascotian* of the late 1820s and 1830s carried the activities of "The Club", an informal organization of journalists and politicians. Howe's reporting of their "meetings" offers a humorous slant to the stern constitutional debates that surrounded the struggle for responsible government. Upon occasion, the wit was not even thinly veiled. In the *Colonial Patriot* of October 7, 1829, we find an editorial entitled "Bishop's Horsetails and Chaplain's Whiskers". Written while the editor, Jotham Blanchard, was in jail, it derided King's College and the bishop of the Church of England, the Reverend John Inglis. The latter had visited King's College in Windsor to curb a breakdown in discipline and a threatened revolt by students. While inside the building some prankish students " ... shaved the bishop's horses' tails in the neatest manner imaginable". The incident gave Blanchard, noted for his sarcasm, a fine opportunity to pour ridicule on the attempt by the Church of England to monopolize higher education in Nova Scotia.

It has to be admitted that, apart from large libraries and archives, files of papers such as the *Colonial Patriot* or the Chatham *Gleaner* are difficult to find. Thus in 1959 the Canadian Library Association began microfilming all important newspapers. If your school or regional library has a microfilm reader it will be possible for you to investigate a wide variety of newspapers ranging from Joseph Howe's famous *Novascotian* to more obscure journals such as the Sackville (N.B.) *Borderer* 1865-70, the Harbour Grace *Standard* 1863-73, the Summerside *Progress* 1866-72, or the Digby *Courier* 1874-1948. Lack of a microfilm reader should not completely handicap your research. In the nineteenth century even very small communities such as Canning, Sherbrooke, or St. Peter's in Nova Scotia boasted newspapers. Was this true of your area? If so, scour the neighbourhood and try to locate some copies. Even a single issue or a scrapbook of old clippings will be of value. Failing this, some of the larger newspapers such as the Halifax *Chronicle-Herald* produce facsimile copies of early editions and these may be useful in your research.

Before moving on to discuss the literary heritage of Atlantic Canada it would be prudent to pause and consider some of the pitfalls encountered in the use of primary source materials. Historical research is never clear sailing and facts have a habit of being very elusive. Tracking down a solitary item can be most time-consuming, yet the effort is balanced by the satisfaction of finding the correct answer to a vexing question. One should be wary of the temptation to accept blindly printed material simply because "it was in the paper". The historian's attitude toward evidence should be one of continual scepticism. Is the account complete in all its details? Was the writer an eyewitness or was information obtained second-hand? Is there evidence of bias? Rigid political or religious views are always suspect. Can you corroborate one piece of evidence by another? These are questions to ask yourself as you tackle research in primary source material. For an interesting account of historical detective work, read the *Collections New Brunswick Historical Society*, XIX (1966): 17-38, and learn how J. C. Medcof unravelled details concerning the loss of the barque *Genii* at New River, New Brunswick, in 1869.

The difficulties encountered in this type of investigation should never deter you. In the critical examination of facts lies much of the enjoyment of local history, for written proof has a unique value in making the past come alive. Experience will cause you to agree with the conclusion: "The original document is, in a sense, more true than any textbook can hope to be; for the writer, though he may have been misguided, biased or mistaken, at least lived through the events of which he speaks; and whatever his shortcomings, he was in certain respects better informed about the times and conditions in which he lived than is the interpreter writing years afterward".[5]

The use of literature as documentary evidence takes us into a completely new field. The primary source materials thus far described "tell what happened"; literature, our most available secondary source, "takes us inside the happening and by means of our imagination we become a part of it."[6] The best way to understand this relationship is to read two excerpts from the pen of Thomas H. Raddall, a novelist of the first rank, who is also a good historian. First, read Raddall in this latter role as he describes conditions in Nova Scotia during the American Revolution. You will find the account in *The Path of Destiny* (Toronto: Doubleday Canada Ltd., 1959), 73-87. The same material was reprinted in *Maclean's Canada* (Toronto: McClelland and Stewart, 1960), 80-4, under the title "How George Washington Lost Canada". A typical lesson in history, the article describes the background and conflict of forces that made the years 1775-83 so momentous for Nova Scotians. It is a vivid, well-written account, although facts are treated in purely historical fashion. We are told what happened and to a certain extent why. There are obvious limits to the straight historical account, however.

> History can only make her pictures and rebuild the past out of the things she can save from a shipwreck; she will piece together just as much of the bottle as the sea washes up on the shores. The memory of the world is not a bright shining crystal, but a heap of broken fragments, a few fine flashes of light that break through the darkness. And so, history is full of tales half told, and of tunes that break off in the middle; she gives us snatches from the lives of men, a peep at some corner of a battlefield, just enough to make us long for a fuller vision.[7]

Next, turn to Raddall, the master of historical fiction, in his story in *Stories from Atlantic Canada* (Toronto: Macmillan, 1973), 1-23. "At the Tide's Turn" describes how Martin Bunt, in the imaginary town of Oldport, fared during the same trying period. In this rendering, the author takes you "inside the happening" and explores the impact of the war on everyday people. Which account is the more revealing, the more interesting? From the historical or literary standpoint it really does not matter, for both versions are of equal excellence. What Raddall has done is translate the historical account in terms of fiction. The events are not distorted or camouflaged; they are portrayed in another vein and with a different objective. This time the author reinforces our understanding of past events so that we see not only "what" and "why" but, equally important, "how". Finally, take the evolution of this account full circle by reading an eyewitness version from the pen of Simeon Perkins—a flesh-and-blood justice of the peace, merchant, politician, and privateersman of Liverpool. This is to be found in *The Diary of Simeon Perkins* (Toronto: Champlain Society, 1948), 177-266. Before long you will recognize that Martin Bunt and Simeon Perkins have something in common.

With an abundance of tales "half told and tunes that break off in the middle", the region has frequently been a resource for historical fiction. In addition to Raddall, Will R. Bird, Hugh MacLennan, Evelyn Eaton, E. M. Richardson, and Charles Bruce are among those who have deliberately recreated the past of Atlantic Canada. There can be little doubt as to the genuine appeal of this type of writing, and consideration of its role in the study of local history is vital. History all too often becomes bogged down with wars, rumours of wars, and the records of kings, queens, and politicians. The novelist stops us short with the reminder that history is also about ordinary people. *His Majesty's Yankees*, set, as are so many of Raddall's tales, in Nova Scotia in the 1770s, amply demonstrates the point. The author shows clearly what it was like to live in a revolutionary storm centre. Following a privateering attack on Liverpool, the hero, David Strang, comments:

> Ay, the British flag was ours, by the simplest rule of arithmetic, and all this gunpowder was blowing us apart from the America we had known. What the outcome would be not one of us could guess, though we knew the deep sources of American strength and saw the weakness of the King's in the very presence of the privateers, attacking our town under the nose of the Halifax admiral. ... My father had seen that today's events would prove a sign and portent for the ... hitherto neutral Yankees of the whole south shore.[8]

The dramatic events of the American Revolution have attracted many writers. Among the best is an American, Kenneth Roberts, whose approach to historical writing closely parallels that of Raddall. Read *Oliver Wiswell* for a graphic description of the Loyalist side in the conflict. Roberts clearly reveals his motive in writing:

> It was to tell exactly how the Loyalists felt about everyone and everything, as well as what they did. They had strong feelings about the Declaration of Independence, and if I couldn't clearly convey what they thought and why, readers would keep on thinking that they didn't think. .... All I cared about was painting a complete and truthful picture of the Loyalist side of the American Revolution. I had to explain that Wiswell was a man of principle, a fighter. Like all the rest of those unfortunate Loyalists, he was by nature loyal, not a weak-spined opportunist. .... [9]

By concentrating on a single individual (for example, the fictional Oliver Wiswell) a novelist can do things impossible for the historian. In fiction, the writer is freed from the constraints of balance and proportion; he can intensify an episode by interpreting it through a blend of fiction and fact. Yet, in utilizing history, the author should never rewrite it. Again, the point is made clear by Raddall.

If you are going to interfere with the truth, with history, to the extent of introducing some fiction, you owe history something for the liberty you are taking, and that is to make sure of your facts. Then your reader is not only going to be entertained by a story, he is going to learn something true about the time of which you write.[10]

Sometimes the career of a person who actually lived may serve as a central theme. Thus, the crotchety, stubborn J. W. F. Des Barres, one-time governor of Cape Breton and later of Prince Edward Island, soldier, surveyor. and artist, becomes a novelist's medium in *An Earl Must Have a Wife* by Will R. Bird. However, Bird does more than retell Des Barres's story—he recreates the dying days of the eighteenth century in London and Nova Scotia and describes some of the eccentricities of British colonial administration. To do so with credibility, it was necessary for him to read "more than a thousand letters written by Des Barres or addressed to him" and where there were gaps in the record he had to fill these "on the basis of knowledge acquired from existing archive material and published works as well as on the basis of reasonable conjecture".[11] To form an opinion of how well Bird accomplishes this task, check his fictional account with that of a scholarly historian. See G. D. N. Evans: *Uncommon Obdurate: The Several Careers of J. F. W. Des Barres* (Toronto: University of Toronto Press, 1969).

There remains for consideration the novel or short story that is not outwardly historical, but from which we also may learn. What better place to gain understanding of nineteenth-century life than through the pen of T. C. Haliburton and the "perambulations" of Sam Slick? (See *Stories From Atlantic Canada*, 28-33.) Life in a typical Newfoundland outport community (Bay Roberts) is detailed in a nineteenth-century novel, Robert Lowell's *New Priest in Conception Bay* (Toronto: McClelland and Stewart, 1974). The works of L. M. Montgomery have remained on best-seller lists for over a half-century and thousands of her books still sell annually. Why? Nostalgia? Human interest? Tourist promotion? Perhaps, but it should also be noted that Montgomery was a perceptive reporter with an eye for detail. In many short stories and in some of the novels (it would be foolish to pretend all are of equal merit) we have a genuine portrait of early-twentieth-century rural life.

Will R. Bird is well known for his historical novels dealing with the Yorkshiremen of the Chignecto Isthmus. However, some of his best writing arises from personal experiences in the First World War. See *Ghosts Have Warm Hands* (Toronto: Clarke, Irwin, 1968). Easing his book on a diary kept during 1914-18, Bird depicts the courage, horror, and humour of war and its impact on a generation of Maritimers. Serving with him in the 42nd Royal Highlanders were a group of Newfoundlanders—only one of whom survived Passchendaele. During the long nights in the trenches Bird encouraged the men to talk "about their home life, their villages and what they did for a living". A half-century later, in a type of fictional memoir, *Angel Cove* (Toronto: Macmillan of Canada, 1972), Bird gives an account of a way of life that has all but vanished from Atlantic Canada. Or again, compare Ernest Buckler's outstanding novel of rural Nova Scotia, *The Mountain and the Valley*, with a novel based on outport Newfoundland, *Tomorrow Will Be Sunday* by Harold Horwood. Both authors convey the sense of place and regional identity so characteristic of the literature and the art of Atlantic Canada (see page 160). Buckler writes:

> In the Nova Scotia country, almost specifically in the country where I live, you get the universals more than you do almost anywhere else. You don't have to wander all over the bloody world and explore every nook and cranny to find out how people behave. . . . In a small community like this, you have a representation of every kind of psychological mode. The whole macrocosm is here in microcosm.[12]

Narrative poetry, or poetry that tells a story, is one of the oldest forms of literature. History and fiction have always been combined through this medium and it is not unusual that the stirring episodes in the history of Atlantic Canada have also left their mark on the poetry of the region. As with historical fiction, however, we may be misled. Those who turn to poetry looking for straight history will, more often than not, come away disappointed. Discounting folk songs and ballads (because of their importance they merit separate consideration), "most people go to poetry because in its own way it may provide insight into history . . . the poet uses historical materials as a symbol or structuring principle in order to make a personal statement of his own." It is clear that in narrative poetry based on historical themes we are dealing with two distinct categories. In the "poeticized form of history" a story is retold in verse; in "historically based poetry" historical data are used as a source of metaphor and symbol.[13]

Andrew Merkel's poem *"Tallahassee"* is an example of the first type. Based on careful archival research and investigation of contemporary records, it recounts one of the most thrilling episodes of the American Civil War. During the early 1860s blockade runners of the Confederacy (the South) became a common sight along the coast of Atlantic Canada. Maritimers had a ringside seat and followed closely every move of the war at sea. The *Tallahassee*, the fastest ship in the Confederate navy, was renowned among Federalist (Northern) vessels. Her skipper was Captain John Taylor Wood, a former colonel in the Confederate army, a grandson of Zachary Taylor, the twelfth president of the United States, and a nephew of Jefferson Davis, president of the Confederacy. (For a link between Taylor and Atlantic Canada see page 27.) The exploit that inspired Merkel's poem began in August 1864, when a shortage of coal forced the *Tallahassee* to seek haven in the port of Halifax. In hot pursuit and waiting outside the harbour entrance were two Northern gunboats. According to international law Taylor had twenty-four hours to take on supplies. Units of the Royal Navy were on hand to see that no munitions went on board and that all ships left within the prescribed time. Merkel's poem, based on accurate sources, will tell you how the *Tallahassee* "escaped ... late that moonless night", completely outwitting her pursuers.

Atlantic Canada's most distinguished interpreter in poetry is without question E. J. Pratt.

Tide and wind and crag,
Sea-weed and sea-shell.
And broken rudder—
And the story is told
Of human veins and pulses,
Of eternal pathways of fire,
Of dreams that survive the night,
Of doors held ajar in storms.[14]

Much of Pratt's poetry is historically based and deeply rooted in the environmental influences of his native Newfoundland. Born the son of a Methodist clergyman at Western Bay northeast of Carbonear in 1883, he spent his first twenty-four years on the island before "emigrating" in 1907 to assume an academic career in Toronto. Although the remainder of his life was spent inland. the early years in outport communities such as Moreton's Harbour left an imprint later reflected in his poetic outpouring. One of his major preoccupations, the struggle of life against the sea, is a theme that re-echoes through poems such as "The Cachalot". Here, "a sperm whale in the pitch of prime" is pitted against a Nantucket whaling barque. Two longer narrative poems deserve a careful reading if one is to capture the full impact of the poet's approach. Significantly, both recount tragedies at sea. The best known, "The Titanic", focuses attention on the clearly defined conflict between human values and the "blind menace of the sea". "The Roosevelt and the Antinoe" is based on the rescue of the crew of the

... British freighter, "Antinoe".
Don't know position. Sixteen hours ago,
Rough latitude—North forty-six and ten,
Rough longitude—thirty-nine, five-eight.
Been hove-to ever since; the present rate
Of drift to East, two knots (approximate).[15]

E. J. Pratt has great stories to tell and this brief introduction may encourage the reader to dip into his *Collected Poems* (Toronto: Macmillan of Canada, 1958). While there are many reasons for Pratt's popularity, among them are certainly his sense of colourful detail and his painstaking research of topics. Only someone thoroughly familiar with the seal fishery could write "The Ice-Floes" or describe "The Shark" thus:

His fin,
Like a piece of sheet-iron,
Three-cornered,
And with knife-edge,
Stirred not a bubble
As it moved
With its base-line on the water.

His body was tubular
And tapered
And smoke-blue,
And as he passed the wharf
He turned, . . . [16]

or treat the idiosyncracies of the 1920s with such wit and verve as in "The Witches' Brew". While we may not totally accept the verdict of the German historian Jacob Burckhardt that "history finds in poetry not only one of its most important but one of its purest and finest sources",[17] it must be admitted that the medium yields, to those who search, evidence, insight, and meaning. A knowledge of the poetry of those already mentioned and others such as Bliss Carman, Charles G. D. Roberts, Charles Bruce, and Alden Nowlan will help toward a fuller understanding of the region that provided them with so much inspiration.

November 14, 1607, is a date of significance in the history of Atlantic Canada; it saw a "first" theatrical production not only for the region, but for the entire North American continent. Marc Lescarbot, lawyer and author, whose *Histoire de la Nouvelle France* is an important source on early Acadia, wrote the script "Le Théâtre de Neptune" to mark Poutrincourt's return to Port Royal. In the play, a nautical tableau, the god Neptune is surrounded by a court of Tritons and Indians who welcome the returning explorers and praise the colony's leaders. Cannon were fired, trumpets sounded, and Lescarbot reported that the audience was suitably impressed. An abridged version of the play may be found in the *Nova Scotia Journal of Education*, March 1939, 275-82. While not a drama in the strict sense, *L'Ordre de Bon Temps* (see page 108), also organized by the resourceful Lescarbot at Port Royal, had all the characteristics of a theatrical production. To combat boredom and long isolation from France he conceived a plan whereby each day one individual was responsible for the menu and meal preparations. The dinner was preceded by a ceremonial procession in which the food was carried to the table:

> At the dinner the steward with napkin on shoulder, staff of office in hand and collar of the order round his neck, led the van. The other guests in procession followed, each bearing a gift. After grace in the evening, he resigned his insignia to his successor, and they drank to each other in a cup of wine. It was the steward's duty to look to supplies, and he would go hunt or fish a day or two before his turn came and add some dainty to the ordinary fare.[18]

Andrew Merkel has written a poem, "The Order of Good Cheer", that will give you more details on the organization of what has been described as the oldest social club in North America.

A love of drama is instinctive in all of us and we can easily appreciate the part played by events such as those organized by Lescarbot at Port Royal. While the theatre did not arrive until much later, the pioneers of the region were imaginative in developing their own dramatic and social activities. Thus the "building bee"—a gathering of people to construct a house or barn—and the "milling frolic"—when home-woven blankets were waulked or filled (worked until a nap was raised on the surface)—became occasions of song and dance and mime. In Newfoundland the practice of mumming or janneying—to act or play in a mask or disguise—while still found, was more prevalent in earlier days. Evolving from this tradition the text of three mummers' plays ("St. John's", "Change Island", and "Salvage") may be found in *Christmas Mumming in Newfoundland* (Toronto: University of Toronto Press, 1967). More detail on this subject as it relates to folklore and local history will be found in Chapter 9.

Larger towns and cities attracted travelling players and saw the erection of theatres. Halifax newspapers were advertising forthcoming productions as early as 1768 and the prevalence of play-going was causing unfavourable comment in the press. Until the first regular theatre was built in 1789, the Pontac Inn saw double duty and more than a hundred different plays, operas, and farces were produced during the last fifteen years of the eighteenth century. The presence of the military in large numbers accounted in part for the popularity of live theatre, and early St. John's, Saint John, Fredericton, and Charlottetown newspapers contained frequent references to dramatic productions. Only during the present century have writers emerged to give us drama conveying a sense of the historical past. Drama means action and it is not complete until the words are spoken and acted. Should the play excel, the problem depicted and the attitudes conveyed will have a universal appeal. Further, if it is grounded in a particular historical episode we may well come away with a heightened understanding of the past.

The Highland Clearances in Scotland, comparable to the Expulsion of the Acadians or perhaps to the plight of some of the Loyalists, provides a ready-made background for an excellent play, *The Blood Is Strong*, by Lister Sinclair. In the northern Highlands, in Sutherlandshire, Ben Bhraggie rises 1,300 feet above the blue-green waters of Dornoch Firth. Here is to be found a red sandstone effigy of George Granville Leveson-Gower, first Duke of Sutherland, second Marquis of Stafford, third Earl Gower, and fourth Lord Gower of Sittenham. Despite his many titles the Duke, an Englishman, lives on in infamy wherever Scottish Highlanders have settled, because in large measure he was responsible for dispossessing thousands of them in favour of raising sheep. Defenceless against such a landlord's power, many Highlanders migrated to northern Nova Scotia, Cape Breton Island, and Prince Edward Island. Between 1790 and 1850 over one hundred emigrant ships landed at the port of Pictou alone. Change and dislocation were not limited to Sutherlandshire: the entire Highland area and neighbouring islands were affected by the imposition of a sheep economy. This displacement of people provides the background for *The Blood Is Strong* and the play conveys, as could no other means, the hardship and travail " . . . which is the same no matter where people come from, or where they are going or when."[19]

The twentieth century has seen ample evidence of the emotional shock associated with eviction and emigration. While the Highland Clearances and the problems of pioneer life are used by Sinclair as a frame of reference, the meaning is clear. In comprehending this play, we grasp a fact of history very basic to every Scottish Highlander, Acadian, or Loyalist. There are bonds in adversity. Drama can also reflect the atmosphere of a period more vividly than other written accounts. The love of land and the inherent sentimentality of the Celtic people is captured in *The Blood Is Strong*. The play concludes with Murdoch MacDonald saying to his daughter Kate: "When I go to the lobster beach and look over the water now, I think I'm just beginning to make out the hills of Scotland again. . . . One of these days my sight's going to clear up so that I'll see your mother again, a girl in Glen Sligachan. That'll be the day, Katie, that'll be the day."[20]

One of the best-known contemporary playwrights in Atlantic Canada is Dr. A. L. Murphy of Halifax. A number of his plays, including *Thy Sons Command* and *You're Calling Me Michael*, have been produced locally, and in addition he has written widely for radio and television. You will enjoy reading *The First Falls on Monday* (Toronto: University of Toronto Press, 1972), which is illustrative of his work in historical drama. Newfoundland, through the writing of Michael Cook, Edward (Ted) Russell, and E. R. Procunier, has been the setting for several plays with local themes. Cook's *Colour the Flesh the Colour of Dust* depicts the "seamy side" of early St. John's, while *Tiln* concerns two aging seamen who "just may be" the only inhabitants left on earth. Russell, a one-time magistrate, civil servant, politician, and salesman, is well known for his radio character "Uncle Mose", a homespun philosopher and commentator on the Newfoundland way of life. *The Hangashore* and *The Holdin' Ground* are among his most frequently produced plays. Procunier's *The Strength of Love*, set in the fictional outport of Peace Harbour, returns to the theme of man's endless conflict with the sea and the impact of the sea on those who daily must risk their lives to follow it. His *The Moonless Night* considers a recurring topic in the fiction of the region: a young man leaves home, "does well", and then returns—often with surprising consequences. Both plays are in E. R. Procunier: *A Knife to Thy Throat and Nine Other Plays* (Toronto: The Book Society of Canada, 1962). L. M. Montgomery explores a variation of the same subject in a short story, "The Brother Who Failed", found in *Further Chronicles of Avonlea* (Toronto: Ryerson Press, 1953), 107-22. Charles Bruce has also captured the essence of the exiles' return in *People From Away*: "For what he saw now was that it was not a story, it was not finished. It was life and going on, and he was part of it. He had returned from the land of venture. But somehow he was one of them. His thoughts turned in on this, in flashing dream. The curious revelation . . . that Currie Head and Boston were not separate worlds, but extensions of the same thing."[21]

Plays such as these deserve to be better known in the region that inspired them. All are worth study, and if your school has a drama club you might consider producing a play that centres on life in Atlantic Canada. Those by E. R. Procunier are particularly appropriate for high-school production. A helpful book is E. Conrad and M. Van Dyke: *History on the Stage* (New York: Van Nostrand Reinhold, 1971).

A contemporary resurgence of interest in Acadian history and culture has given rise to an increased literary output. For this, much of the credit must go to Antonine Maillet, a native of Buctouche, New Brunswick, and a professor at Laval University. Mme Maillet first achieved national attention with her play *Les Crasseux*, a dramatic parody on life in Acadia. This initial success was later to be eclipsed by *La Sagouine*, a triumph of the demanding art of monologue. The sole character, La Sagouine, an elderly charwoman, is described as " . . . a woman of the sea, daughter of a cod fisherman, wife of a fisherman of oysters and smelts". When the census-taker asks her "citoyenneté pis nationalité" she replies:

> C'est malaisé à dire. . . . Je vivons en Amarique, ben je sons pas des Amaricains. Non, les Amaricains, ils travaillont dans des shops aux Etats, pis ils s'en venont se promener par icitte sus not côtes, l'été, en culottes blanches pis en parlant anglais. Pis ils sont riches, les Amaricains, j'en sons point. Nous autres je vivons au Canada; ça fait que je devons putôt être des Canadjens, ça me r'semble.
>
> . . . Non, je sons pas tout à fait des Français, je pouvons pas dire ça: les Français, c'est les Français de France. Ah! pour ça, je sons encore moins des Français de France que des Amaricains. Je sons putôt des Canadjens français, qu'ils nous avont dit.
>
> . . . Ça se peut pas non plus, ça. Les Canadjens français, c'est du monde qui vit à Québec. Ils les appelont des Canayens, ou ben des Québecois. Ben comment c'est que je pouvons être des Québecois si je vivons point à Québec? . . . Pour l'amour de Djeu, où c'est que je vivons, nous autres?[22]

La Sagouine, by combining wit and satire, relying heavily on folk history and the language and idiom of the seventeenth century, succeeds in symbolizing the modern Acadian renaissance. The best way to appreciate the popularity of *La Sagouine* is to obtain a copy and read it in the original. However, be prepared to use the glossary provided, for La Sagouine speaks a French that is foreign even in Quebec. In this return to the patois, or dialect, of old Acadia, Maillet underscores the point that Acadians are *not* French Canadians. Professor Melvin Gallant of the University of Moncton (a Prince Edward Island Acadian) has given expression to this difference by commenting: "Our origins were different, we grew up in different regions . . . and they have never seen the sea like we have."[23] Explore the poetry and songs of Raymond LeBlanc, Calixte Duguay, and Donat LaCroix for further examples of the search for an Acadian identity.

Reading *La Sagouine* is not the only experience posing difficulty in translation and interpretation. It is necessary that we be aware of regional characteristics in language. There are words and phrases common to the whole Atlantic region, and within the area, patterns of speech exclusive to certain districts may be found. Thus the same word may have a totally different meaning in Lunenburg and Notre Dame Bay.

Ralph Waldo Emerson once referred to language as "an archive of history". This suggests the question, "How can a study of language development complement local history?" The point will become clear if we try a simple test:

1. Can you define the following words? aboiteau, ballaceter, liveyere, peavey, sloven, stagehead.
2. What is a woodboat? a fishing admiral? a glitter storm? a barrel man? soft sawder? moose muffle? screech? rappé pie?
3. If someone asked you to locate the following, what would you look for? Richibucto geese, Malpeques, Digby chicken, Pictou twist, a Robertson raft, Labrador tea.

All of the above words or expressions have a particular meaning in Atlantic Canada. Some are not found elsewhere, while others, although not totally exclusive, have strong regional associations. Aboiteau (sometimes spelled abbatteau, aboideau, or bito) refers to the sluice gate in the dykes found along the Bay of Fundy. Used first by the Acadians and undoubtedly of French origin, its exact etymology or source is unknown. An ingenious feat of engineering, the aboiteaux permit fresh water to drain out at low tide, automatically closing with the incoming tide to prevent salt water from flooding the dykelands.* If you were unable to identify any of the other words or phrases in the test, check *A Dictionary of Canadianisms on Historical Principles* (Toronto: W. J. Gage Ltd., 1967). This valuable reference work should be in every school library. Inquire among the older residents in your home community to see if you can establish some distinctive local words or speech patterns. Sometimes distinctive words and phrases may be associated with a particular industry. Louise Manny (ed): *Songs of Miramichi* (Fredericton: Brunswick Press, 1968) contains a valuable glossary of words common to northern New Brunswick and closely connected with lumbering. Check to see if these are known and understood in your part of Atlantic Canada. See also page 70 for a discussion of the impact of the sea on language.

Most of the serious research in this field has been undertaken by Memorial University, and their *Regional Language Studies* are of special interest. One area, Carbonear, has been extensively studied and linguistic experts have concluded that Newfoundlanders generally use English in "a superior and more logical manner"[24] than is common elsewhere. In 1971 a sampling of Canadian high school students (at the Grade IX level) were questioned about their vocabulary, pronunciation, and grammar. Results of this study are now appearing in print and, as we might expect, wide variations exist. You may be interested in comparing some of the national results with interpretations common in your own community. See *The English Quarterly*, Canadian Council of Teachers of English, 5 (1972), 47-104. One of the best accounts of the English language in Canada is Mark M. Orkin: *Speaking Canadian English* (Toronto: General Publish-

*A detailed discussion of Acadian dyking methods is to be found in Andrew Hill Clark: *Acadia: The Geography of Nova Scotia* (Madison: University of Wisconsin Press, 1968).

ing Co., 1970). From this brief survey it can be seen that "Where records are lacking or inadequate, the historian can use the spoken language as an artifact that provides objective, unique and valuable evidence of otherwise undocumented ideas and practices."[25] While it would be wrong to count too heavily on this type of investigation (for authoritative interpretation requires a lifetime of study) words can nevertheless provide us with an informative "archival source".

If we are to understand local history at a level more profound than mere surface events and a listing of data, we must probe deeply. The traditional approach in history gives us a glimpse of past events but it too often withholds the touch of direct experience. It is here that documentary evidence and literature can perform a useful service. Primary sources—of whatever kind—take us back to the actual text, the eye-witness account, the contemporary opinion, the bedrock of historical writing. Beyond this, literature has its place both for the incidental information revealed and the provision of the atmosphere or climate of a bygone age. Even after making full allowance for its shortcomings, "there is no better way of acquiring the necessary familiarity with a section of the past, with its ideas and outlook, than prolonged immersion in literature. This sense of period is something that the historian must acquire if he is to get full value out of his more direct historical sources."[26] For local history in Atlantic Canada literary sources have another value. The novelist, the playwright, or the poet does not merely reproduce the past any more than the artist copies nature. "After memory comes experience . . . and reflection upon this experience." A close study of the writing of an E. J. Pratt or a Thomas Raddall will go far in revealing the regional identity so characteristic of Atlantic Canada.

FOR READING AND REFERENCE

Because of the sweep of material covered in this chapter (particularly literary sources) it is difficult to devise a meaningful bibliography that does not run to hundreds of entries. As a starting-point, you are encouraged to read widely in *Atlantic Anthology, Island Prose and Poetry: An Anthology, By Great Waters*, and *Stories from Atlantic Canada*. From there, go on to sample as much additional prose and poetry as possible.

BIRD, WILL R. (ed.): *Atlantic Anthology*. Toronto: McClelland and Stewart, 1959. Fiction, non-fiction, and poetry are combined to present an interesting literary cross-section of all four provinces.

GRAHAM, ALLAN (ed.): *Island Prose and Poetry: An Anthology*. Charlottetown: Irwin Printing Co., 1973. Collected by the Prince Edward Centennial Commission Literary Committee, this important anthology covers entries in English, French, and Gaelic—the three major languages of Atlantic Canada.

NEARY, PETER, AND O'FLAHERTY, PATRICK (eds.): *By Great Waters*. Toronto: University of Toronto Press, 1974. A complete anthology of the best in the literary heritage of Newfoundland and Labrador.

THOMPSON, KENT (ed.): *Stories from Atlantic Canada*. Toronto: Macmillan of Canada, 1973. An important collection of short stories and fictional excerpts ranging from Haliburton to Buckler. The book emphasizes contemporary writing in the region.

Archives—Mirror of Canada's Past. Toronto: University of Toronto Press, 1972. Provides an overview of the rich resources of Canada's national archives.

PUBLIC ARCHIVES OF NOVA SCOTIA annually publishes collections of documents and monographs of topics relating to the history of the province. See also PANS: *Manuscripts: A Preliminary Short Inventory*, Halifax, 1972.

THE ARCHIVES of the other three provinces also publish documentary material and inventories of sources. Particularly helpful is *We Have News for You*, produced by the Newfoundland and Labrador Provincial Archives, and *Museum Memo*, a publication of the New Brunswick Museum.

NEW BRUNSWICK MUSEUM, Archives Division: *Inventory of Manuscripts*, Saint John, 1967, and Provincial Archives of Newfoundland and Labrador, *Preliminary Inventory*, St. John's, 1970, are also essential.

All important collections of manuscript source materials are indexed in *Union List of Manuscripts in Canadian Repositories*, Public Archives of Canada, Ottawa, 1968.

SUGGESTIONS FOR FURTHER RESEARCH

1. Harold Horwood, in his novel *Tomorrow Will Be Sunday*, has one of his characters say: "No, Christopher, . . . when you grow up here you're a separate breed forever. You may become a professor at a great university, or a research scientist, or something that I can't guess at, but I know one thing, you'll be a Newfoundlander and a bayman to the end of your days." What is the meaning of this passage? Does it apply to other areas of Atlantic Canada? Can you find additional expressions of a "regional identity" in the literature of Atlantic Canada?

2. No literary figure has done more to publicize Nova Scotia than Henry Wadsworth Longfellow. His poem *Evangeline*, published in 1847, was reputed to have "reached almost every literate home in the United States". More recently, the image portrayed by Longfellow has been assailed by critics. Historians have pointed out that the Expulsion was largely a New England rather than an English venture as depicted by the poet, and Mme Antonine Maillet has gone further: "If Longfellow had actually lived a while among the Acadians, without doubt he would have chosen a mother of twelve children instead of his virginal heroine to symbolize the Acadian woman." Read *Evangeline* from the historical standpoint and assess the manner in which Longfellow blended fact and fiction. For historical detail on the Expulsion of the Acadians see the bibliography on page 20. How Longfellow came to write the poem is discussed in Father Arthur Landry: *La Société Historique Acadienne* III, Bulletin 3 (avril-mai-juin 1969): 112-17. See also John Frederic Herbin, *History of Grand Pré* (Kentville: Kentville Publishing Co., 1969), 154-61.

3. Humour and satire have always held a prominent place in the literature of Atlantic Canada. See Thomas McCulloch: *The Stepsure Letters* (Toronto: McClelland and Stewart, 1960), and T. C. Haliburton: *The Sam Slick Anthology* (Toronto: Clarke Irwin, 1969). Compare the approach of McCulloch and Haliburton with that of Ray Smith in "Cape Breton Is the Thought Control Centre of Canada", to be found in *Stories from Atlantic Canada*, or of Antonine Maillet in *La Sagouine*. How does each reflect the period and audience for which it was written?

9. Folk Songs
and Folklore

A major navigational hazard in the North Atlantic is the iceberg, for often only one-eighth to one-third of its mass is visible above the surface. Similarly, in the study of local history much necessary information and detail is invisible. There are attitudes and undercurrents of thought and emotion, quite crucial to the understanding of a particular event, that are never recorded in official documents. Our research can, however, be enriched by a study of the "hidden history" inherent in folk songs and folklore. Historians often place reliance on a newspaper editorial, when in fact it may reflect the opinion or bias of but one individual, the writer. On the other hand, the mere survival of a particular folk song or item of folklore says something about the popular acceptance of its message. While few would go as far as the Scottish patriot Andrew Fletcher: "Give me the making of the songs of a nation and I care not who makes its laws",[1] the folk heritage can throw light on past events and provide a frank expression of the character of a region. Unfortunately, radio, television, and recordings have eroded the place of folk music and today it is rare to find true folk singers. Thanks to the "research in time" of W. Roy MacKenzie, Elisabeth Greenleaf, Maud Karples, Helen Creighton, Louise Manny, Kenneth Peacock, Edward Ives, and others (see bibliography, page 154) we have a good cross-section of the folk-song heritage of Atlantic Canada. Songs depicting important events, political satire, racial characteristics, seafaring life, and lumbering are among the categories of major interest. Examples drawn from all four provinces will illustrate this theme.

MacEdward Leach, an international authority on folk music, once wrote: "If a folklorist should be given the opportunity to create an ideal region, he could hardly do better than to duplicate Newfoundland."[2] Comparative isolation, along with settlements composed of a single ethnic group, has helped to provide a favourable environment for the creation and preservation of folk music. Some songs originated overseas, others found their way to Newfoundland from Canada and New England, and still others developed locally. In a land where people are "wedded with the sea and their children's eyes change colour with it",[3] the focal point is obvious. Voyages afar, shipwrecks, sealing expeditions, ghostly apparitions, misled maidens, and duped sailors have provided a well-stocked storehouse for the balladeer. The most detailed collection is to be found in Kenneth Peacock's *Songs of the Newfoundland Outports*, a 1965 publication of the National Museum of Canada.

Upon occasion folk songs may have a very practical application. Elisabeth Greenleaf relates that while visiting Newfoundland in 1929, " ... as the S.S. *Clyde* gingerly entered the narrow rocky channel of Fogo Harbour",[4] the captain recited a portion of "Wadham's Song". Written in 1756, this song was placed on the Admiralty records in London as the best guide to a portion of the Newfoundland coastline. Using a copy of the *Newfoundland Pilot* (see page 57) and a nautical chart or topographic map (Cape Bonavista to Fogo), see if you can locate some of the navigational hazards mentioned in the song:

Wadham's Song

From Bonavista Cape to the stinking Isles
The course is North full 40 miles;
When you must steer away North East
Till Cape Freels, Gull Island bear NNW.

Then NNW 33 miles
Three leagues off shore lies Wadham's Isles;
Where of a rock you must take care
Two miles SSE from Isles it bears.

Then NW by West, 12 miles or more
There lies Round Head on Fogo Shore;
But NNW seven or eight miles
Lies a sunken rock near the Barracks Isles.

Therefore, my friend, I would you advise
Since all those rocks in danger lies,
That you may never amongst them fall
But keep your luff and weather them all.

As you draw near to Fogo Land
You'll have fifteen fathoms in the sounding sand;
From 15 to 18 never more
And that you'll have close to the shore.

When you abreast of Round Head be
Then Joe Batt's Point you'll plainly see;
To starboard then three or four miles
You'll see a parcel of damned rugged Isles.

When Joe Batt's Arm you are abreast
Then Fogo Harbour bears due West;
But unkind Fortune unluck laid
A sunken rock right in the trade.

So NNW you are to steer
Till Brimstones Head doth plain appear
Which over Pilley's Point you'll see
Then off that danger you are free.

And as you draw within a mile
You'll see a house on Syme's Isle;
The mouth of the channel is not very wide,
But the deepest water is on the larboard side.

When within Syme's Point you have shot,
Then three fathoms of water you have got;
Port hard your helm and take care
In the mid channel for to steer.

When Pilley's Point you are abreast,
Starboard haul and steer SS West
Till Pilley's Point covers Syme's Stage
Then you are clear, I will engage.

Marine tragedies, from the exploits of Captain William Jackman "off rugged Labrador" in 1866 to the torpedoing of the S.S. *Caribou* in Cabot Strait during the Second World War, have claimed the attention of local songwriters. "The Southern Cross", "The Wreck of the Steamship Ethie", and "The Greenland Disaster" were all written in this tradition. Compare the last-mentioned with E. J. Pratt's poem "The Ice Floes", which depicts the same tragedy. Pratt was living in St. John's in 1893 and witnessed the return of the *Greenland* with her flag at half-mast. Alongside hundreds of others he stood in the crowded street listening to the tolling of the church bells during the funeral services for the victims. Try to find newspaper accounts of these disasters or others like them. When the factual style of newspaper reporting is contrasted with the folk version we can understand why these songs have had such widespread appeal.

Perhaps the greatest compliment to be paid Newfoundland folk songs is that so many have found ready acceptance wherever people gather to sing. While they do not always mean what mainlanders think they mean, they possess an irresistible appeal. " . . . a sheer love of naming objects produces songs that seem riotous, knobbly catalogues offered to someone who does not believe in the external world. In fact, for most of Newfoundland's severe history, that world was not much worth believing in; so the songs have a resolute look at some of the better objects. The rest is imported keening, languishing and suspense . . . ."[5] The best way to gain an appreciation of these folk songs is to sing them, or at the very least to listen to some of the records listed in the bibliography. Perhaps your school glee club might be interested in arranging a concert of Newfoundland folk songs.

When we cross over to Nova Scotia certain similarities and contrasts become apparent. The predominant theme of the sea is still there and familiar Irish and English tunes are again encountered. However, a new dimension in the form of Scottish music and song is noticeable. Just after the *Hector* set sail from Loch Broom in July 1773 for Pictou, a stowaway, John McKay, was discovered. Since McKay was an experienced piper, the passengers offered to share their rations in order that he might remain on board. Thus they were entertained during the long passage across the Atlantic and it was to the strain of the pipes that the Highlanders landed on September 15, 1773. From that point onward, the "rantin' pipe", the "tremblin' string", and the Gaelic song have been an integral part of the folk inheritance of New Scotland.

If we know little else about the racial background of a community, the prevailing folk songs will sometimes betray the land of origin of the people. Again, as with so many other historical clues, care must be exercised, since folk music is both popular and portable. Not infrequently songs and ballads common to a given area are simply local adaptations of borrowed tunes. There can, however, be no mistaking the Gaelic folksongs of Cape Breton. A sense of the historical and that incurable Celtic disease—homesickness, combined with lusty humour, make them of interest even in translation. The best collection, *Gaelic Songs of Nova Scotia* by Helen Creighton and Calum MacLeod, a publication of the National Museum of Canada, 1964, contains nearly one hundred examples. In one, "The Woman Who Lost Her Gaelic", ridicule is poured on a girl who emigrated to Boston, "put on airs", and lost—or refused to use—her native tongue. Meanwhile, her lover was not idle:

... You have grown indifferent toward me
since you became a stylish lady
and you departed to another country.
Although I paid attention to you I did
not concentrate completely upon you.
The maiden of my love is tending cattle
In Little Breton, In Little Breton.
May you stay in John O'Groats house* forever,
And may maledictions descend upon yourself
and your kind who become arrogant and smart.
When you visit here you will be dressed in
a new suit and bonnet;
Gaelic will be brushed aside and you will
be called a Yankee,
You perpetrator of devastation, You perpetrator
of devastation ... [6]

In Cape Breton "the blood is indeed strong". A good illustration of an historical incident immortalized in song is provided by the Highland Clearances. After over a century and a half this experience is still remembered:

Fuadach Nan Gàidheal

1. Gur a mise tha tùrsach,
    Ag Caoidh cor na dùthcha,
    'S nan seann daoine cùiseil
    Bha cliùiteach is treun;
    Rinn uachdarain am fuadach,
    Gu fada null thar chuantan,
    Am fearann chaidh thoirt uapa,
    'S thoirt suas do na féidh.

1. Sad am I mourning for the state of the country, and the old, scrupulous people who were worthy and courageous. Landlords evicted them far over the seas; their lands were taken from them, and given up to the deer.

2. 'S e sud a' chulaidh-nàire,
    Bhi faicinn dhaoine làidir,
    "'G am fuadach thar sàile
    Mar bhàrrlach gun fheum";
    'S am fonn a bha àlainn,

---

*The outline of John O'Groats house may still be traced near Duncansby Head in the extreme north of Scotland. In this house "John O'Groats built an eight-sided room with a door to each side and placed an octagonal table therein ... to settle a question of precedence in a family quarrel." See *Brewer's Dictionary of Phrase and Fable*.

> Chaidh chur fo chaoirich bhàna,
> Tha feanntagach 's a' ghàradh,
> 'S an làrach fo fheur.

2. It was, indeed, an object of shame to see strong people being evicted over the ocean like a useless tramp, and Cheviot sheep being placed to graze on the beautiful land. There are nettles in the garden, and the ruins are covered with grass.

> 3.   Far an robh móran dhaoine
> Le 'm mnathan is le'n teaghlaich,
> Chan'eil ach caoraich-mhaola
> Ri fhaotainn 'n an àit',
> Chan fhaicear air a' bhuailidh
> A' bhanarach le buaraich,
> No idir an crodh guaillfhionn,
> 'S am buachaille bàn.

3. Where there used to be many people with their women-folk and families, there are now only hornless sheep to be found in their place. No longer do you see the milk-maid with her spancel, or even the white-shouldered cattle and the fair-haired herdsman.

> 4.   Tha'n uiseag anns na speuran,
> A' seinn a luinneig ghleusda,
> 'S gun neach ann 'g a h-éisdeachd,
> 'N uair dh'éireas i àrd;
> Cha till, cha till na daoine,
> Bha cridheil agus aoibhneil,
> Mar mholl air latha gaothaidh,
> Chaidh 'n sgaoileadh gu bràth.

4. The lark is in the firmament singing its tuneful song, yet nobody is present to listen to her when she ascends the heights. The people will never return, never return, who were hearty and cheerful. They have been dispersed for ever like chaff on a windy day.[7]

From Creighton and MacLeod: *Gaelic Songs in Nova Scotia,* 1964. Source: The National Museum of Man of the National Museums of Canada. Reproduced by permission of Information Canada.

The folk-song heritage of Nova Scotia has had a significant influence on the literary output of the province. Archibald MacMechan, Will R. Bird, and Thomas Raddall, to mention only three writers, have drawn extensively upon this inheritance. As an illustration read "Blind McNair", a short story by Raddall, to be found in *Tambour and Other*

Stories (Toronto: McClelland and Stewart, 1945), 371-88. For " . . . although they sing ballads no more, nor will you hear a chantey, since the chanteymen have vanished and tall grass shines where once the ship-yards lay under a snow of chips and shavings . . . ",[8] the appeal remains. A number of ballad operas drawing on the same tradition have been written. *L'Ordre du Bon Temps* by Louvigny de Montigny and Healey Willan is based in part on Acadian folk songs—a reminder that the first permanent European settlers in Nova Scotia carried with them the traditions of old France. "I remember," wrote Marc Lescarbot, "that on the fourteenth of January 1607, of a Sunday afternoon we amused ourselves with singing and music on the river Equille. . . . "[9] Adaptations of French folk songs such as "Vive les Matelots", popular in the early-seventeenth century, are incorporated in *L'Ordre du Bon Temps*. A steadfast faith and courage in the face of adversity have always been hallmarks of the Acadian people. "Ave, Maris Stella", an ancient Latin *cantique*, has been sung by Acadians since the founding of the colony. Tradition has it that King Louis XIII suggested this hymn as a special anthem and it is still so regarded by the Acadians of Atlantic Canada.

A folk song found in many lands and guises is "The Broken Ring". In fact, the story of the returned lover matching parts of a ring may be traced as far back as Greek mythology.

> Give me the ring that rests on your finger;
> Break it in twain, our love to seal;
> Each a half shall carry until we marry,
> Until at an altar we both do kneel.

You will find several variations of this song in Helen Creighton and Doreen Senior: *Traditional Songs from Nova Scotia* (Toronto: Ryerson Press, 1960), 134-40. Using this ancient ballad as a focal point, Don Wetmore (librettist) and Trevor Jones (composer) have written a folk opera, *The Broken Ring*. The music is based on typical Nova Scotian folk songs and ingeniously combines the legendary *Saladin* Mutiny of 1844 with the broken-ring theme. Full details of the *Saladin* incident are contained in Archibald MacMechan: *Old Province Tales* (Toronto: McClelland and Stewart, 1924), 207-38. On Harbour Island in Guysborough County (N.S.) is located a neck of land called Saladin Point. Can you discover the connection between this place name and the mutiny?

The desire to caricature, satirize, and ridicule has frequently provided motivation for the composition of folk songs, or what might be better described as folk poetry. Especially has this been true in the political field. In Atlantic Canada politics have always been uppermost, to the extent that for many years "every boy and every gal born into the world alive" was either "a little liberal or else a little conservative".[10] Thus, letters-to-the-editor columns in nineteenth-century newspapers often contain "political poetry". In addition to exposure through the press, some of the better-known verses (e.g., those dealing with Confederation) were given wide circulation as broadside ballads. Printed on one side of a large sheet of paper, or broadside, they sold for a few pennies on street corners. Not all of these writers, many of whom are anonymous, limited their output to political matters. George Story has written of St. John's (though it is equally applicable to other parts of the region): "An incident, a ceremony, a remark . . . immediately begat a poetic epistle."[11] Typical of these local poets was New Brunswicker Michael Whelan (1858-1937). See Louise Manny and James R. Wilson: *Songs of Miramichi* (Fredericton: Brunswick Press, 1970) for examples of his works. Although the tradition is dying, letters in verse may still be found in the editorial pages of the St. John's *Evening Telegram*.

The question may be asked, "Of what value to local history are these bits of rhymes and verses?" Only a few can stand the test of true poetry, while many are simply parodies of well-known works (Hamlet's "To be or not to be" speech may be cited as one overworked model). The answer is provided by Edward Ives, whose research has contributed so much to our understanding of the folk heritage of Atlantic Canada. Writing about Lawrence Doyle, the farmer-poet of Prince Edward Island, he concluded:

> Part of his response to life was to interpret it for others by making songs about it, and through his songs he has given us many, remarkably sharp pictures of his world—what caught his fancy, what tickled him, what angered him, what the neighbours were like and what his horizons were. Furthermore it is a special kind of look at a way of life gone by. What it was it was, and what it was nothing else will ever be again.[12]

One political song, essentially political satire, is "Prince Edward Island Adieu", attributed by Ives to Lawrence Doyle. Sometimes called "The History of Prince Edward Island", it summarizes in capsule form the history of the province. Two of its twelve verses will be sufficient to convey the message:

> Come all ye hardy sons of toil
> Pray lend an ear to me
> Whilst I relate the dismal state
> Of this our country
> I will not pause to name the cause
> But keep it close in view:
> For comrades grieve when they must leave
> And bid this Isle adieu.

There is a band within this land
Who live in pomp and pride;
To swell their stores they rob the poor;
On pleasures' wings they ride.
With dishes fine their table shine,
They live in princely style.
They are the knaves who made us slaves,
And sold Prince Edward Isle.

For a detailed analysis of this popular song, read Chapter V in Edward Ives: *Lawrence Doyle: A Study in Local Song-Making* (Orono: University of Maine, 1971), 61-86.

The vehemence of the debate over Confederation (whether in all four colonies in the 1860s and '70s or in Newfoundland during 1948-9) inspired local poets in many parts of Atlantic Canada. Newfoundland's "Come Near at Your Peril—Canadian Wolf" is perhaps the best-known example. Nowhere, however, was this tradition more prevalent than in Nova Scotia. Here, the poetic outpouring conveyed in dramatic fashion how many felt regarding this emotion-tinged issue. "Lines suggested by the legislature passing the confederation resolutions with such haste" (*Acadian Recorder*, March 25, 1867), "Anti-lyrics" (to be found in the *Morning Chronicle*, 1867-8), and "The Lullaby" represent a tradition of satirical verse which, if nothing else, gave yet another cutting edge to the sharp debate that prevailed.

Hush my babes, be still and trusting;
    Sooth your fears and soundly sleep.
My biggest bubble's almost bursting,
    But soothing syrup's blessed cheap.

Sleep soft dupes and trust in Tupper;
    Retrenchment's but a naughty dream.
The sad effect of too much supper,
    He never thought of such a scheme.[13]

Reprinted by permission of *The Dalhousie Review*, Dalhousie University, Halifax.

New Brunswick shared a similar heritage in folk songs and poetry; however, because of the significance of lumbering, songs associated with this industry assume a special importance. Understandably, the Miramichi River valley provided the inspiration for many lumberjack songs. See Manny and Wilson: *Songs of Miramichi*. Moreover, their popularity over the years prompted the establishment of a highly successful folk festival, thereby assuring a continuing interest in this music and song. Two ingredients, tragedy on the river and in the woods, associated with a natural catastrophe—the Miramichi Fire of 1825, continued to give abundant source of incident for the balladeer.

> This is the truth, that now I tell you
>   For mine eyes in part did see
> What did happen to the people
>   On the banks of the Miramichi.
> The seventh evening of October
>   Eighteen hundred twenty-five,
> Two hundred people fell by fire;
>   Scourged those that did survive.[14]

The Miramichi Fire has been described as the worst disaster that ever befell the area. Study the folk-song versions to be found in *Songs of Miramichi* (145-51) and compare these accounts with that of any standard history text. Note the map that depicts the extent of the fire in J. C. Webster: *Historical Guide to New Brunswick* (Fredericton: Government Bureau of Information, 1941), 62. If you have access to newspapers of the period you will find these a source of detailed information—not only on the fire, but on the rescue and relief operations that followed.

One of the most popular New Brunswick ballads tells of a young Prince Edward Islander* who was crushed to death by a falling log near Boiestown, New Brunswick, in 1881. It is of special interest for two reasons. The song has been recorded in Newfoundland, Nova Scotia, Prince Edward Island, New Brunswick, and Maine, illustrating the portability of this type of ballad. Further, its widespread fame indicates that such songs know no boundaries. Other folk songs depicting incidents in the history of Atlantic Canada have become well known in Maine—a point that emphasizes the interdependence of the two areas. None the less, it would be wrong to assume that relations between Maine and New Brunswick have always been cordial. For a long time the international boundary was in dispute and this prompted the so-called "Aroostook War" in 1839. The difficulties became celebrated in song on both sides of the border. A detachment of the American army was stationed at Houlton, Maine, in readiness to

---

*The victim, variously called Emery, Hembly, Emberley, etc., was in reality Peter Amberley (or at least his family was so known in Prince Edward Island). His grave, near Boiestown, was marked in 1963 by a marble monument. See illustration in *Songs of Miramichi*, 214. For text of one folk song on "Peter Emberley" see *Songs of Miramichi*, 160-3. See also H. Creighton: *Folksongs from Southern New Brunswick* (Ottawa: National Museum of Man, 1971), 231-3.

. . . lick the redcoats anyhow,
And drive them from our border;
The loggers are awake—and all
Await the General's order;
Britannia shall not rule the Maine,
Nor shall she rule the water;
They've sung that song full long enough,
Much longer than they oughter.[15]

For their part, the Woodstock *Times* avowed the determination of the New Brunswickers, " . . . with bayonet and cheer", to "make them stand clear."[16] Check a standard history text or encyclopedia and see how despite "all sound and fury" the bloodless Aroostook War was settled.

Thus it is that folk songs and folk poetry, although they cannot be regarded as authoritative history, can provide information that will help explain the past and augment our knowledge of it.

Standard dictionary definitions of folklore tell us that it concerns the traditional beliefs, customs, tales, or sayings that have been orally preserved among a people. On first reading it may appear that the inclusion of such material in this book is to deny all that has been stressed about accuracy and objectivity. The claim that Lake Utopia, New Brunswick, is inhabited by a serpent rivalling Scotland's Loch Ness monster; the custom in outport Newfoundland of children and adults dressing up in weird costumes and going janneying at Christmas-time; the belief of some people in phantom ships; the use of ancient home remedies; the search for buried treasure—these may be interesting, but are they history? Perhaps not in the traditional sense. All of the examples mentioned do form part of the heritage of Atlantic Canada; consequently, if we are to gain full understanding and appreciation of the roots of this culture, the folk inheritance is worthy of consideration.

Those who are sceptical should recognize that folk traditions are not dead. Although we live in the space age, time-honoured beliefs are all about us.

Hex signs on barns are on their way out, but amulets hang from rear-view mirrors of automobiles. Haunted houses are still with us, but more immediate concern is directed toward "jinx" or "death" cars. Kissing games in the parlour are giving way to kissing games on the highway. The legendary warriors with invincible swords have become legendary warriors in jet-propelled aircraft, and the invincible swords themselves have become mysterious death or disintegration rays . . . monsters have been crowded out of the newspapers by flying saucers.[17]

If nothing else, a study of folklore can provide a sense of balance and those seemingly absurd concepts of earlier days may not be so ludicrous after all. Despite this, there is a tendency among many people to discount all references to folklore as nonsensical. Equally unfortunate is the opposite view, which naïvely accepts as valid every tall tale that is told. There is much to be gained from a study of folklore, yet we should not blind ourselves to the fact that a great deal that masquerades as "the way of our forefathers" may well be classified as "fakelore". Memories can be shaky, deliberate deception is not unknown, and some oral traditions are grounded in fiction. To check and double-check must be the standing motto of everyone with an interest in this field.

To begin, folklore provides us with basic information on customs and traditions that, in some cases, have survived centuries of time and a trans-atlantic crossing. These may be of interest for their own sake; however, they can also tell us something about the kind of people who first settled Atlantic Canada and even, upon occasion, help pinpoint a country or a place of origin. Then, too, a local legend or firmly held tradition may be a clue to the verification of an incident through documentary or archae-ological evidence. The tale that "there *is* something buried out there" ought not to be discounted. Local traditions may be clues to attitudes and prejudices that once prevailed. The surviving elements of these concepts may also help one to understand contemporary attitudes and beliefs. It is evident then that the study of folklore has a special place in local history—a point emphasized by the American historian, Richard M. Dorson.

> The union between the historical and the legendary is firmest at the level of local history. The local historian is concentrating on a well defined and bounded community, with its own strong sense of identity and continuity, of roots and past—a much stronger sense than the nation as a whole possesses of its history. Within the county and the township borders the family names and local landmarks perpetuate a history that is visible and immediate and borne in mind rather than buried in history books. Local history is in a very large sense traditional history. [Today] . . . where the facts are endlessly stored in print, and the populations are crammed in vast cities, the personal sense of history has all but vanished—save in the local community.[18]

To further understand what is meant by folklore and this "personal sense of history", you should sample two books by Dr. Helen Creighton, one of the region's authorities in the field. *Bluenose Ghosts* (Toronto: Ryerson Press, 1957), is a collection of stories that many Nova Scotians like to tell "when the lamps are lighted and long shadows haunt home and countryside". *Bluenose Magic* (Toronto: Ryerson Press, 1968), a more specialized book, deals with popular beliefs and superstitions current in Nova Scotia. Although the material is limited to one province, there is much that is shared by New Brunswick, Prince Edward Island, and Newfoundland. Charles W. Dunn: *Highland Settler: A Portrait of the Scottish Gael in Nova Scotia* (Toronto: University of Toronto Press, 1953) is also a very useful reference, since it describes how emigration affected the Scottish folk culture. Before discussing some suggestions on the collecting of this material, a few examples will illustrate the scope of folklore in local history.

Midway between North and South Gut, St. Ann's on Cape Breton Island is the only Gaelic College in North America. Each summer since 1939, courses have been offered in Higland arts, crafts, dancing, and pipe music, as well as in the Gaelic language and song. Here too during August the annual Gaelic Mod, a week-long festival of Scottish culture, is held. Obviously such an institution may be credited with the preservation of much of the language, traditions, and culture of old Scotland. However, traces of Scottish folklore may be found in other parts of Atlantic Canada. The Miramichi, northern Nova Scotia, Prince Edward Island, and the Codroy Valley of Newfoundland also share this heritage. If your community was founded by Scots you may find that people still hold *ceilidhs* in the tradition of their ancestors. It is on occasions such as this that the tales of the supernatural, of the *sithichean*, or little people, will be told, old folk songs sung, and the walls echo to the sound of music and dancing. Read the chapter entitled "The Ceilidh" in *Loch Bras d'Or* by Margaret MacPhail (Windsor: Lancelot Press, 1970) for a description of one such gathering. There is no better way to sample that blend of revelry and reverence so characteristic of the Scot. "Ghosts across the Atlantic" in Neil MacNeil's *The Highland Heart in Nova Scotia* (Toronto: S. J. Reginald Saunders, 1958) is confirmation of another Scottish trait, an addiction to the mystical and the supernatural.

This addiction is by no means limited to the Scots. The Irish settlers of New Brunswick have also handed down many fascinating tales. One ghost story that is firmly entrenched in the folklore of the Miramichi centres around the "whooping ghost" of the Dungarvon River. The alleged murder of a cook in an isolated lumber camp became celebrated through its retelling and, so the story goes, his ghost periodically returned accompanied by a whooping or shrieking sound. According to Louise Manny, historian of the Miramichi, a parish priest "felt seriously enough about the matter to go to Dungarvon and read the church service of exorcism [a formal act to expel evil spirits]. It is said that after this the ghost was heard no more."[19] For a sampling of the ballads that recount this story, see *Songs of Miramichi*, 78-85. Throughout Atlantic Canada, from Port-au-Port peninsula, Newfoundland, to Cheticamp, Isle Madame, Clare, or Argyle in Nova Scotia, to the north shore of New Brunswick, there are common elements in the folklore of the Acadian people. Although territorially a part of Quebec, the inhabitants of the Iles de la Madeleine in the Gulf of St. Lawrence have much in common with the Acadians—in fact, many are of Acadian origin. You will find Père Anselme Chiasson's book, *Les Légendes des Iles de la Madeleine* (Moncton: Aboiteaux, 1969), of particular interest in making a comparative study of Acadian folklore.

A folk tradition of particular interest is mumming, or janneying. Especially prevalent in Newfoundland, the practice may also be found in parts of Nova Scotia. During the twelve days of Christmas it is customary for men and women, boys and girls to don disguises and visit the homes in their neighbourhood. The verb "to mum" means both "to mutter" and "to be silent", and the word "mummer" apparently is derived from one or both of these meanings. The synonymous word "janneying" is peculiar to Newfoundland and the term, if not coined there, probably originated in the West Country of England.[20] The custom is an ancient one and is traceable to the Middle Ages, proof once again of the value of Newfoundland as a laboratory of folklore and tradition. The authoritative book on the subject, *Christmas Mumming in Newfoundland* (Toronto: University of Toronto Press, 1969), contains the following description:

> Janneys wear all sorts of garments—anything outlandish that they feel will not be identified. Some cover their boots with brim (burlap) bags tied around their legs and hands are usually covered since their peculiarities are known. People wrap themselves in quilts, drape themselves in tablecloths and put on odd garments. Mummers may walk with a stoop or change their gaits as mannerisms and postures are easily identified in a close community. The face is often covered by a veil and grotesque rubber masks are a recent introduction. ... When janneys come to the door they knock loudly and impressively. People are not obliged to let them in and many do not. ... Sometimes janneys step dance ... and those in the house attempt to ascertain their identity.[21]

Mummers occasionally perform plays and often these centre around the legend of St. George and the dragon. Texts of typical plays may be found in *Christmas Mumming in Newfoundland*, 187-207. Perhaps your school dramatic society might be interested in reviving one of these ancient plays. November 5 (Guy Fawkes Day), Pancake Night (the eve of Lent), and St. Patrick's Day are among those festive days marked by ancient customs and traditions. Are any of these marked in your community? Each folk tradition encountered is part of the culture that has been handed down from other generations. As such, each custom has an interesting history and tracing its evolution will add to our total understanding of any community.

At this stage, a most obvious question presents itself: "Where does one begin?" The answer is straightforward—with yourself. Do you know any tales or legends that relate to the early history of your neighbourhood? Can you remember hearing ghost stories, tales of phantom ships, or tragedies? Are you able to list any old proverbs, sayings, or beliefs—relating possibly to the sea or the weather? After having thought through these questions, the next step is to repeat these and similar inquiries among family and friends. More often than not your interest will spark a chain reaction until the problem may be not a scarcity, but an abundance of material.

The way of life once characteristic of Atlantic Canada is fast disappearing, yet much of it can still be preserved through recording interviews with older people. The vast majority will never write memoirs, nor is it likely that many will leave behind detailed correspondence or diaries that provide so much valuable information about the famous. (See Chapter 12.) Yet these people will often be glad to share their reminiscences with you. Details of the changes witnessed during the lifetime of an elderly person may be especially valuable for the light they can throw on folk history. Occupational changes, skills and crafts once prevalent, local words and dialect, and superstitions and beliefs are just a few of the interesting categories you may encounter. Old recipes and home remedies can reveal information about the ethnic background of a community. To illustrate: can you identify the following traditional recipes, common to various parts of Atlantic Canada? Each is identifiable with one of the major racial strains of the region:

Cock-a-leekie	Finnan Haddies
Dutch Mess	Pâté à la Râpure
Poutines Râpées	Brewis
Kohl Cannon	Sally Lunns
Bannock	Solomon Gundy
Sailor's Duff	Fanikaneekins

There is a sense of great urgency about folklore research, for if this information is to be salvaged at all, the time to start is now. Along the way you will not only encounter expressions of the culture of Atlantic Canada, and meet fascinating people, you will come away with a heightened appreciation of the pre-automobile, pre-television, pre-space-flight world, for "Folklore [is] a preservation of those things which the people of the world hold dear. It provides a key to understanding a way of life of a people, a sort of distilled essence of their values and experiences. To know these well is to know the people who made them."[22]

The material is yours for the searching and the asking.

FOR READING AND REFERENCE

A. Folk songs

CREIGHTON, HELEN, AND SENIOR, DOREEN: *Traditional Songs from Nova Scotia*. Toronto: Ryerson Press, 1960. See also Helen Creighton: *Maritime Folksongs* (Toronto: Ryerson Press, 1962); (with Calum MacLeod): *Gaelic Songs in Nova Scotia* (Ottawa: National Museum of Canada, 1964); *Songs and Ballads from Nova Scotia*; (New York: Dover Publications, 1966); *Folksongs from Southern New Brunswick* (Ottawa: National Museum of Man, 1971).

FOWKE, EDITH; MILLS, ALAN; AND BLUME, HELMUT: *Canada's Story in Song*. Toronto: W. J. Gage Ltd., 1961.

GREENLEAF, ELISABETH, AND MANSFIELD, GRACE: *Ballads and Sea Songs from Newfoundland*. Cambridge: Harvard University Press, 1933.

KARPLES, MAUDE: *Folk Music from Newfoundland*. Toronto: Oxford University Press, 1934.

LEACH, MACEDWARD: *Folk Ballads and Songs of the Lower Labrador Coast*. Ottawa: National Museum of Canada, 1965.

MCCAWLEY, STUART: *A Book of Songs and Come All Ye's of Cape Breton and Newfoundland*. Glace Bay: Brodie Printing Service, n.d.

MACKENZIE, W. ROY: *The Quest of the Ballad*. Princeton: Princeton University Press, 1919. See also *Ballads and Sea Songs from Nova Scotia* (Hatsboro, Pa.: Folklore Association, 1963).

MANNY, LOUISE, AND WILSON, JAMES R.: *Songs of Miramichi*. Fredericton: Brunswick Press, 1968.

PEACOCK, KENNETH: *Songs of the Newfoundland Outports* (3 vols.). Ottawa: National Museum of Canada, 1965.

WELLS, EVELYN KENDRICK: *The Ballad Tree*. New York: Ronald Press, 1950.

B. Recordings

Canada's Story in Song, sung by Alan Mills, with notes by Edith Fowke, Folkways FW 3000 (two 12-inch L.P.s).

Folk Songs of Canada, sung by Joyce Sullivan and Charles Jordan, Hallmark CS3.

My Life Recording Canadian Indian Folklore, by Marius Barbeau, Folkways FG 3502.

Folk Songs of Acadia, sung by Alan Mills and Hélène Baillargeon, Folkways FW 6923.

French-Canadian Folk Songs, sung by Alan Mills, Folkways FW 6929.

Folk Songs of Newfoundland, sung by Alan Mills, Folkways FW 8744.

Songs of the Maritimes, sung by Alan Mills, Folkways FW 8745.

Newfoundland Folk Songs, sung by CJON Glee Club, RLP 84, London Records (two 12-inch L.P.s).

Across Canada with the Travellers, Hallmark 659.

Traditional Folksongs of Nova Scotia, sung by Diane Oxner, AMLP 4006, London.

C. Folklore

CREIGHTON, HELEN: *Folklore of Lunenburg County.* Ottawa: National Museum of Canada, 1950. See also *Bluenose Ghosts* (Toronto: Ryerson Press, 1957); *Bluenose Magic* (Toronto: Ryerson Press, 1968)

DUNDES, ALAN: *The Study of Folklore.* Englewood Cliffs, N.J.: Prentice-Hall, 1965.

DUNN, CHARLES W.: *Highland Settler: A Portrait of the Scottish Gael in Nova Scotia.* Toronto: University of Toronto Press, 1953.

EMMERSON, GEORGE S.: *Rantin' Pipe and Tremblin' String*, Montreal: McGill-Queen's University Press, 1971.

EVANS, GEORGE E.: *Ask the Fellows Who Cut the Hay.* London: Faber and Faber, 1961 (English Folklore).

HALPERT, HERBERT, AND STORY, G. M. (eds.): *Christmas Mumming In Newfoundland.* Toronto: University of Toronto Press, 1969.

IVES, EDWARD D.: "Twenty-One Songs from Prince Edward Island", *Northeast Folklore*, V, 1963. See also *Larry Gorman, the Man Who Made the Songs* (Bloomington: Indiana University Press, 1964); *Lawrence Doyle: A Study in Local Song Making* (Orono: University of Maine Studies, 1971).

MACNEIL, NEIL: *The Highland Heart in Nova Scotia.* Toronto: S. J. R. Saunders and Co., 1958.

SUGGESTIONS FOR FURTHER RESEARCH

1. Folk songs are more often the result of difficult times than of prosperous times. Study carefully the Newfoundland folk songs "A Great Big Sea Hove in Long Beach" and "The Merchants of Fogo". What deductions can you make about life in the outports during the time these were written? Can you date these songs? A period in history that inspired many folk songs was the War of 1812-14. Search the collections listed in the bibliography and see how many of these songs you can find. On the basis of this evidence, what impact did the war have on the British North American colonies?

2. Dr. Helen Creighton has pointed out that in Atlantic Canada "the supernatural is not a subject talked about for the sole purpose of entertainment . . . it is a part of a way of life." (See pages 44-5 in Chapter 4.) Are there ghost stories associated with your community? Have these been incorporated in folk songs? Remember that ghost lore is everywhere and some of the best tales of the supernatural are set in unlikely places. For two examples, read "The White Horse of Merigomish", a railroading story by R. G. Jefferson, in the *Atlantic Advocate*, XLVII, 11 (August 1957): 47-51, and "The Phantom Dog Team" by Henry Paddon in the same magazine, LXII, 7 (March 1972): 25-8.

3. (a) *Historic Newfoundland*, a publication of the Newfoundland Tourist Bureau, lists sayings, figures of speech, weather lore, folk medicines, and omens common to that province. Study this list and ascertain how many of these are common to your locality. Can you add further examples?

   (b) The art of cookery is characterized by traditions and customs that have been handed down for generations. Make a survey of your community and see if you can locate some traditional recipes. You will find the following cookbooks useful references for this project: Hilchey, Florence: *A Treasury of Nova Scotia Heirloom Recipes* (Halifax: Nova Scotia Department of Agriculture, 1967); Hunt, Peter: *Cape Cod Cook Book* (New York: Gramercy Publishing Co., 1954); Nightingale, Marie: *Out of Old Nova Scotia Kitchens* (Halifax: Petheric Press, 1970); *Dutch Oven: A Cook Book of Traditional Recipes from Lunenburg* (Lunenburg Progress Enterprise, 1953); *Perkins Hearth Cook Book* (Liverpool: Zion United Church, 1959); *From the Gristmill—Oat and Wheat Recipes* (Halifax: Nova Scotia Department of Agriculture, 1970); and *Recipes of Newfoundland Dishes* (St. John's: Memorial University, 1971).

10. Art and Architecture

Throughout this book, words are used to convey something of the history of Atlantic Canada from pre-historic days, through the period of European settlement, down to modern times. Words tell the story of people, the famous and the infamous; they portray the meanings of place names, sometimes obvious though often hidden, or make known the legacy of the sea "in sailor's song and rousing tale". Beyond the printed page, much of the development of the region may also be interpreted through a study of the surviving art and architecture—by historians who are silent and wordless until we break the code and decipher the message. The paintings, etchings, and drawings, along with the buildings from any given period, literally "roll back history" and provide what authors of science fiction like to call a time capsule of a bygone age.

What can we learn through the study of such works of art? Just as much of our knowledge of older civilizations is derived from these sources, so it is equally true of more recent history. The artists of Atlantic Canada have made a significant contribution to our understanding of the past by providing a valuable record of early times. Consequently, the sketches of topographical painters such as Richard Short and Thomas Davies, who in the 1750s made a number of accurate drawings of Halifax and area, and Col. J. F. W. Des Barres, who during the years 1763-73 illustrated maps of the eastern seaboard with coastal views and sketches of Louisbourg, Halifax, and Annapolis, have been frequently reprinted. The better-known William Henry Bartlett (1809-54) was responsible for many Canadian engravings, including scenes of the Atlantic area. While Bartlett sketched on location, the final product was completed in London and he was not above inserting an occasional waterfall or exotic tree to "improve" the picture. These artistic liberties to the contrary, the work of Short, Davies, Des Barres, Bartlett, and others is important as a form of documentation and we are fortunate that many of the early visitors to Atlantic Canada were draftsmen or amateur artists. J. M. S. Careless: *The Pioneers: The Picture Story of Canadian Settlement* (Toronto: McClelland and Stewart, 1968) contains reproductions of a number of sketches and engravings illustrating scenes in Atlantic Canada. Particularly noteworthy is a series of water colours "prepared like a modern publicity brochure to lure the adventurous immigrant".[1] The location in question was Stanley, New Brunswick, founded in 1835 as a project of the New Brunswick and Nova Scotia Land Company.

In other instances paintings are significant because they tell the story of an event or episode. We are indebted to Edward John Russell (1832-1906), a New Brunswick marine artist, for his accurate drawings of early shipbuilding and paintings of many famous ships. In addition, Russell sketched numerous scenes in and around Saint John, including a remarkable on-the-spot portrayal of the great fire of 1877. You may learn more about his career by reading Huia G. Ryder: *Edward John Russell—Marine Artist* (Saint John: New Brunswick Museum, 1953). Beyond these examples, the artist makes another and more intangible contribution. He *selects* elements of life and filters them through his own experience and perception. The true work of art is not a mirror image or a picture-window on life, for the artist does not attempt to include everything. He deliberately emphasizes some qualities and de-emphasizes others. To truly understand any painting we require time to search for an inner meaning, to become aware of both form and content. Art offers those interested in local history not merely documentary evidence, it also provides, or should provide, an aesthetic experience.

Study carefully the reproduction of Robert Harris's famous painting, *A Meeting of the School Trustees*. The original now hangs in the National Gallery in Ottawa. It would be quite possible for a modern photographer to pose five people in a setting similar to that of *A Meeting of the School Trustees*; however, the result could never convey the human qualities or the flavour of the time as did the artist. Look again at the picture and study the puzzled looks on the faces of the trustees. What might have been the object of the interview—a raise in salary? some item of local controversy? or is it an expression of the early women's liberation movement? The meaningful work of art must challenge the mind and delight the eye, or, as John Dewey once wrote, "If all meaning could be adequately expressed by words the art of painting would not exist."[2] Harris, although born in Wales, grew up in Prince Edward Island.* After working as a

---

*For details on his career see Moncrieff Williamson: *Robert Harris: An Unconventional Biography* (Toronto: McClelland and Stewart, 1970). An extract from his own book, *Some Pages from an Artist's Life*, may be found in *Island Prose and Poetry: An Anthology* (Charlottetown: Irwin Printing Co., 1973), 51-7.

"A Meeting of the School Trustees" by Robert Harris.

surveyor and a portrait painter in his native province, he studied art in the United States and England and rose to become one of Canada's outstanding artists. An important collection of Harris's work may be seen in the art gallery of the Confederation Centre in Charlottetown. In addition, a number of his paintings adorn All Souls Chapel of St. Peter's Anglican church, also in Charlottetown. Harris's best-known painting, a study of the Fathers of Confederation, was used on Canadian postage stamps in 1917 and again in 1927.

Should you live near Fredericton, Saint John, Sackville, Charlottetown, Halifax, or St. John's try to visit an art galley and seek out paintings by artists of Atlantic Canada. The works of Alex Colville, Tom Forrestall, Miller Brittain, Jack Humphrey, John Cook, Alan Wylie, Julius Zarand, Christopher Pratt, and David Blackwood are among the most outstanding. Next best is to refer to the books listed at the end of the unit, many of which contain reproductions of paintings by area artists. Another useful way to gain a deeper understanding of local history is to study the sketches and drawings of C. W. Jefferys. Although not a native of the Atlantic provinces, he knew the region well and devoted much of his artistic career to illustrating aspects of its history. Particularly notable is the book *Sam Slick in Pictures* (Toronto: Ryerson Press, 1957), with text by T. C. Haliburton and incomparable pen portraits of early pioneer life by Jefferys.*

The aspect of life in Atlantic Canada least understood, even by those who live there, is the "regional identity" of the area. There *are* qualities that set the Maritimer apart from other Canadians; many people have sought to explain what has been called the "Nova Scotianess" of Nova Scotians or with equal truth the "Newfoundlandness" of Newfoundlanders. Itinerant tourists from the nineteenth century onward, royal commissions by the dozen, inquiring journalists and probing sociologists, native sons and immigrants, have all had their turn at the explanation game. None has found a totally satisfactory answer. Perhaps they have been looking in the wrong places, for one authority on Canadian art has written:

> The spectator should be made aware of a particular flavour that is generalized within the painting of this region. It is a flavour that without question distinguishes between the painting of this area and that of any other area in Canada. Almost without exception the characteristic flavour seems to be a general and deep felt involvement with the region. Removed from the turmoil and upheaval of the art world, the chances of seduction by passing fads are distinctly lessened. It is as though the distance in space had achieved the equivalent and often to be desired distancing in time, thus permitting a somewhat cooler and more reasoned appraisal of what is new and up to the moment.[3]

If we let it, the contemporary art of Atlantic Canada has much to tell us. Tom Forrestall, who formerly divided his time between Fredericton, New Brunswick, and Upper Clements, Nova Scotia, and now resides in Dartmouth, is one artist (among several who might be cited) who exemplifies this "general and deep felt involvement with the region". Not only is he an outstanding painter, with a subtle sense of organization and near-flawless technique, he also possesses "a profound sense of place". Of his work, which portrays central New Brunswick and the Annapolis Valley, one critic has written:

> The sense of place is more than the sum of many acutely perceived incidents. It is the feel of the whole: the colours, shapes, sizes and textures of forms, the quality of light and space around them. What is more, these things are images of greater proportions in that they stand for sets of values, patterns of life and structures of society in a given

---

*Much the same has been done for the architectural heritage of Nova Scotia through the publication by the Heritage Trust of the sketches of L. B. Jensen. (See bibliography at the end of this chapter.)

area. . . . Tom Forrestall is both a local historian and a minor poet.[4]

The next time you visit an art gallery look especially for paintings and water colours by Forrestall. When an artist such as he paints a landscape, he conveys something quite different from what the average person might see in the same scene. He arranges, simplifies, and highlights and in so doing turns our attention to special items. For example, his paintings are rarely landscapes in the traditional sense—instead, he "paints the spaces defined by buildings . . . he is a master of architectural values . . . through knowing Forrestall's work one can appreciate the architecture of the Maritimes."[5] For an interesting commentary on his approach to painting read "Amerikay's Last Mystical Plowboy" by Alden Nowlan in the *Atlantic Advocate*, September 1971. A reproduction of a Forrestall painting, "Along the Fence", may be seen on the cover of the December 1969 issue of the same magazine.

Fortunately, when we turn to the architectural heritage of the region, we have examples at hand in every community. What can old buildings reveal to us? To begin, the lumber, brick, or stone used in construction will indicate the materials and skills once available. Their use may provide a clue concerning the origins of the builders and first owners. Thus, the stone cottages of Pictou, similar to those found in northern Scotland, are clear evidence of a Highland heritage. Similarly, the stone structures of the Douglastown-Chatham area, although fewer in number, confirm the early Scottish development of the Miramichi.* A particular architectural style often illustrates a connection with other places and other times. In parts of Prince Edward Island one may find cottages built of sandstone with distinctive eyebrow gables reminiscent of the thatched gables to be found in England, a reminder that many early colonists emigrated directly from Britain. Throughout the Annapolis Valley and in numerous coastal villages of all four provinces we may find excellent examples, sometimes dating from the eighteenth century, of New England architecture. What does this tell us about New England influence on the region?

As expressions of a bygone age, buildings can have an emotional impact as they speak for their own time. A visit to the Simeon Perkins house built in 1766 in Liverpool, Nova Scotia, where the "Samuel Pepys of Nova Scotia" wrote his famous diary, will help us to understand not only Perkins, but also the early colonial period that he described so well. The lives of our ancestors are often revealed as much by their homes as

---

*Among the most outstanding of the Miramichi stone buildings are the Miramichi Golf and Country Club, Bushville; MacDonald House, Bartibogue; The Seaman's Hospital, Douglastown; MacTavish Farmhouse, South Esk; Willard House, Newcastle; Wyse House, Douglastown; Rankin House, Kouchibouguac; and Williston House, Chatham.

by their writings. Even structures that have undergone alteration, so that at first glance their architectural merit is concealed, can tell us of the connection between survival and change and of passing fads in building. Why have some styles endured while others remain only in isolated examples? The answer to this question leads us beyond the study of single buildings to take a look at streetscapes and the overall pattern of architectural development. Buildings large and small, humble homes and elegant mansions, parish churches and great cathedrals, structures architecturally outstanding and those that are not, all reveal concealed history. Let's explore!

The beginning of any continuing form of architecture in Atlantic Canada, other than the primitive settler's cabin,* dates from the middle of the eighteenth century. Halifax was founded in 1749, the New England Planters arrived in numbers during the 1760s, and the area finally became British in 1763. Many New Englanders brought with them the sawn lumber, glass, hardware, mortar, and bricks necessary to build their new homes. Thus the "Cape Cod" style was introduced and may be found in its many forms from Campobello to the Avalon peninsula. Simply defined, a Cape Cod house is a single-storey frame structure with pitched roof coming down to the first-floor ceiling level. Three types may be found: the "half house" with two windows to the side of the door; the "three-quarter house" having two windows to one side of the door and one on the other; and the "full cape", usually one and one-half storeys high with a centre door flanked by two windows on either side. Another variation is the "saltbox", not so common in Atlantic Canada, yet still to be found. This one-and-one-half- or two-storey house with a long rear roof line is so called because of its resemblance in shape to the old colonial saltboxes.

The arrival of the Loyalists saw the introduction of the Georgian style,† again with New England adaptations. In the early part of the nineteenth century, the usual Georgian house consisted of two storeys, two rooms deep. The front-door opening might be either square- or round-headed; the windows with heavy hung sashes usually contained twenty-four panes of glass. The interior normally had a central hall plan, and doors and windows were made elegant with applied mouldings. In time the pure

---

*No Acadian buildings dating from the pre-1755 period survived the Expulsion.

†No attempt is made in this unit to follow rigid classifications of architectural style, for even the experts disagree on naming the various sub-categories. In the interest of simplicity basic generic terms such as "classical" or "gothic" will be used. Other terms, e.g., "Georgian" or "Victorian", which refer to chronological periods as well as architectural styles, are utilized in line with common practice. For more detail and definition of architectural terms see "Styles of Building" in T. Ritchie: *Canada Builds 1867-1967* (Toronto: University of Toronto Press, 1967), or any standard encyclopedia.

The Nova Scotia Communications & Information Centre

An example of "salt-box" architecture at Lower Granville, Nova Scotia, believed to date from the early-eighteenth century.

New Brunswick Travel Bureau

This traditional Loyalist house, built in Saint John in 1810 by David Merrick, has been restored and refurnished. Can you find examples of other buildings that exhibit the same clean lines?

Georgian style was followed by the Classic or Greek revival, although this trend was more noticeable in public buildings. St. Andrews, New Brunswick, and Sherbrooke and Arichat, Nova Scotia, have notable examples of courthouses in this design. These structures are characterized by columns and architraves, friezes and cornices, all in imitation of the Greek temple. About the same time Gothic revival architecture, noteworthy for its pointed windows, arches, and high steep roofs, entered the Atlantic provinces. In fact it is still not uncommon to find buildings with a combination of both Greek and Gothic characteristics. This style was initiated when local builders began attaching pieces of Gothic ornament to the exterior of churches and houses of Georgian proportions. Gothic church architecture will be discussed later in the chapter.

Toward the end of the Victorian period many public buildings such as post offices and railway stations were characterized by a mixture of adapted styles—Roman, Italianate, and French. These buildings, many of which still remain, can be identified by low, rounded arches, squat towers, and masonry of red sandstone or brick. More attractive were the private homes of the period, which usually did not incorporate so many extremes in style. Some undoubtedly were ugly and ornate; however, these homes, often painted brown, russet, or moss green, were high-ceilinged and spacious—qualities frequently lacking in more modern construction. Every part of Atlantic Canada possesses buildings, both public and private, betraying marks of this period. The town of Amherst is notable for a large number of late-Victorian buildings that are still functional and in a good state of repair. It is a matter of interest that until the 1960s Victorian architecture (especially the form with an overabundance of decorative woodwork, or "gingerbread") was the subject of scorn; now, restoring and refurnishing houses of this period has become an absorbing hobby for many.

While the development of architecture in Atlantic Canada runs parallel to that of neighbouring New England, other external influences were at work. Buildings in the region (particularly in the pre-1867 period) present an interesting blend of styles common both to New England and the British Isles. As one would expect, the overseas tradition is best exhibited in the administrative and governmental buildings of the period. The region can boast of an unusual share of such structures, notable for their sense of proportion and dignity. The legislative buildings in Halifax (1819), Charlottetown (1848), and St. John's (1850) amply demonstrate these qualities. Province House in Halifax, the oldest legislative building in the country and one of the best examples of Georgian architecture, served as a model for the others. Not only is there a common heritage in the architecture of these three buildings, but the two in Halifax and Charlot-

Nova Scotia Communications & Information Centre

Wm. B. Hamilton

Newfoundland & Labrador Tourist Development Office

The Harvey Studios Ltd., Fredericton

The legislative buildings in Halifax, Charlottetown, St. John's and Fredericton.
All, with the exception of that at St. John's, continue to be used for their original purpose.

tetown were constructed from sandstone quarried at Wallace, Nova Scotia. The Colonial Building in St. John's, built in the Classical tradition, although no longer the seat of government has been restored to serve as the provincial archives. On the occasion of its official opening, the building was described in the *Royal Gazette* of February 5, 1850:

> The façade of the building, which forms the principal entrance, consists of six massive columns of the Ionic order, which are finely proportioned and surmounted by a pediment containing the Royal Arms, highly relieved. A flight of ten steps extending nearly the whole length of the front, which is eighty-eight feet, leads to a magnificent hall, thirty by twenty feet, from which a grand staircase conducts by a corridor on either side, to the public galleries of the Council and Representative Chambers, to the Legislative Library, and to the Committee Rooms of both branches. A screen of columns of the Ionic order lines the corridors and gives a noble appearance to the hall. The columns support a quadrangular dome, with a beautiful lantern, which admits a sombre but a sufficient light. At either side of the hall is a vestibule leading to the respective chambers of legislation—to the President of Council's, Speaker's, and Clerk's Rooms. The Chambers are particularly beautiful, and of similar dimensions and construction. . . . The exterior of the building is all faced with cut limestone [from Cork, Ireland]. The windows and doors are neatly trimmed with appropriate mouldings, and the entabulature of the portico is continued all round and forms a very fine projection under the roof. The site commands an extensive view of the suburban country and of the ocean, and good streets lead to the town from it at all sides. The building reflects the highest credit on the architect, Mr. James Purcell, who was also its designer.

Descriptions such as the above and the photographs on page 165 do not completely answer two important questions: "What makes a building great?" and "Of what importance is design?" Alan Gowan in *Looking at Architecture in Canada* suggests that the answer may be psychological rather than practical.

> . . . columns and cornices do nothing to support the structure; it would stand quite as well without them. Their real purpose is to articulate the structure; that is, to organize it visually as a set of neatly coordinated elements readily comprehensible to the mind. . . . In the presence of architecture like this, a man can feel only comfortable and confident. To make him feel this way is the real function of design."[6]

Thus good architecture, like a great work of art, expresses an inner truth, a hidden meaning—it has something to say to us and we are the better for it. To grasp the full significance of this idea, compare pictures of the region's legislative buildings with the unfortunate egg-crate design of many late-twentieth-century public buildings. This should not be taken to mean that *all* modern architecture is lacking. Confederation Centre in Charlottetown and the City Hall in St. John's are among noteworthy examples of contemporary architecture. The sad part is that much present-day building makes us far from "comfortable and confident".

A happier continuing heritage may be found in church architecture. Here the problem is one of selection. All four Atlantic provinces have many churches that combine architectural merit and historic interest. In Halifax consider St. Paul's, the oldest Protestant church building in Canada, and St. Mary's Basilica with its towering granite spire and pillars of polished Aberdeen granite. In Sydney there is historic St. George's. In St. John's the Garrison Church of St. Thomas, and the Catholic Basilica of St. John the Baptist with its twin towers dominating the skyline. The list is endless! Before studying the diagram on page 172 and applying it in your own community, it will be helpful to take a close look at several representative churches both large and small. In this way you will gain a better idea of the major "watch points".

Christ Church Cathedral in Fredericton, designed by the English architect Frank Wills,* is a good example of the Gothic tradition. The basic plan is that of the late-thirteenth-century parish church in Snettisham, Norfolk. Built during 1846-53, this cathedral has a subtle sense of balance that sets it apart. The walls of warm, mellowed rubble stone with carved free stone adornments, the oak doors and stained-glass windows, and a massive hammer-beam roof of eleven bays, are some of its key features. Unlike many churches in downtown areas, Christ Church is enhanced by its superb location near the Saint John River. Indeed, so successful were the architect and builders that to step inside is to be mentally transported to the great Gothic churches of late medieval England.

Another outstanding example of the same style is the Newfoundland Cathedral (Anglican) in St. John's. There has been a church at or near this location since 1720; however, the present structure dates from 1843. At first the nave alone was completed, only to be destroyed by the fire that swept the city in 1846. It was at this stage that the famous English architect Gilbert Scott was engaged to design a new building. Choice of the Gothic style was deliberate, as the cathedral historian Dr. A. C. Hunter has written:

*A small country church at Burton, N.B. (attributed to Wills), illustrates many of the same characteristics as Christ Church, although it is of wooden construction and on a smaller scale.

New Brunswick Travel Bureau

New Brunswick Travel Bureau

Newfoundland & Labrador Tourist Development Office

Cathedral of the Immaculate Conception in Edmundston, N.B., Greenock Church in St. Andrews, N.B., and the Roman Catholic Basilica in St. John's, Nfld. What architectural traditions are represented in these buildings?

This was the age of Gothic renascence in England. A later generation learned to mock Gothic, calling it insincere, unoriginal, mere copying; and it is true the vaulted and pinnacled town halls and railway stations of the nineteenth century are ridiculous, but there is yet to be discovered a style that will manifest more perfectly the fervour and aspirations of the Christian faith. We can be but grateful to Scott for planning the new church in the early English Gothic. He was content with the centuries-old tradition of Western Europe. The building was to lie East and West in the form of a cross; it was to have a nave and aisles. In English fashion it was to have no apse [arched or domed recess at the end of the church] but was to enjoy the lightness and airiness given by a big clerestory.[7]

By 1850 the new nave was completed, but no further construction was undertaken during the next thirty years. Building was resumed in 1878 and the choir and transepts were ready for dedication seven years later. Then, in 1892, another disastrous fire swept the city. Only the cathedral walls survived. In spite of these setbacks, work was begun again; the cathedral was rebuilt in stages, proceeding to the magnificent structure we know today. Unlike Christ Church, the Newfoundland Cathedral is crowded by nearby buildings and some of its chief architectural glories are found within. Perhaps the most outstanding is the reredos, the ornamental design covering the wall behind the altar. Carved in almost-whitestone, the overall effect is heightened by the surrounding fire-blackened walls. There are a number of interesting stained-glass windows—should you visit the cathedral at night, you will see the beauty of the Gothic window tracery. The essential problem in studying a great building such as Christ Church or the Newfoundland Cathedral is time. Fortunately, most large churches have printed guides and these should be obtained in advance of any visit. Then, as a result of leisurely study you will be able to see that such structures are not only places of worship for believers or things of beauty for the artist, but meaningful combinations of both.

Architectural and historic interest is not confined to large cathedrals. The small, white-spired churches that dot the landscape have their own appeal and are worthy of attention. Since many of these belong to denominations other than Roman Catholic or Anglican, it is useful to distinguish some differences in religious outlook—differences that in turn are reflected in architecture.

In the Roman and Anglo-Catholic view, a church is pre-eminently the House of God. God is literally present on the altar; it follows, therefore, that a church is a good deal more than an ordinary building. Its architecture should demonstrate the Presence within—it should be a kind of tangible theological proof of God. But the Protestant view is different ... it is essentially a place where people can meet to hear their personal experiences of God explained in sermons, and put into relation with the sum of Christian experience everywhere. Its architecture, then, is not a symbolic expression but a practical means to an end: which means that the primary requirement of a Protestant church is an interior arranged so that everyone can see and hear plainly.[8]

The qualities mentioned as characteristic of Protestant church architecture are exemplified in the early Congregational meeting-houses erected by the Pre-Loyalist Planters and recognizably New England in appearance. Two eighteenth-century meeting-houses in Nova Scotia may be cited as illustrations. The oldest, erected at Barrington in 1765, was used both for town meetings and for congregational worship. The plain exterior of the building with windows in two rows, combined with the internal arrangement of seats and galleries, serves to focus attention where it was intended—on the pulpit. Another New England meeting-house in similar style, but of the Baptist denomination and dating from 1791, is to be found at Lower Granville, Nova Scotia. This church has significance aside from its architectural interest, for it witnessed the

Nova Scotia Information Service

The Protestant tradition in church architecture is illustrated in the Old Meeting House in Barrington, Nova Scotia.

formal organization of the Baptist Association of Nova Scotia in 1800. The well-known Presbyterian meeting-house at Grand Pré (basically completed in 1811 but with the tower and graceful spire added in 1818) is in the same tradition. Read the *Diary of Deacon Elihu Woodworth* (Watson Kirkconnell, ed., Wolfville Historical Society, 1972) for an interesting glimpse of the early life of this old church. Another example in slightly different architectural style (with a hip roof) is the Free Meeting House of Moncton erected in 1821. Although the eighteenth-century meeting-house tradition with its hand-hewn timbers and lack of ornamentation may seem austere, there is beauty in the symmetry of design. If these buildings were cut in halves or quarters the sections would be identical, for matching proportions and complementary angles are their leading features.

Not all of the early Protestant churches were as lacking in decoration as the first meeting-houses. Many that date from an early period compare favourably with the finest in church architecture. A good illustration is Greenock Church in St. Andrews, New Brunswick (see page 168). Completed in 1824, this strikingly beautiful church is two storeys high and has always been painted white. A gallery occupies two sides and the southwest end is supported by ten pillars of solid bird's-eye maple. The facing of the gallery is of the same wood combined with mahogany and is finished in panel work of artistic design. The focal point is undoubtedly the carved pulpit which rises to the height of the gallery. On the outside of the large tower a carved representation of an oak tree may be seen and underneath the tree is the date of the church and its name—so designated because Greenock, Scotland, was the birthplace of the church's chief benefactor, Captain Christopher Scott. St. John's Presbyterian Church in Belfast, Prince Edward Island, also dating from 1824, is another architectural gem. The builder of the church, Robert Jones, was a native of Paisley, Scotland, who emigrated to Prince Edward Island in 1809. The crowning feature of this structure is the tower, inspired by a design based on a church by Sir Christopher Wren.* St. John's also shows traces of the Gothic revival in church architecture and is one of many examples of "carpenter gothic" in Atlantic Canada. Other examples may be found in Lunenburg, Nova Scotia (St. John's Anglican Church), St. Andrews, New Brunswick (United Baptist Church), Malpeque, Prince Edward Island (United Church), and Pictou, Nova Scotia (First Presbyterian Church). It is of interest that many early churches, particularly those of Prince Edward Island, were designed by William Critchlow Harris, brother of the more famous artist Robert Harris. See "Maritime Architect William

*St. Dunstan's-in-the-East, London, England. Unfortunately this church was destroyed during the air raids of the Second World War.

Harris", *Atlantic Advocate*, 6 February 1974, 37-41.,

There are some 1,500 churches in Nova Scotia alone, and thus all that can be done in this chapter is to give a bird's-eye view of a few outstanding examples. Should you live near any of the churches mentioned, try to arrange a visit, for all are worthy of close study. Beyond this, use the diagram below to conduct an examination of the church buildings of all faiths to be found in your community. In a few instances, in larger centres, you will be able to locate religious structures belonging to non-Christian groups. Although these are seldom old in the historic sense, they tell us something of our inheritance from other lands.

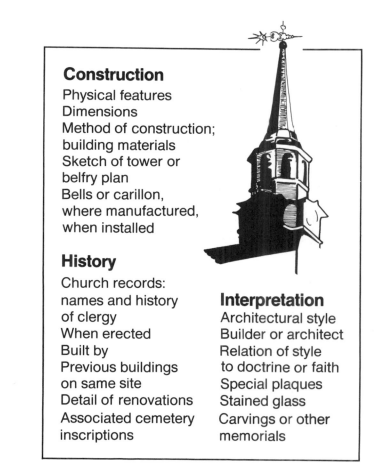

Construction
Physical features
Dimensions
Method of construction;
building materials
Sketch of tower or
belfry plan
Bells or carillon,
where manufactured,
when installed

History
Church records:
names and history
of clergy
When erected
Built by
Previous buildings
on same site
Detail of renovations
Associated cemetery
inscriptions

Interpretation
Architectural style
Builder or architect
Relation of style
to doctrine or faith
Special plaques
Stained glass
Carvings or other
memorials

Can you identify the oldest house in your community or on your street? In recent years, and particularly since 1967, there has been a renewed interest in domestic or house architecture. During centennial year a number of historical associations arranged to identify and mark all houses built before 1867. Occasionally, as you drive about the countryside, you may see a sign denoting a "Century Farm", indicating that a particular location has been in one family for at least that period of time. During 1973 the Prince Edward Island Federation of Agriculture inaugurated a scheme to identify the "farm families of the century" to mark the anniversary of that province's entry into Confederation. On the national level a Canadian inventory of historic buildings was launched in 1970. This means that efforts will be made to record architectural and historic details concerning all habitable and usable buildings that predate 1880 in eastern Canada and all pre-1914 survivors in the west. A standard form designed to register all important items has been drawn up and the information coded for a computer. If you live in an old house and the survey is complete for your area, somewhere in Ottawa there is a computer card that can give a researcher, at a moment's notice, the basic architectural and historical information concerning the structure.

The purpose of the national inquiry is twofold. It serves to pinpoint with accuracy the older and more interesting buildings and to provide through a central data bank speedy information to help answer basic questions. Should this building be retained? Is it worth restoring? Is it unique from the standpoint of age or style? If the answers are yes, then action may be necessary to save the building from demolition.

Another sign of growing interest in the preservation of historic buildings has been the information of Heritage Trust organizations in all parts of Atlantic Canada. Sometimes these are province-wide, as in Nova Scotia and Newfoundland; in other cases, as in Fredericton and Pictou, they are organized on a local level. The aim of the Heritage Trust of Nova Scotia, organized in 1959, is fairly typical of such associations. It strives " ... to promote, foster and encourage interest in and preservation of buildings and sites of an historic, artistic and cultural nature within the province; to acquire and preserve buildings and sites which are appropriate to this end and to encourage and assist in the preservation and acquisition thereof."[9] New Brunswick has provided for the protection of its architectural and historical heritage through the medium of a Historical Resources Administration which became operative on May 1, 1967. It includes a central administration responsible for all historic resource matters, it co-ordinates activities related to museum development, and it has conducted a survey of historic sites and structures. The New Brunswick legislation is a model for other provinces. This interest in the identification and preservation of old buildings prompts the question "Why?" One answer is simply that many of these structures should be preserved for their artistic or aesthetic merit. Another reason, sometimes overlooked, is that old houses are, literally, social records of a bygone age.

Atlantic Canada is fortunate that many early buildings have survived their major enemies—fire and developers. Even so, the record is not without blemish. Examples can be cited in all four provinces where those without a sense of history have demolished outstanding examples of early architecture. To be fair, even the most avid historian would have to admit that not all old buildings can or indeed should be saved. The only way an intelligent decision can be made is to (a) know something of the history of architecture and (b) be able to assess what is historically and architecturally worth saving. For a host of reasons, many of an economic nature, some buildings of historic interest must be torn down. In such cases demolition should only be done after careful consideration and proof that renovation is out of the question. Oddly enough, there are times when renovation is more economical than wreckage. Read *A Sense of Place*, a publication of the Heritage Trust of Nova Scotia, which describes an imaginative plan to save an entire street once described as "among the finest in British North America".

As a class project in your own community, try to compile an inventory of all pre-1900 buildings. If you live in a large city or consolidated school district, you may want to limit the area covered. The task is not something that can be completed quickly; dating old buildings can be both difficult and time-consuming. However, if you cover the details outlined in this chapter, study the references listed at the end, and follow a standard inventory, you should be able to complete the task in a reasonable period of time. One word of warning. It is seldom wise to take an owner's opinion as to date. One who has interviewed hundreds of people, seeking such information, has written: "Do not infer that a date will not be supplied you; it will be given gladly. It will be given in all sincerity and innocence. . . . It will be wrong."[10] An overstatement, but perhaps, basically true. Information from any source should always be double-checked. Apart from documentary evidence, no single item can be relied upon in dating houses. Helpful sources of information are early maps such as those found in historical atlases published in the late-nineteenth century. Old directories and school and municipal records may need to be consulted. If you are on the track of something of extreme historic interest, a search of primary sources such as deeds, wills, estate inventories, and census records may have to be undertaken. Your teacher will be able to advise you on this point.

Architectural details should be easily obtained except in instances where renovation and remodelling have obscured the original design. Much of this research will need to be conducted on location: hence it would be wise to familiarize yourself with details of the various architectural styles. Study pictures and old photographs and test your knowledge before starting to compile the inventory. Visits to such places as the Kings Landing Historical Settlement in New Brunswick and the Sherbrooke Village Project in Nova Scotia can also be of assistance, for gathered in one location you may study varied and excellent examples of early architecture. In a number of cases old buildings of architectural interest have been converted into museums and are more readily examined than structures in private hands. The Queens County Museum, Gagetown (N.B.), dating from 1786 and the birthplace of Sir Samuel Leonard Tilley; Balmoral Grist Mill, 1830, at Balmoral (N.S.); Randall House Museum (1836), at Wolfville; the Albert County Museum, 1845—"the museum in a jail" at Hopewell Cape (N.B.); the Strathgartney Homestead, 1846, at Strathgartney (P.E.I.); and La Vieille Maison at Meteghan (N.S.) are unique and interesting examples.

When assessing a building from the historical and architectural standpoint it is useful to follow a systematic pattern. Again, it is unwise to base decisions upon a single clue. Doors in older homes were often changed for "modern" styles, the charming 20- or 24-paned windows replaced with larger panes or picture windows, lean-to's and ells added to original structures, fireplaces bricked up, and so on. First, look carefully at the exterior of the building. Observe its general style, proportions, and overall construction. Windows come next. Usually, the older the house, the smaller the panes. Exterior and interior doors, fireplaces and chimney locations, hardware patterns, width of floor boards, and even the kinds of nails used may help with identification. By careful observation of a wide variety of details you should be able to reach a conclusion regarding the architecture and age of the structure.

The linkage of history and architecture through a study of government buildings, churches, and homes is fairly obvious. Not so evident are other structures that also speak of the past. Old mills, abandoned factories, and even the lowly barn may be included in this category. The covered wooden bridge was once found in many parts of Atlantic Canada; today only New Brunswick can claim this heritage. The covered bridge has survived in New Brunswick, in part, because the province has more rivers and streams than any area of comparable size on the continent. In fact, there is a community in New Brunswick called Covered Bridge, located on the Nashwaak River not far from Fredericton. It is the site of the first such structure in the province, although the original bridge was destroyed in 1911. Various reasons have been advanced to explain the building of covered bridges. The most common, to protect the timbers and make the bridge last longer, has validity; however, beyond this there is a sound engineering argument. The truss construction on each side, along with

Covered bridge, New Brunswick.   New Brunswick Travel Bureau

bracing across the top, resulted in a stronger bridge. Once built, it was only logical to add a proper roof with shingles to protect the timbers from the weather. So skilful were the early builders that some covered bridges have stood for as long as eighty years.

Unless you live in New Brunswick it will not be possible for you to study a covered bridge at close hand. You can, however, find some of the same construction techniques in older barns and storage sheds. Like the covered bridge, the old-style barn is becoming an endangered species as methods of farming change. Large, mass-produced factory-type structures with metal roofs are replacing the wooden structures that once dotted the countryside. Although it might appear that the lowly barn is lacking in architectural appeal, a closer study will reveal otherwise. Some things to watch for are the roof's pitch, shape, and material, the location and spacing of doors and windows, the size of boards, and the type of beams used in construction. Occasionally you will find a "saltbox" barn, shingled and with unequally pitched roof, that is yet another example of the continuing New England influence. If you are fortunate you may discover an octagonal barn, of which a few examples exist in Atlantic Canada.* Octagonal buildings were popularized in the latter part of the nineteenth century by Orson Fowler, an American phrenologist (one who studies the

*Note the illustration in *Seasoned Timbers* (Halifax: Petheric Press, 1972); also, sketches of barns to be found on Prince Edward Island in *Canadian Antiques Collector* (P. E. I. issue, 1973), 63-5. Even fences may be used as a basis for historical study; see Harry Symons: *Fences* (Toronto: Ryerson Press, 1958).

shape of the skull in an effort to determine character) with an interest in architecture. Houses were also built following the same basic design. Can you locate such a house or barn in your community?

A number of developments now under way in Atlantic Canada permit the study not only of individual buildings but also of villages and street-scapes. One of these, the Kings Landing Historical Settlement in New Brunswick, is designed to preserve in living tableau life as it was in the Saint John River valley between 1790 and 1870. When completed, the community will have over sixty buildings, including ten dwellings, a smithy, a cooperage, two mills, a bridge, a horse ferry, a church, an inn, a village hall, and an operating farm. In apparent paradox, Kings Landing Historical Settlement exists today because of the construction of the Mactaquac Power Project and the subsequent flooding of a wide area of the Saint John River valley. A number of buildings of historic interest, in the path of the project, were either dismantled or moved to the site intact. The principle behind the Sherbrooke Village Restoration Project in Nova Scotia is much the same, except that in this case few buildings had to be moved. Today we can step back a hundred years and sample the life-style of a typical prosperous nineteenth-century village. Here one finds on a compact fifty-acre site a general store, courthouse, jail, church, manse, school, houses, and outbuildings. Aside from general interest, Kings Landing and Sherbrooke are important for another reason—both

New Brunswick Dept. of Tourism

Kings Landing Historical Settlement in New Brunswick. Look for evidence of early agricultural practices in your own community.

are attempts to preserve, restore, and re-create the living aspects of the past. Spinning, dyeing, weaving, quilting, blacksmithing, and wood-working traditions are among the nineteenth-century crafts that are being revived along with the building restoration.

These two projects have been mentioned in some detail because of their size and scope; there are several others worthy of attention. The Lower St. George Street development in Annapolis Royal (unique because of a number of eighteenth-century buildings), Granville Street in Halifax, the Guard House—part of the Fredericton Military Compound, and the commemorative Highland Village at Iona on Cape Breton Island are additional examples. The centenary of Prince Edward Island's entry into Confederation was marked by the establishment of a major historic site in each of the three counties of the province. In New Brunswick, plans are under way to reconstruct a typical Acadian village, and the Newfoundland Historical Trust is spearheading efforts to preserve Quidi Vidi on the outskirts of St. John's. This village, which has changed little in over two centuries, contains buildings dating from the middle of the eighteenth century. The restoration of the old Court House at Upper Woodstock, New Brunswick, is of special interest because it was rescued and returned to its former dignity largely through local initiative. When obtained by the Carleton County Historical Society in 1962 it had been used for a half-century as a barn and storage shed. "Two windows in the south end were replaced by a barn door, a large section of the back wall had been removed to allow access to what was no longer a court room but a barn floor. The balconies were down, beams, posts, railings and all . . . ."[11] Today, after a decade of painstaking research, hard labour, and removal of hay mows, false ceilings, and added partitions, we can enjoy a classic example of mid-nineteenth-century colonial architecture. Thus we see evidence in all corners of Atlantic Canada of a renewal of interest in our architectural heritage.

History becomes a living reality through a study of art and architecture. Just as a knowledge of geology can alert us to our physical surroundings and make them more meaningful, so an understanding of art and architectural styles provides insight into local history. From the broadest standpoint architecture, once called "frozen music", is art. It is an important part of our environment, it is an expression of creativity, and it provides a basic medium for the study of the many influences that have moulded life in Atlantic Canada. Moreover, knowledge of this field can open up new possibilities of study and activity, and may well provide a career for some who read this page. In this age of leisure and the shrink-ing work-week, people have more time for hobbies and avocational interests. The tremendous appeal of museums and historic sites of all kinds bears out this interest. Restoring antique furniture and furnishings, studying costume and design, acting as a guide or consultant, or exploring the wider field of historical restoration are just a few career possibilities that may evolve from an interest in the art and architecture of the past. Let us hope that through them we may recapture the craftsmanship of our forefathers that is our heritage.

FOR READING AND REFERENCE

A. Art

BARTLETT, W. H : *Canadian Scenery Illustrated*. Toronto: McClelland and Stewart, 1969.

COLGATE, WILLIAM: *Canadian Art, Its Origin and Development*. Toronto: Ryerson Press, 1943.

DOW HELEN: *The Art of Alex Colville*. Toronto: McGraw-Hill Ryerson, 1972.

DUVAL, PAUL: *Canadian Drawings and Prints*. Toronto: Burns and MacEachern, 1952. See also Paul Duval: *Canadian Water Colour Painting* (Toronto: Burns and MacEachern, 1954) and *Four Decades: The Canadian Group of Painters* (Toronto: Clarke, Irwin, 1972).

HARPER, J. R.: *Painting in Canada: A History*. Toronto: University of Toronto Press, 1966. See also J. R. Harper: *Early Painters and Engravers in Canada* (Toronto: University of Toronto Press, 1970).

HUBBARD, R. H.: *An Anthology of Canadian Art*. Toronto: Oxford University Press, 1959. Also, *The Development of Canadian Art* (Ottawa: National Gallery, 1964) and *Thomas Davies in Early Canada* (Oberon Press, 1972).

JEFFERYS, C. W.: *Canada's Past in Pictures*. Toronto: Ryerson Press, 1964. Also, *Sam Slick in Pictures* (Toronto: Ryerson Press, 1957) and "The Formative Years: Canada 1812-67", *Imperial Oil Review*, LI, July 1967.

KERR, D. G. G., AND DAVIDSON, R. I. K.: *Canada: A Visual History*. Toronto: Thomas Nelson and Sons, 1966.

PIERS, H.: "Artists in Nova Scotia", *Collections Nova Scotia Historical Society*, XVIII: 101-65.

ROSS, MALCOLM: *The Arts in Canada*. Toronto: Macmillan of Canada, 1958.

SPENDLOVE, F. ST. G.: *The Face of Early Canada: Pictures Which Have Helped To Make History*. Toronto: Ryerson Press, 1958.

WILLIS, N. P.: "Excerpts from the Bartlett Prints", *Atlantic Advocate*, LVIII, 6 (February 1968): 61-3, 65-7.

B. Architecture

BARBEAU, MARIUS: "Types des Maisons Acadiennes", *Le Canada Français*, XXIX: 35-43.

BIRD, W. R.: "Some Historic Houses of Nova Scotia", *Canadian Geographical Journal*, LVII, 2 (August 1958): 62-5.

CAPREOL, JEAN: "The Bridges of New Brunswick", *Atlantic Advocate*, L, 10 (May 1960): 51-4.

GOWANS, ALAN: *Looking at Architecture in Canada*. Toronto: Oxford University Press, 1958. Also, *An Architectural History of Canadian Life* (Toronto: Oxford University Press, 1966).

HILL, ISOBEL L.: *Fredericton, New Brunswick*. Fredericton: York-Sunbury Historical Association, 1967.

HUBBARD, R. H.: "An Architecture for All Seasons", *Transactions Royal Society of Canada*, Section 2, VIII (1970): 41-49.

JENSEN, L. B.: *Vanishing Halifax*. Halifax: Petheric Press, 1968. Also, *Nova Scotia Sketch Book*, 1969, and *Wood and Stone—Pictou, Nova Scotia*, 1972, same publisher.

KIRKCONNELL, WATSON: *Wolfville's Historic Homes*. Windsor: Lancelot Press, 1967.

MACRAE, MARIAN: *The Ancestral Roof: Domestic Architecture of Upper Canada*. Toronto: Clarke, Irwin Ltd., 1963.

PERKINS, CHARLOTTE: *The Romance of Old Annapolis Royal*. Annapolis Historical Association, 1934.

RITCHIE, T.: *Canada Builds: 1867-1967*. Toronto: University of Toronto Press, 1967.

TWEEDIE, R. A., COGSWELL, F., AND MACNUTT, W. S. (eds.): *Arts in New Brunswick*. Fredericton: Brunswick Press, 1967 (covers art as well as architecture). For similar coverage of Newfoundland, see J. R. Smallwood: *The Book of Newfoundland*, St. John's, 1967, vols. III, IV.

C. General

The Canadian Antiques Collector, VII, 1, 1972, featuring Nova Scotia; VIII, 1, 1973, featuring Prince Edward Island.

Volume VI of the *Draft Master Plan for the City of St. John's*: "The Essential St. John's".

Publications of the Nova Scotia Heritage Trust: *Founded Upon a Rock*, 1967; *A Sense of Place*, 1970; *Seasoned Timbers*, 1972; *Country Roads*, 1973, for Pictou Heritage Trust; Halifax: Petheric Press.

Annual Reports Historical Resources Administration (New Brunswick).

Preserving Historic St. John's: Submission to the Public Commissioner on Plan 91, Newfoundland Heritage Trust, April 1972.

Pioneer Gardens, Toronto: Holt, Rinehart and Winston, 1972.

Heritage Canada Quarterly and other publications of Heritage Canada, P. O. Box 1358, Station B, Ottawa, Ontario.

SUGGESTIONS FOR FURTHER RESEARCH

1. "Some people think of history only in terms of pioneer settlers in log cabin settings, forgetting the gradual evolution toward a 'more civilized' way of life. The elegance and opulence of the late Victorian and Edwardian periods had their place in the history ... [of Atlantic Canada]."[12] Make a detailed study of the furniture and furnishings that might be found in such a home in your community during the late-nineteenth and early-twentieth centuries. Visits to local museums, antique shops, and attics will help in this project.

2. After you have completed this study you might like to carry the project one stage further by writing a play that centres around a house, a church or some other building of historic and/or architectural interest in your neighbourhood. If you stage the play you will, of course, need to research extensively in the field of costume and design—one of the fascinating byways of history.

11. Economic Development

Over the years, economic problems have loomed large in Atlantic Canada. The period since 1867 has been a time of industrial readjustment, brought about largely by technological change. The economy of the mid-nineteenth century, based on a close integration of coastal trading, shipbuilding, and lumbering, was shattered as wood, wind, and water were replaced by steel, steam, and new forms of energy. If this were not enough, there continued to be a steady emigration, largely to New England and central Canada. We naturally search for an explanation. The instant reaction is to blame all economic ills on Confederation and the coinciding decline of shipbuilding and shipping. Certainly, a century ago, most parts of Atlantic Canada enjoyed a level of prosperity that compared favourably with the rest of the country. Not so today. While it is true that many individual locations are experiencing an economic boom, general advancement is not characteristic of the region. Delving into the history of key industries, investigating the reasons behind the economic dislocation, and considering the related problem of adequate transportation and communication, are therefore necessary in order to gain a balanced view of the local history of Atlantic Canada.

Economic problems are always complex—a fact borne out by the time and ink consumed in various attempts to find answers. In all, since 1867, Atlantic Canada has seen 102 federal investigations and 44 joint federal-provincial studies. What did these inquiries concern? To take but two major industries, agriculture and fishing, the list seems endless.

AGRICULTURE

General Studies: Farm finances, farm practices, farm income, farm production costs, co-operative ownership of farm machinery, preferences for farm products, agricultural statistics, Atlantic agriculture.

Special Studies: Apples, potatoes, poultry, hogs, dairying, sheep, blueberries, strawberries, milk marketing, fruit and vegetable marketing, egg marketing, peas processing.

Investigations into: land settlement, land use, rural children, rural population trends, co-operatives, food consumption, marshland reclamation, marshland utilizations.

FISHING

General Studies: Labour productivity in the fishing industry, credit needs of fishermen, small fishing boats, salt fish processing and marketing, herring exploitation, fishing gear, fisheries development, the future of the fishing industry.

Special studies: Fishing methods, fish curing, the herring industry, sword-fishery, lobster fishery, oyster fishery, sport fishery, deep-sea fishery, ground-fish industry, crab fishery, shell fishery, eel fishery, shrimp fishery. (The lobster industry alone was studied in 1898, 1902, 1909, 1927, 1930, 1952, 1955, 1956.)[1]

A similar inventory might be compiled for other aspects of the economy. In the twenty-year period from 1925 to 1945 no less than five royal commissions analysed the economic prospects of Nova Scotia. Small wonder that Maritimers sometimes have the feeling that they spend most of their time on the stage of a microscope. Taking a balanced view, it is apparent that the economic state of Atlantic Canada is a combination of geographic and political factors (a situation that further emphasizes the close relationship between geography and history; see Chapters 4 and 5).

On the geographic side, the area juts well out into the Atlantic and is considerably distant from potential markets in central Canada. With the exception of Newfoundland-Labrador, the region is not heavily endowed with natural resources. Since the boundaries of Nova Scotia, New Brunswick, and Prince Edward Island were fixed, there has been no opportunity for a northward expansion as was the case with Ontario, Quebec, and the west. Study an atlas (for example, Kerr's *Historical Atlas of Canada*) and note the extent to which certain provinces have increased in size since 1867. There is a possibility that offshore mineral resources may counteract this disparity; however, the jurisdiction of these rights is claimed, in part, by the federal government.

"OF COURSE I'M KEEPING SABLE ISLAND"

OIL ON SABLE
Daily Paper
OTTAWA KEEPING ISLAND—Trudeau
NOVA SCOTIA PRESSES CLAIM

"I'VE ALWAYS LOVED SABLE ISLAND."

"WHERE **IS** SABLE ISLAND?"

Oct. 7th 1971:   Nova Scotia
discovers oil — and Ottawa
discovers Nova Scotia.

Cartoon by Chambers courtesy Halifax *Chronicle-Herald*

Though geographical factors have been influential, many would argue that national policies have had an even more detrimental effect on the region's economy. This belief persists, despite the willingness of federal and provincial governments to search for an economic utopia. Before 1867 individual provinces had the freedom to adopt a customs and tariff policy that reflected the economic realities of the day. It is strongly felt by many Maritimers that the disadvantages of the federal protective tariff policy (adopted in 1879 and basically continued since then) have far outweighed any advantages. For example, many manufactured items could be imported more economically by water from New England, yet Canadian tariff policy forces the Maritime consumer to purchase such goods in central Canada. Maritimers have been compelled to buy in a protected market, while continuing to sell their principal produce in open competition. Only a few industries, such as coal and steel, have been subsidized to any extent by federal tariff policy.

Obviously, the situation is not quite as simple as the above portrayal would indicate, for it fails to recognize the positive role of federal policies and services. Nor does it take into account the fact that even if Nova Scotia, New Brunswick, and Prince Edward Island had remained outside Confederation and retained the right to arrange their own fiscal policies, the golden age was coming to an end. Reciprocity with the United States and the American Civil War, both of which had contributed to prosperity, were over and the provinces needed outside capital for vast public expenditures such as railways. Dr. Murray Beck, speaking of Nova Scotia, has written "Only a delay of two or three years in the entrance of the province into federation could have afforded convincing proof that the basic conditions of their former happy state had vanished."[2] Although editorials in the newspapers of Atlantic Canada still frequently hark back to the "good old days" and often draw an unflattering picture of the economic benefits of Confederation, it must be recognized that the picture has changed in recent years. Particularly since 1927, the overall economic imbalance has been partially rectified by successive federal governments. Regional incentive grants, tax rebates, and special freight-rate considerations are examples of positive national policies that are working to the advantage of the region.

A typical royal commission appointed to investigate the economic ills of the region was that of 1926-7, the Duncan Commission, so named for its chairman, British industrialist Sir Andrew Duncan. Look into the findings of the Duncan Report and note its major recommendations. What impact did they have on the region?

Where do economic factors tie in with local history? In the first place, it is necessary to have some knowledge of the total picture before moving on to more detailed studies of specific industries and developments in particular communities. In this sense Atlantic Canada may be regarded as a unit, for although Newfoundland remained outside Confederation until 1949 it was beset by many of the same difficulties as its neighbours. If we take manufacturing as an illustration, we may find in almost every corner of the region evidence of once-thriving factories and plants that no longer exist. Some failed for internal reasons, others because the goods they turned out were too expensive, and still others became victims of national mergers and outside competition. Study newspapers and other records of fifty or a hundred years ago and see if you can account for the failure of such industries in your own community.

It is worth noting that some businesses have thrived, withstanding all the perils that have swept others away. For over a century, one such industry has prospered in St. Stephen, New Brunswick, in direct competition with similar plants in other parts of the country. In 1872 James Ganong purchased a small bakery and began producing bread, cakes, and candy. Some time later he was joined by his brother Gilbert, and Ganong Bros. entered the candy and chocolate business in earnest. Although everything was hand-operated in the beginning, the firm turned to steam-powered equipment as early as 1884. Four years later, in defiance of all geographic disadvantages, their products were being sold in Vancouver. Arthur Ganong, son of the founder, in time took over management of the firm and is credited with producing in 1910 the first chocolate bars sold in North America—Ganong's "Nut Milk" and "Evangeline Cream" bars.

As a contrast to the previously mentioned project on industries that have failed, compile a list of firms in Atlantic Canada, such as Ganong's, that have been able to develop a national market for their products. How do you account for their success?

While manufacturing brings into sharp focus some of the economic advantages and disadvantages of the region, it is the primary industries—agriculture, fishing, lumbering, and mining—that have been the mainstay of Atlantic Canada. Two of these—agriculture and the fishery—will be surveyed in brief to provide a research pattern that may be applied to the industries in your particular location. Agriculture had its beginnings in Atlantic Canada at Port Royal in 1606. According to Lescarbot's account the tiny colony produced "fair wheat, rye, barley, oats, peas, beans, hemp, turnips and garden herbs". In addition, pigs, sheep, hens, and pigeons were kept and it is believed that some apple trees were planted. During the ensuing years, farming moved northward to the Minas Basin as the Acadians began to reclaim additional land from the sea. Eventually their settlements spread to Cobequid Bay, the north shore of Nova Scotia, and the Isthmus of Chignecto. Because the dyked land was fertile, many varied crops were grown. Wheat, peas, barley, and rye were produced in quantities sufficient to supply (secretly, after Acadia became British in 1713) part of the requirements of the garrison at Louisbourg. In retrospect, the main agricultural legacies of the Acadians were the dyking of vast acreages of marshland and the planting of fruit trees which indicated the fruit-farming potential of the Annapolis Valley. With the Expulsion in 1755, progress was halted for a time.

The New Englanders who followed continued to farm the fertile acres of the Annapolis and Cornwallis valleys, although they found it necessary to enlist the aid of Acadian prisoners in maintaining the dykes. Recognition of the importance of agriculture came as early as 1765, when the first exhibition was held at Windsor. A plaque erected by the Historic Sites and Monument Board summarizes the story.

Commemorating the first agricultural fair in Canada, authorized on the creation of the township of Windsor in 1764 and held at Fort Edward

Hill, May 21, 1765. Prizes were awarded for creditable exhibits of cattle, horses, sheep, hogs, grain, butter, cheese, and homespun cloth. In 1766 the trustees of the fair received a royal charter which was renewed in 1815. Since that date the fair has had an uninterrupted existence.

Despite this early progress, agriculture at the beginning of the nineteenth century was still comparatively limited. In New Brunswick, farming was eclipsed by the profits to be made in shipbuilding and lumbering, while in Prince Edward Island progress was retarded by the land question (see page 15). Newfoundland, then as now, was prevented for obvious geographic reasons from developing agriculturally. In 1815 John Young, a Scotsman keenly interested in farming, arrived in Halifax. Three years later a series of letters published in the *Acadian Recorder* over his pen name, "Agricola", caught public imagination. In all, thirty-eight letters were published, covering every conceivable phase of up-to-date agricultural practice. Printed later in book form, *The Letters of Agricola* provided impetus to agriculture. A central agricultural society was organized with branches in the various counties and interest in a more scientific approach was developed. See J. S. Martell: *The Achievements of Agricola and the Agricultural Societies* (Halifax: Public Archives Nova Scotia Bulletin, II, 2, 1940).

Later, in 1849, the New Brunswick government invited James F. W. Johnston, an English agricultural expert, to visit that province and make an analysis of its farming potential. His book, published in 1850, performed much the same role as Agricola's letters in Nova Scotia. More than a century later, Johnston's *Report on the Agricultural Capabilities of the Province of New Brunswick* is fascinating reading and provides an excellent description of farming practices of the day. Unfortunately, copies of the book are difficult to locate; however, a summary may be found in Anita Lagrace: "Origin of the Agricultural Society of New Brunswick" in *Collections New Brunswick Historical Society*, XVIII (1963), 166-79.

While some farming was carried on in Ile-St. Jean (modern Prince Edward Island) during the Acadian period, and on occasion supplies were shipped to Louisbourg, it was some time before the agricultural possibilities of the "Garden of the Gulf" were fully exploited. In addition to the nucleus of the Acadian population (many of whom escaped the Expulsion) the French left "some euphonious names on the map and a basic stock of animals, seeds, fruit seedlings, and weeds for the blessings and curses of the settlers of the next two centuries."[3] Potato farming is inevitably associated with Prince Edward Island and the first record of planting dates from the early 1770s. By 1821 Walter Johnstone, in his *Letters Descriptive of Prince Edward Island*, reported that islanders were "exporting livestock of all kinds, grain and potatoes to Newfoundland, and grain, pork and potatoes to the Miramichi, and grain and potatoes to Halifax." Read Andrew Hill Clark's *Three Centuries and The Island* (Toronto: University of Toronto Press, 1959) for a comprehensive treatment of the evolution of agriculture in Prince Edward Island.

Books such as those mentioned above are valuable; however, a better impression of farming as it was carried on in the nineteenth century can be gained through a visit to the Kings Landing Historical Settlement in New Brunswick or the Ross Farm at New Ross, Nova Scotia. The latter project is designed to depict a farm of the last century in its actual day-to-day operation. Should a visit to either of these locations be impossible, study carefully J. Lynton Martin's *The Ross Farm Story*, a publication of the Nova Scotia Museum. In addition to providing a wealth of information on early agriculture, the booklet is well illustrated and depicts many nineteenth-century farming implements. If you live in a rural area, investigate your own community and see how many examples of old farming tools and implements you can uncover. Read *Men of the Soil*, published in 1967 by the Nova Scotia Federation of Agriculture. This book records the history of 380 farms (from all parts of the province) that have remained in the same family for at least a century. Perhaps this will interest you in writing a history of your family farm.

Near the coast of the Avalon peninsula, northeast of Bay de Verde, lies Baccalieu Island. Derived from the old Basque word *Baccalaos*, or cod, this place name (along with others) documents the fact that it was the cod fishery that first brought the Basques, Portuguese, Spaniards, French, and English to these shores. From the very beginning fishing has maintained its importance. As early as 1672 Nicolas Denys gave a detailed description of the cod fishery and reported that from 200 to 250 vessels annually "set sail and went by the Grace of God to find the Grand Bank". At first the cod fishery was conducted offshore; however, in time many ships, instead of remaining on the Banks for a season, sought some sheltered harbour—usually on the coast of Newfoundland. Here racks, or flakes, were set up, fish was cured, and the crews had a change from the long months at sea. No effective provision was made to totally prevent settlement, however, and fishermen did establish year-round residence. By the eighteenth century the Newfoundland fishery was largely controlled by England and France and the whole question was becoming an important consideration in Anglo-French diplomacy. Because of long-standing tradition, France had claimed a portion of the Newfoundland coastline. However, the Treaty of Utrecht in 1713, which gave France the right to dry fish on a portion of that coast, did not settle matters and the "French Shore Question" remained a controversial issue until the twentieth century.

During the early 1800s the so-called ship, or bank, fishery experienced a decline and the fast-emerging inshore fishery offered increased opportunity. Its progress was paralleled by the development of the new sealing and whaling industries, each of which provided valuable winter employment. Sealing was important both for the revenue it produced and for the subsequent stimulus to shipbuilding in all parts of Atlantic Canada. At about the same time still other fleets began to appear in the harbours and coves of Newfoundland. While some of these vessels were equipped for sealing, others sailed each summer to the Labrador, thereby following a pattern similar to that of the first fishermen who had sailed annually from England to the Grand Banks.

Meanwhile, on the south shore of Nova Scotia, something of a racial transformation was taking place. Many of the original settlers deliberately selected this area because of its close proximity to the fishing banks. Certainly this was a prime motivation for the New England migration to settlements such as Yarmouth, Barrington, Liverpool, and Chester. One major group, the "Foreign Protestants" of Huguenot, Swiss, and German origin (who settled Lunenburg County), were natives of central Europe with no tradition of a seafaring life. The newcomers very quickly adapted to their environment and soon made the Lunenburg fishing fleet world-famous.

One indicator of the importance of the industry is the amount of time devoted to the topic in international diplomacy. From 1783, when the new United States was recognized as an independent nation, to the present day, fishing rights in the north Atlantic have been a matter of debate. In the early period fishermen from the British North American colonies found it difficult to compete with the Americans, for it was alleged the latter openly violated the territorial waters of the region. Negotiations on this issue were carried on in 1818, 1854, 1871, 1874, 1887, 1898, and 1911—to name only the major agreements. How did the fishermen of Atlantic Canada fare as a result of these deliberations? A standard history text or the *Encyclopedia Canadiana* will provide the answer. Throughout much of our region's history Canadian-American relations can be summarized in four words: conflict over fishing rights.

While the fishing industry as a whole provides a convenient backdrop for a study of Canada's dealings with her nearest neighbour, there is much to be gained from a local study of it. In accounting for the evolution of the fishing industry in your community, it will be helpful if you centre your attention on three major points (1) *The People*: Compare the life of a fisherman of today with that of one in the early 1900s. How has his life-style been affected by technological developments in the industry? Why have fishing communities changed more slowly than others? Why has it become necessary to relocate some of these? (2) *The Produce*: Has the local fishery always been dependent on one type of fish? How has the industry diversified over the years? With what results? Have markets and demand fluctuated? Has the industry been able to cope with change? Have laws regarding conservation and pollution had a bearing on the industry? Has the co-operative movement made an impact? (3) *The Equipment*: Investigate changes in the construction of vessels and gear. Try to locate old photographs, sketches, and models to illustrate significant developments. Assess changes in the processing of fish. How do present-day methods differ from those of 1900?*

Communities removed from the coast also have a stake in this industry, for much of the total economy of Atlantic Canada is dependent upon what happens on the "Blue Prairie". The fishery and associated industries have seen dramatic changes over the years, and this has had far-reaching effects. To cite one example, from Grand Manan along both sides of the Bay of Fundy, on the Atlantic coast of Nova Scotia, in the Northumberland Strait, in the Gulf of St. Lawrence, and on to the Labrador, lobsters abound in such numbers that they are sometimes called "crawling gold". However, they are not as plentiful today as formerly. Around Chaleur Bay during the mid-nineteenth century lobsters were used as fertilizer on the land, while at Shippegan and Caraquet they were gathered in quantity from among the rocks and pools left by the outgoing tide. In the late 1860s and early 1870s when the meat began to be preserved in tins, the industrial possibilities of lobstering became apparent. By the turn of the century there were 227 canneries in Prince Edward Island alone, and in 1910 the entire region could claim around 700. Today only a handful are left. Can you account for this dramatic change?

In your investigation of the rise and fall of these and other enterprises, look carefully for old ledgers, records, and accounts associated with early firms. Unfortunately, many have been lost; however, it is possible that you may stumble across a cache of such papers. If you do, handle them with care, for old records are invaluable in charting fluctuations in wages, salaries, and the prices of commodities and services in days gone by. In 1969 the Business Archives Council of Canada was established to locate such items and the Killam Memorial Library at Dalhousie University was named an official repository. The Campbell papers, detailing the activities of an old shipping and lumbering firm in Weymouth, Nova Scotia, is one example of a recent acquisition. Each of the provincial archives possesses

---

*The writer is indebted to Mr. Ross Bussey, Port-de-Grave, Newfoundland, for many of the above suggestions.

valuable records concerning the commercial life of Atlantic Canada. Check their inventories and see if any relate to your community. For leads on this type of research check the article "The General Store" by Marie Nightingale in *Nova Scotia Historical Quarterly*, II, 1 (March 1972). Utilizing the records of a general store, it provides a picture of life during the years 1876-7. Of equal interest is the chapter on "The Ships Business" in Stanley Spicer: *Masters of Sail* (Toronto: McGraw-Hill Ryerson, 1968). Memorial University has recently launched a more ambitious undertaking—the establishment of a centre for the study of Maritime history. A team of historians is gathering, as far as possible, all documents relating to the history of shipping, commerce, and fisheries in the North Atlantic. While still in its initial stages, the centre will eventually be a major resource for serious research in all aspects of Maritime history.

Space has permitted merely a brief analysis of the background of two industries, agriculture and fishing. The reader interested in more detail on these or other industries is directed to the suggestions for reading and reference on page 200.

Because labour relations, transportation, and communication are basic to all aspects of the economy, and because history has been more silent in these areas than in others, a discussion follows of their implications for local studies.

June 11 is Miners Memorial Day in Cape Breton. Few people know that until 1939 it was called "Davis Day" in honour of William Davis, one of the many coal miners who became involved in the early union struggles against the British Empire Steel and Coal Corporation. Davis was killed in an uprising near New Waterford on June 11, 1925, and since that time the day has symbolized the long struggle for union rights and recognition. The story really began forty-six years earlier, in the summer of 1879, when secret meetings were held nightly in a woods near Springhill, Nova Scotia. The local mining company had posted a notice declaring a reduction in wages of four cents per ton—the second such decrease in a short span of time, despite the fact that the price of coal remained high. Collective bargaining worked; the company capitulated and from this humble beginning the Provincial Workmen's Association began. The movement grew, but so did the determination of management to block its progress. Later strikes and threats of strikes frequently led to bloodshed. Springhill, Pictou County, and Cape Breton (the chief coal-producing areas during the half-century that followed the first attempt at unionization) all witnessed confrontations between management and labour. Sometimes the militia was called in to quell the strikes and upon other occasions more "subtle" means were used. The cynical attitude of those in authority is best summarized in the words of J. E. McClurg, a vice-president of BESCO. Referring to the strike of 1925, he said "We hold the cards, things are getting better every day they stay out. Let them stay out two months, or six months, it matters not, eventually they will come crawling to us. They can't stand the gaff."[4]

The implication behind this comment indicates the stranglehold BESCO possessed over the lives of the workers. The company owned the stores from which groceries and supplies were purchased. These were obtained on credit and the amount was deducted from the worker's pay. Similarly, many of the homes were company houses and rent too was subtracted at source. The stores, called "pluck me's" (a phrase borrowed from Scottish miners who laboured under frighteningly similar conditions), typified the conflict that frequently contributed to strike action. Investigate the sorry events of 1882, 1904, 1909-10, 1922, 1925, and 1930—the years of the most violent strikes—and in the process you will learn something of the heroes of the Cape Breton labour movement. These include J. B. McLachlan, arrested and tried* for seditious libel; Dan Livingston, a close associate of McLachlan and an early union organizer; and Forman Waye, who was elected M.L.A. for Cape Breton County in 1920 and became a spokesman for labour in the Assembly.

Not surprisingly, there is a close connection between the labour movements in Cape Breton and Bell Island, Newfoundland. Labour in both areas was struggling against primitive working conditions and battling the same corporation, BESCO, which was employing identical tactics in an effort to suppress the trade union movement. The first union, the Wabana Workmen's and Labourer's Union, was organized in 1900 by Thomas St. John, who became its first president. Almost at once the workers went on strike, demanding parity with BESCO's pay scale at Sydney. When the company attempted to break the strike by importing non-union employees, fighting broke out and St. John was arrested. Eventually the strike terminated on neutral ground at Kelligrews (the settlement became known as the Treaty of Kelligrews) with E. M. Jackman, another union organizer, representing the workers. In Newfoundland, as in Cape Breton, union-versus-management strife reached a peak in the 1920s and efforts were made to prevent joint action by Cape Breton and Newfoundland workers. In October 1923 Joshua Humbers, a union representative from Bell Island, was refused entry to Canada, being stopped by immigration officials at North Sydney as a dangerous "labour agitator". Read Norman Crichton's novel *The Camerons* (New York: Alfred A. Knopf, 1972) for a descriptive account of the birth pangs of the labour movement in the coal-mining areas of Scotland. A comparative study with the events of the

*As was Joseph Howe; however, unlike Howe, McLachlan was imprisoned.

1920s in Cape Breton will reveal that the *dramatis personae* was the same.

Coal mining in Atlantic Canada, as in other parts of the world, has been declining in importance. The quality of the coal mined, the distance from markets, and competition from other forms of energy have been contributing factors. Meanwhile, one of the most important schemes aimed at strengthening the economy of Atlantic Canada has been the suggested harnessing of the tidal power of the Bay of Fundy. Contrary to public opinion the idea is not new, having been advanced as early as 1915. Of interest, too, is the fact that the successful Rance River Tidal Project in France is located in an area not far from the ancient homeland of the Acadians who settled the Fundy region and first stemmed the tides by building dykes. Look into the potential impact of the Fundy scheme on both the economy and the ecology of the region. Some useful references are Duncan Fraser: "Planned Fundy Tidal Project in 1915", *Halifax Chronicle Herald*, January 23, 1971; John Connor: "La Rance: Tethering the Tide", *Halifax Chronicle Herald*, March 2, 1971; Charles MacLennan: "A Workable Scheme for a Fundy Power Centre", *Halifax Chronicle Herald*, April 15, 1972. The *Atlantic Advocate* frequently features articles on tidal power.

On April 7, 1967, a sixteen-foot open boat with six men and a symbolic sack of potatoes set out from Borden, Prince Edward Island, en route to Cape Tormentine, New Brunswick. An historical re-enactment of a once-common practice, the event not only dramatized the dependence of Prince Edward Island on links with the mainland, it served as a reminder of the crucial role of transportation and communication in the economic life of Atlantic Canada. The original ice boats, used in winter crossings of the Northumberland Strait from 1827 until 1917, weighed about eight hundred pounds and were equipped with a small sail, oars, and special runners on the underside of the hull. When open water was found, sails, oars, and paddles were used. But when ice blocked the passage the crew would haul the boat over the ice using heavy leather straps attached by chains along each gunwhale. The ice boats would leave Cape Traverse, Prince Edward Island, at dawn and the crossing, depending on weather, tide, and ice conditions, could take from four to eight hours. In 1970 the Historic Sites and Monuments Board erected a memorial to honour the ice-boat crews. For an interesting account of this early form of transportation read "The Strait", Chapter XV, in Lorne C. Callbeck's *The Cradle of Confederation* (Fredericton: Brunswick Press, 1964).

During the nineteenth century, before the advent of the railway and for a longer period in areas not served by rail lines, transportation was largely by water. The many towns and villages that dot the shoreline of Atlantic Canada were served at first by coastal trading schooners, until the increase in population demanded regular communication. New Brunswick, well endowed by nature with navigable rivers, was fortunate, and these internal waterways played an important role in opening the interior of that province. See *Johnny Woodboat* by George MacBeath (Ottawa: Museum Restoration Service, 1969) for a descriptive account of the woodboats that once plied the Saint John River. One of the earliest interprovincial links (operating on a regular basis) connected Saint John with Digby and Annapolis Royal on the Nova Scotia side of the Bay of Fundy. The first steamboat in the region, the *General Smythe*, was a paddle-wheel boat that in 1816 began a weekly round trip on the river between Saint John and Fredericton. Later her machinery was transferred to the *St. John*, the first steamboat to navigate the Bay of Fundy. In 1832 there was an unsuccessful attempt to establish steamboat service between Fredericton and Woodstock; however, this objective was achieved on April 30, 1837, when the *Novelty* made her maiden trip. Meanwhile, the death knell for the sailing ship was struck when the *Royal William*, sailing from Pictou, crossed the Atlantic by steam power. Seven years later Samuel Cunard founded the first regular transatlantic steamship line, with the *Britannia* making the trip from Liverpool to Halifax in twelve days and ten hours.

Transportation by land remained backward as the stagecoaches (where they existed) bumped over rough and ill-defined roads. Nova Scotia in 1815 possessed only two highways capable of accommodating stage-coaches—the so-called Great Road from Halifax to Windsor, and the Old Cobequid Road from Halifax to Truro with an extension to Pictou. In 1825 a coach road was opened between St. John's and Portugal Cove, Newfoundland, becoming the first official "highway" in that colony. By the 1830s Nova Scotia's Great Road has been extended through the Annapolis Valley, and the Royal Western Stage Coach Company ran three times a week between Halifax and Annapolis. The trip took sixteen hours, excluding an overnight stop.

Of first importance in developing better communications in Atlantic Canada was the advent of intercolonial telegraph and cable lines. Early in 1848 construction began on a telegraph line from Saint John to meet at the American border another extending from Portland to Calais. For a period during 1849 news from Great Britain to the United States was brought across the Atlantic by Cunard steamers to Halifax. From here it was dispatched to Digby Gut via the north shore of the Annapolis Basin by riders who changed at Kentville. To save time, fresh mounts were provided every twelve miles of the 144-mile route. The news was then relayed to Saint John by steamer and on to its ultimate destination by telegraph. The completing of overland lines from Halifax to Saint John

cancelled the need for this service and Atlantic Canada entered the telegraph age. Plans for cable connections with Prince Edward Island and
Newfoundland became the next step. Eventually, after an unsuccessful
attempt in 1855, a cable was laid in 1856 to connect Cape North with
Cape Ray. From Cape Ray (near Port-aux-Basques) a telegraph line
already led to St. John's. The final step came ten years later, on July 27,
1866, when the *Great Eastern* landed the first successful transatlantic
cable at Heart's Content, Newfoundland, thus linking Atlantic Canada
with Britain and the rest of the world. For nearly a century—until modern
technology rendered such operations unnecessary—Heart's Content
remained a major communications relay station.

The 1830s and '40s were years when agitation for the construction of
railroads began to mount. The first rail line in Atlantic Canada was built
by the General Mining Association and opened in 1839. It connected
Albion Mines (Stellarton) with the ship-loading ground at Dunbar Point
near New Glasgow, a distance of six miles. One of the original locomo-
tives, the *Samson*, may still be seen in the New Glasgow Museum. The
grand opening in September 1839 created a stir, as a contemporary newspaper reporter witnessed:

> One of the most novel and imposing spectacles ever witnessed in this
> portion of the world, took place on Thursday last [September 19, 1839]
> on the premises of the General Mining Association. ... The event
> which this exhibition was designed to commemorate was the running
> of the locomotive carriages for the first time on the completion of the
> first section of the new Rail Road. ... The most important part of the
> ceremony, the running of the locomotives, was to take place at 2 o'clock.
> The intervening time was spent in examining their construction and
> admiring these most astonishing monuments of human ingenuity. ...
> The locomotives, are three in number, and are called—the *Hercules*, the
> *John Buddle* and the *Samson*. On this occasion the first two only were
> called into active service.
>
> At the appointed hour the carriages were cleared of the crowd and
> filled with those whom the Association had sent tickets of admission
> to. In a few minutes both trains were in motion—the *Hercules* taking
> the lead having a train of 35 carriages, containing about 700 people.
> The *John Buddle* with an equal number followed. It was a wonderful
> sight to see these splendid efforts of human mechanism, at the magic
> touch of the engineers "walking it off like a thing of life" at a speed
> varying from 10 to 20 miles per hour.[5]

The individual most responsible for the promotion of railroads was
Joseph Howe. A tour of Nova Scotia had convinced him of the need for

improved transportation and he set about to use every means, politically and editorially, to achieve this objective. One of his early converts, T. C. Haliburton, took up the cause in *The Clockmaker*. According to Sam Slick:

> ... Let them make a railroad to Minas Basin and they [the citizens of Halifax] will have arms of their own to feed themselves. If they don't do it, and do it soon, I guess they'll get into a decline that no human skill will cure. The only thing that will make or break Halifax is a railroad across the country to the Bay of Fundy. .... This railroad will beget other useful improvements. It will enlarge the sphere and the means of trade, open new sources of traffic and supply, develop resources, and what is of more value, perhaps, than all, beget motion.[6]

Initial enthusiasm to the contrary, progress was still slow. The sceptical had to be convinced, sources of capital found, and bickering over possible routes resolved. A line was proposed from St. Andrews to Quebec but the Ashburton Treaty of 1842 awarded Maine much of the territory through which it was to run. Two other routes were suggested. The "European and North American" was to connect Halifax with Saint John and Portland, hopefully diverting some transatlantic traffic from Boston and New York. The second proposal was to link Halifax, Truro, the Miramichi, and the Matapédia Valley with Quebec. Strenuous efforts were made to interest outside capital in these projects, but to no avail. See H. H. Folster: "Story of Old New Brunswick Railways", *Collections New Brunswick Historical Society*, XVII (1961): 54-61, and C. W. Anderson: "The St. Andrews and Quebec Railway", *Collections New Brunswick Historical Society*, XIX (1966): 53-8. Good coverage of the history of railroading in Nova Scotia will be found in David E. Stephens: *Iron Roads: Railways of Nova Scotia* (Windsor: Lancelot Press, 1972); see also Bruce Macdonald: *The Guysboro Railway 1897-1939* (Antigonish: Formac Ltd., 1973).

A few short railway lines were constructed during the 1850s. Windsor and Truro were linked to Halifax and a line was constructed from St. Andrews to Woodstock with a spur to St. Stephen. Another, a portion of the proposed "European and North American", was built from Saint John to Shediac and opened for traffic August 5, 1860. However, major developments were not complete until after Confederation. Can you suggest reasons for this? Search local records and newspaper accounts to ascertain when the rail lines nearest your home were built. Look for proposed railway projects, many of which were abandoned almost before they were started. For example, in Nova Scotia the Stewiacke Valley and Lansdowne Railway, incorporated on May 11, 1886, failed shortly thereafter. Can you find other examples of railway dreams that failed to become realities?

Probably the most ambitious unfulfilled project in Atlantic Canada was the Chignecto Ship Railway. As early as 1822 the government of New Brunswick considered building a canal across the isthmus to connect the Bay of Fundy with the Northumberland Strait It was obvious to anyone who consulted a map that such a canal would make economic sense by reducing the distance between Saint John and ports on the St. Lawrence. The major difficulties in the path of such a project were the high tides and the silt-laden waters of the Bay of Fundy. The man who came forward with a scheme to solve these problems was Henry George Clopper Ketchum. A native of Fredericton and graduate of King's College (later U.N.B.), where he earned the first diploma in civil engineering in 1862, Ketchum had a remarkable career in railroading. He served first on the building of the Sao Paulo Railway in Brazil, returning to New Brunswick in 1865 to become construction engineer on the rail line between Moncton and Amherst. Still later he was chief engineer on the construction of the Fredericton-to-Edmundston route.

Ketchum's solution was a ship railway with tracks and equipment sufficiently strong to transport an ocean-going ship and cargo across the isthmus, a distance of seventeen miles. Practicable as the project may have been from an engineering standpoint, it was destined never to be completed. In 1888 a company launched by Ketchum undertook construction and continued until July 1891, when work was halted. Look into this amazing engineering feat and establish the reason for the collapse of Ketchum's dream. Today, little evidence of the Chignecto Ship Railway remains, although more than half of the line was actually completed. In recent years the idea of a Chignecto Canal has been advanced, largely spurred on by a campaign launched in the editorial pages of the *Atlantic Advocate*. Investigate the pros and cons of this controversial project, which has sparked almost as much debate as Ketchum's ill-starred plans of nearly a century ago.

The railway came late to both Prince Edward Island and Newfoundland and in retrospect more problems were created than were solved. In 1871 a railway act passed the Prince Edward Island legislature, calling for the construction of a railway from Georgetown at the eastern end of the island to Alberton in the west. Branch lines were eventually built from Mount Stewart to Souris and from Alberton to Tignish. Unfortunately for the province, it did not have the population or resources to support such an ambitious plan. The major contribution of the railway was "to settle the island's future (see Chapter XI in F. W. P. Bolger: *Prince Edward Island and Confederation*, Charlottetown: St. Dunstan's University Press, 1964). The financial impasse caused by over-expenditure on railways was one of the main reasons for the island's entry into Confederation in 1873.

Newfoundland was to wait another decade before its railway saga began to unfold. In 1880 the Newfoundland legislature recommended that a start be made on a narrow-gauge line from St. John's to Conception Bay. Unlike residents of other parts of Atlantic Canada, where there was considerable enthusiasm for railways, many Newfoundlanders registered violent opposition. At Foxtrap (near Kelligrews) local landowners, fearing that they might be dispossessed of their land, resorted to hurling sticks and stones at the workers and thereby halted construction. While the five-day "Battle of Foxtrap" was eventually settled, it was none the less the forerunner of more trouble. The major problems occurred when attempts were made in the 1890s to push the railway 546 miles westward to Port-aux-Basques. Sparse population, high cost of construction, and government intrigue all conspired to create a railroad in search of a country. For more details check "The (Almost) Great Train Robbery" in St. John Chadwick: *Newfoundland: Island Into Province* (Cambridge: At the University Press, 1967), 83-98.

Atlantic Canada has always been, because of its geographic location, a stepping-stone between the Old World and the New. There remains for us to consider the field of aviation and to note some of the "firsts" chalked up by the region. At Baddeck on February 23, 1909, the *Silver Dart*, piloted by J. A. D. McCurdy (later to be named lieutenant-governor of Nova Scotia), became the first heavier-than-air machine to fly in the British Commonwealth. Behind this event was the creative genius of Alexander Graham Bell. While he is usually remembered as the inventor of the telephone, to limit his achievements thus is, in the words of one authority, " . . . to seriously underrate his genius . . . he was the Leonardo da Vinci of the modern age with a restless curiosity that probed into many fields." A visit to the tetrahedral Bell Museum at Baddeck or the reading of a selection of the countless books and articles about the man will convince us of the truth of this statement. On June 14, 1919, Captain John Alcock and Lieutenant Arthur Brown took off from Lester's Field near St. John's. Sixteen hours and twelve minutes later they landed at Clifden, Ireland, to complete the first transatlantic flight. From then until the supersonic age Newfoundland, by virtue of its North Atlantic location, was to figure prominently in aviation links between the hemispheres. It must also be remembered that eighteen years earlier, in 1901, a scant few miles from where Alcock and Brown's famous flight began,

> Signor Marconi announced tonight [December 12, 1901] that he had received electrical signals across the Atlantic Ocean from his station in Cornwall, England. Signor Marconi arrived a week ago and selected Signal Hill, at the entrance to the harbour, as an experimental station and moved his equipment there. There is much speculation here as to the practicability of this scheme of wireless telegraphy. Marconi is satisfied, however, that great surprises are in store for the world. . . . [7]

One of the many visitors to the installation on Signal Hill was an eighteen-year-old boy—E. J. Pratt. He was fascinated by what he saw, and wireless telegraphy was later to figure prominently in many of his narrative poems (see page 129).

The heritage of Atlantic Canada has been conditioned over the years by the economic development of the region. Trials and difficulties, triumphs and achievements—all must be taken into account in local history. While the pessimist might agree with the conclusion of the Gordon Royal Commission of 1956 that " ... generous assistance should be given to those people who might wish to move to other parts of Canada where there may be greater opportunity", those of more optimistic bent will surely applaud the vision of Dr. M. M. Coady:

> We have no desire ... to create a nation of mere shopkeepers, whose thoughts run only to groceries and to dividends. We want our men to look into the sun and into the depths of the sea. We want them to explore the hearts of flowers and the hearts of fellow men. ... We desire above all that they will discover and develop their own capacities for creation. [Then] they will usher in the new day by attending to the blessings of the old. They will use what they have to secure what they have not.[8]

FOR READING AND REFERENCE

A. General

BREWIS, T. N.: *Regional Economic Policies in Canada.* Toronto: Macmillan of Canada, 1969.

GEORGE, R. E.: *A Leader and a Laggard.* Toronto: University of Toronto Press, 1970.

MANN, NELSON: "Atlantic Provinces Economic Council", *Dalhousie Review*, XXXV, 4 (Winter 1956): 309-22.

MARTIN, J. LYNTON: *This Land.* Halifax: Nova Scotia Museum, 1972. See also *A History of Everyday Things in Nova Scotia*, a series of pamphlets produced by the Nova Scotia Museum, e.g., "Lumbering", 1969.

WADE, MASON (ed.): *Regionalism in the Canadian Community.* Toronto: University of Toronto Press, 1969.

The Social Significance of the Co-operative Movement, Extension Department, St. Francis Xavier University.

There is a wealth of government publications dealing with this topic: royal commission reports, and *Canada Year Book* and specific studies such as: "A Development Plan for Prince Edward Island", Canada Department of Regional Economic Expansion, 1969. Check the current catalogue of Canadian government publications for details.

B. Industrial

COMEAU, F. G. J.: "The Origin and History of the Apple Industry in Nova Scotia", *Collections Nova Scotia Historical Society*, XXIII: 15-40.

COPELAND, M. NEIL: "The Power and the Glory: Fundy Tidal Project", *Atlantic Advocate*, August 1970, 18-24.

EVANS, G. R.: "Early Gold Mining in Nova Scotia", *Collections Nova Scotia Historical Society*, XXV: 17-48.

GALGAY, FRANCIS: "The Newfoundland Whaling Industry", *Newfoundland Quarterly*, LXII, 3 (Fall 1963): 11-14.

LOUNSBURY, RALPH G.: *The British Fishery at Newfoundland*. Hamden Conn.: Archon Books, 1969 (reprint).

MORROW, R. A. H.: *Story of the Springhill Disaster*. Saint John: Morrow Publishers, 1891.

NEARY, PETER: "Wabana You're a Corker: Two Ballads with Some Notes Towards an Understanding of the Social History of Bell Island and Conception Bay", paper presented to Canadian Historical Association, Kingston, June 1973.

RASKY, FRANK: *Great Canadian Disasters*. Toronto: Longmans Green, 1961.

TAYLOR, J. G.: "Iron Man in Wooden Ships", *Newfoundland Quarterly*, LXIV, 1 (Spring 1965): 6-8.

The Wood Industries of New Brunswick. Fredericton: Provincial Archives, 1969.

The Newfoundland Seal Fishery of the Early Twentieth Century (Kit). St. John's: Memorial University, 1970. See also C. Brown and H. Horwood: *Death on the Ice* (Garden City N.Y.: Doubleday, 1972).

Kings County—An Agricultural Overview. Kentville, Nova Scotia: Department of Agriculture, 1972.

C. Travel and Communications

BEWITT, ROSS: "The First Atlantic Cable", *Atlantic Advocate*, XLVIII, 12 (August 1958): 51-4.

CUSHING, EILEEN C.: "Early Modes of Travel", *Collections New Brunswick Historical Society*, XV (1959): 7-26.

GREEN, H. GORDON: "The Flight at Baddeck", *Atlantic Advocate*, XLIX, 2 (October 1958): 21-9.

MACLAREN, GEORGE: "Communications in the Northumberland Strait and the Gulf of St. Lawrence", *Nova Scotia Historical Quarterly*, I, 2 (June 1971): 101-25.

MARTELL, J. S.: "Intercolonial Communications", in *Historical Essays on the Atlantic Provinces*. Toronto: McClelland and Stewart, 1967, 179-206.

MOON, ERIC: "Air Race from Newfoundland—Alcock and Brown", *Atlantic Advocate*, XL, 11 (July 1959): 45-56.

PARKIN, J. H.: *Bell and Baldwin*. Toronto: University of Toronto Press, 1964.

ROWE, MELVIN: *Heart's Content: Pioneer in World Communications*. St. John's: Provincial Archives, 1972.

STOLTZ, DOUGLAS: "The Death of the Newfie Bullet", *Canadian Rail*, October 1969, 247-58.

WILMOT, ROSS: "The Day They Flew the Silver Dart", *Imperial Oil Review*, XLII, 1 (February 1959): 2-9.

SUGGESTIONS FOR FURTHER RESEARCH

1. From time to time the question of a political union of the four Atlantic provinces has been advanced as a solution to many of the economic problems that beset the area. However, it is probable that if a vote were held tomorrow on the subject, union would be rejected. Why? Would such an idea be feasible from the standpoint of your province? Arrange a class debate on the subject. During 1973, as part of the special centennial celebrations a new organization, "The Brothers and Sisters of Cornelius Howatt", was formed on Prince Edward Island. Who was Cornelius Howatt? This society is opposed to any form of Maritime union. Can you ascertain why? See David Weale: *Cornelius Howatt, Farmer and Island Patriot* (Summerside: Williams and Crue Ltd., 1973).

2. St. John's has been home to the Portuguese fishing fleet (popularly known as the "White Fleet") for hundreds of years. Annually the white hulls, sharp prows, yellow-painted masts, and latticework of sail and rigging have been a familiar sight on the waterfront. Look into the history of this fishing venture and note some of the historical links that bind Portugal to Newfoundland. Reference: Alan Villiers: *The Quest of the Schooner Argus* (London: Hodder and Stoughton, 1958). For another view of the Grand Bank fishery read Rudyard Kipling's *Captains Courageous*. How has the industry changed since this account was written?

3. "No event in the history of Canada has startled the nation and touched the hearts of all more than the terrible calamity at Springhill collieries." The above was written, not in the late 1950s when Springhill was struck twice by disaster, but in 1891 when an earlier explosion took 125 lives. Research the history of mining disasters in Atlantic Canada (not only in Springhill, but in other areas as well) and discover something of the unparalleled heroism associated with mining. A popular recording, *Miner's Songs* by the Travellers, will help set the background and atmosphere. You may also be interested in reading the novel *Pit* by Robert Lait (Toronto: General Publishing Co., 1970), which deals with the impact of a mine disaster on a community in England. Rex Lucas in *Men in Crisis* (Toronto: General Publishing Co., 1970) considers the problem from the sociological point of view.

12. Biographical Studies

Writing in 1914, a Nova Scotian author paid his native Pictou County the following compliment:

> ... Pictou's proudest product is her men and women. In less than a century she has given to the church nearly three hundred clergymen. She has sent forth one hundred and ninety physicians, sixty-three lawyers, forty professors, twenty-six missionaries, eight college presidents. four judges, two governors, two premiers, a chief justice plus a host of journalists, politicians and business men of note and fame.[1]

This comment about a single county in one province might well have been made about many other regions of Atlantic Canada. Only the statistics would require change. Like consolation-award winners, people in Atlantic Canada have for generations extolled the varied careers of their native sons. More often than not it is those who have achieved fame in faraway places who are remembered.* Names such as Bliss Carman, L. M. Montgomery, E. J. Pratt, or Hugh MacLennan—to give only a literary cross-section—are recalled with ease. The unfortunate part of this approach is that it tends to obscure the achievements of those who remained behind or of others who, though born elsewhere, achieved fame through years spent in Atlantic Canada. Further, as a review of this chapter will reveal, there is much to be learned from a study of the lives of people who never achieved fame—or notoriety.

The true beginning of historical events is to be found in the lives of ordinary people, for it is an axiom of history that we cannot

*Biographies of one hundred Maritimers who achieved fame in the United States may be found in J. Ernest Kerr: *Imprint of the Maritimes* (Boston: Christopher Publishing House, 1959).

understand the nature of any group without detailed knowledge of the individuals who compose it. To be complete, history must not be limited to those who reach the top in any field. This is not to be interpreted as meaning that *all* history is biography. Rather, it serves to emphasize that a profitable approach, especially in local history, may be gained through consideration of the careers of those whose contributions, large or small, add to the sum total of the development of the region. An English historian, Herbert Butterfield, once pointed out that if we were to start with a blank, having wiped out all existing historical literature, we could never prevent children from listening to the tales of a grandfather, or discourage inquiries about famous individuals, or stop the retelling of favourite tales about other people.[2] The reason is simple. The love of a good story is inherent in us and few things are of more lasting interest than the lives of individuals who live now, or who once lived in one's own community.

First, a word of caution about sources of information. When you read biographies, and especially autobiographies, be aware that few examples of this literary form are truly objective. If the reader keeps this in mind, checks references carefully, and takes into account opposing viewpoints, he or she will not likely be misled. In short, it is essential to evaluate *all* material studied: "A good biography shows its subject to be a many-sided person; not all good and not all bad. A man of any substance is disliked as well as admired; he argues with other great men of his time about issues and he is sometimes wrong. A good [biographer] is able to portray a man's weaknesses and mistakes without lessening his importance to history."[3] An example is to be found in the numerous studies of the career of Joseph Howe. Although a controversial figure in his own time, Howe as a politician possessed so many popular or charismatic qualities that often writers have painted a picture "larger than life". It is only because of the more objective work of recent historians that we have begun to see this great Nova Scotian in a true light.

What about biographical research on the local level, and especially concerning those whose careers have never merited the attention of historian or biographer? Here, too, one must carefully weigh evidence and check all possible leads and sources. The best advice is found in the directions given to contributors to the *Dictionary of Canadian Biography*. You would do well to read widely in this series—not only will you learn a great deal about famous Canadians, you will absorb something of the proper biographical approach.

Each biography should be an informative and stimulating treatment of its subject, presented in readable form. Its factual information should be precise and accurate, and be based upon reliable (preferably firsthand) sources. Biographies should not, however, be mere catalogues of

"He says his name is Howe and he wants to talk to us about something called **Responsible Government**"

Aug. 2nd 1972: Canada's
Provincial Premiers meet in
Halifax.

Cartoon by Chambers courtesy Halifax *Chronicle-Herald*

dates and events, or compilations of previous studies of the same subject. The biographer should try to give the reader an orderly account of the personality and achievements of the subject, against the background of the period in which he or she participated. ... It is expected that the biographer will attempt, within the space available, to appraise the circumstances shaping his subject's character and career, enumerating the parts played by ancestry, parentage, education, physical and social environment, and other formative influences; that he will make discreet use of relevant anecdote; that he will conclude his biography by an equitable and discriminating evaluation of the subject's strengths and weaknesses, successes and failures, and probable place in Canadian history.[4]

While it is recognized that the majority who read this page are not aspiring biographers, the above passage is still important. It gives an excellent summary of the correct technique in the writing of similar sketches and provides a convenient test to apply to biographies you may read.

Before mentioning various approaches in local biographical study, it will be helpful to review a representative sampling of Maritimers—the well-known and the unknown—native sons and daughters and those born elsewhere. In this way some idea of the scope of biography in local history will be obtained. Also, it is here that biographical study may bridge an historical gap and provide a more rounded approach to your understanding of the region. Those interested in local history should seek out the "forgotten people" of third or fourth rank whose contributions have been overshadowed by the front-liners. No one can deny the importance of Thomas Chandler Haliburton or Charles Tupper, Samuel Leonard Tilley or Lord Beaverbrook, Wilfred Grenfell or Benjamin Bowring in their respective fields. There were, however, others. Most textbooks deal adequately with the early explorers, the major political figures, and the key leaders in business and industry. All too often other fields of importance in any balanced history, such as religion or social development, have been neglected or seldom mentioned.

If you were asked to list the names of the most prominent people of French origin during the colonial period in Atlantic Canada, you might recall Champlain, Poutrincourt, Lescarbot, or La Tour. But have you heard of Le Loutre, Bourg, or Sigogne? To understand the history of the Acadians, from whatever angle, is impossible without reference to the men who were their unofficial leaders during the unhappy years of the middle- and late-eighteenth century. Abbé Jean-Louis Le Loutre arrived in Louisbourg late in August 1737, charged with the task of establishing a mission among the Indians. After a brief interval during which he mastered the Micmac language, Le Loutre moved to Shubenacadie, Nova Scotia, where he established his headquarters. During the next twenty years this priest became the most controversial figure in the entire region. His role as spiritual advisor to Micmacs and Acadians was eclipsed by a personal "guerre éternelle" against the British. While some aspects of his career remain uncertain, it is clear that Le Loutre played a part in inciting the Indians and Acadians to attack British settlements. A few historians have gone as far as to suggest that these non-religious activities were responsible, in part, for the later expulsion of the Acadians. Words such as "fanatical", "bold", "resourceful", "wary", "untiring", "truculent", and "tenacious" have been used to describe Le Loutre. When Beauséjour fell in 1755 he escaped to the Miramichi. Captured later by the British, he was released after the signing of the Treaty of Paris in 1763. Le Loutre devoted the remainder of his life to assisting Acadian refugees in France, most notably through establishment of the settlement at Belle-Isle-en-Mer eight miles off the coast of Brittany. Why have historians dealt so harshly with this man? Ask your teacher for references and try to form a conclusion.

Two other clergymen played influential roles among the Acadians, but the careers of Abbé Jean-Mathurin Bourg and Abbé Jean-Mande Sigogne were in striking contrast to that of Le Loutre. Bourg, the first native Acadian to be raised to the priesthood, was born at La Rivière-aux-Canards (modern Canard, N.S.) on June 9, 1744. The eleven-year-old Bourg, along with his family, was expelled first to Virginia and later to England, eventually reaching France in 1763. He studied for the priesthood at the Séminaire du Saint-Esprit in Paris and upon completion of his studies returned to minister among his people. In 1773 he established a mission near Carleton, Quebec, on Chaleur Bay. From this location Abbé Bourg served as a travelling missionary to the far-flung Acadian community. During the American Revolution he played a key role. Unlike Le Loutre, who spent so much time and energy in harassing the British, Bourg succeeded in preventing the Indians of the Saint John River valley from rallying to the American cause. Later he was transferred to a parish near Montreal, where he died in 1797. Bourg's career raises a fascinating question. Why would a man who had suffered so much during the Expulsion be found on the British side in the American Revolution? Why, for that matter, did most Acadians support the British at this time? A further look into Bourg's career will provide the answer.

As was the case with most clergymen of the period, Abbé Jean-Mande Sigogne was not native-born. He fled from France to England during the early days of the French Revolution and in 1799 volunteered for service among the Acadians in Nova Scotia. Arriving in Halifax on June 20 of the same year, Sigogne proceeded to the southwestern part of the province where most Acadians lived. Among his first acts was the organization of two parishes: Sainte Anne de Ruisseau east of Yarmouth in the Cape Sable district, and Sainte Marie centred at Church Point on the Fundy coast. The latter became his base for missionary activities. Interested in all aspects of community life, Sigogne opened his own school, supplementing it with a Sunday school for adults where the catechism, reading, and writing were taught. Like many other priests he spent time working among the Micmacs. Because he too had experienced the bitterness of exile, Sigogne understood the plight of the returned Acadians.

In addition to his parochial duties, Sigogne served as justice of the peace and worked closely with T. C. Haliburton, who was the representative of the area in the legislature. Haliburton, later to achieve fame as author and humorist, championed the cause of the Acadians and worked for the abolition of the Test Oath that rendered Catholics (and therefore most Acadians) ineligible for public office. Look into the careers of Haliburton and Sigogne and see how this was accomplished. Sigogne remained in the Clare-Argyle region of Nova Scotia until his death in 1844. Still remembered among the people he served so long, Sigogne is often referred to as "the Apostle of the Acadians". The careers of Le Loutre, Bourg, and Sigogne span the history of the Acadians from conquest through expulsion, exile, return, and revival to the point where they regained their basic legal and constitutional rights.

An equally interesting analysis could be made by interpreting local history through the lives of other religious leaders. Four bishops of the Church of England played a major role in shaping the social, political, and religious development of Atlantic Canada: Charles and John Inglis in Nova Scotia, Medley in New Brunswick, and Feild in Newfoundland. Jens Haven, an early Moravian missionary on the coast of Labrador, and the many clergymen sponsored by the Society for the Propagation of the Gospel (such as Frederick Dibblee in the Saint John River valley) have left behind diaries and other accounts of the hardships and achievements of pioneer life. The early founders of the various denominations led many-sided lives and were often forced to battle both religious indifference and the political establishment of their day. This is exemplified in the careers of Rev. Edmund Burke (Catholic), William Black (Methodist), Theodore Harding (Baptist), James McGregor (Presbyterian), and Richard Preston (African United Baptist). One clergyman of more than ordinary interest is Dr. Thomas McCulloch. In 1803 McCulloch emigrated from Scotland to Nova Scotia where his career was noteworthy for its diversity. Aside from religious duties he is remembered as an educator, political reformer, author, ornithologist, founder of Pictou Academy and Pinehill Divinity Hall, and first president of Dalhousie University. Another measure of his greatness may be found in the prominence achieved by many of his students—for instance, Jotham Blanchard, John Geddie, and J. W. Dawson. Consult a biographical dictionary to discover their particular contributions.

When we turn to the late-nineteenth and early-twentieth centuries we find that social development provides another focal point for biographical study. Many men have struggled in a variety of ways to better the standard of living in Atlantic Canada and too often they have been forgotten or overlooked. Let us consider a representative sampling for additional insight into local history. The map of Prince Edward Island is sprinkled with place names of Scottish origin, a point that was discussed in Chapter 3. One reason was the migration in 1772 of a group of 200 Highlanders under the leadership of Captain John MacDonald, Laird of Glenaladale and Glenfinnan. A direct descendant, William Christopher MacDonald, born at Glenaladale in 1831, was later to amass a fortune as founder and developer of one of Canada's largest tobacco companies. A man who neither chewed nor smoked his own products, MacDonald was knighted by Queen Victoria in 1898. (He marked the event by changing the spelling of his name to Macdonald.) Although best known as a benefactor of McGill University and for the establishment of Macdonald College at Ste. Anne de Bellevue, Quebec, he never lost interest in the land of his birth. One of Macdonald's first schemes, undoubtedly a by-product of his upbringing, was the establishment of a Rural Schools Fund. Designed initially to stimulate development of school gardens, the plan was enlarged to include encouragement of crop rotation and the protection of produce against disease. The scheme made possible the establishment of a number of agricultural fairs and inspired other educators, such as Dr. L. A. De Wolfe in Nova Scotia, to launch programs of nature and agricultural study in the schools. Macdonald's second program was designed to improve the quality of education through school consolidation. The first such schools in Atlantic Canada were founded with his financial backing at Kingston, New Brunswick, and Middleton, Nova Scotia, in 1903 and Hillsboro, Prince Edward Island, in 1905. In this effort Macdonald was ahead of his time, and another quarter of a century was to pass before the idea became common. However, the Macdonald School established in Middleton still stands as a monument to these early endeavours. How do you account for Macdonald's deep interest in education? To answer this question it is necessary to know more of his background and Highland heritage. Macdonald's life followed the pattern of the lives of many other Maritimers who accumulated large fortunes only to invest much of them in various enterprises in their native provinces. Names such as Lord Beaverbrook, Sir James Dunn, Isaac Killam, and Cyrus Eaton are probably the most noteworthy in this regard. There were still others who attempted in dramatically different ways to assist in the development of Atlantic Canada, and who were able to accomplish much without leaving their native heath.

South of Catalina on Trinity Bay, Newfoundland, is located a community called Port Union. It is unique in that it is probably the only town in Canada built by a labour union. The establishment of this community takes us back to a group of nineteen men from Herring Neck, Notre Dame Bay, who joined with their leader William Coaker on November 2, 1908, to form the Fishermen's Protective Union. Who was this man Coaker? Born a "townie" in St. John's on November 19, 1871 and a school dropout at eleven, he went on to establish a movement that was to have a dramatic impact on Newfoundland politics during the early 1900s. The most formative period of his career, 1891 to 1901, saw him living on a lonely island in Bonavista Bay. In this isolated existence Coaker came face to face with the hardships endured by outport fishermen. Far worse than the danger of life at sea was their economic bondage and it was this circumstance that spurred Coaker on. Outport life was dominated by a credit or barter system controlled by rich merchants. This meant that little actual money changed hands and the fishermen were always in debt. Coaker determined to change this situation by collective action. Through a unique combination of dogged persistence and unusual powers of persuasion, Coaker managed to enrol some 20,000 fishermen in a fishermen's union. At times his approach bordered on the theatrical as supporters, wearing their symbolic guernseys (close-fitting, roll-necked sweaters), sang:

> *We are coming, Mr. Coaker, men from Green Bay's rocky shore,*
> *Men who stand the snow white billows down on stormy Labrador.*
> *We are ready and a-waiting, strong and solid, firm and bold,*
> *To be led by you like Moses led the Israelites of old.*
> *We are ready for to sever from the merchant servile throng,*
> *We are coming Mr. Coaker and we're forty thousand strong.*[5]

Despite the poetic exaggeration in the song's last line, the approach worked and Coaker's organization was soon a force to be reckoned with. Following creation of the union, Coaker's next step was to develop the Fishermen's Trading Company and initiate the founding of Port Union in 1910. Later he entered politics, a move regarded by many as a fatal mistake. Through an investigation of Coaker's career, make an estimate of his impact on the merchant-dominated economy of Newfoundland. A critic has written: "Coaker was a man who died rich, successful and defeated—by time, by circumstance and most of all by himself."[6] Do you agree?

Another who struggled with many of the same problems but who avoided direct political involvement was Dr. M. M. Coady, a native of North East Margaree, Nova Scotia. Appointed in 1928 as director of the Extension Department of St. Francis Xavier University, Coady was until his death in 1959 a towering figure in Atlantic Canada. To understand his approach and that of the Antigonish Movement which he helped establish, it is necessary to recall the Depression of the 1930s. The preceding decade had been, for much of Canada, a time of comparative prosperity. The collapse of the New York stock market in October 1929 threw the economic system of the United States, and with it that of Canada, into chaos. Although in some respects the primary producers of Atlantic Canada were not as hard hit as the urban unemployed, they had their share of problems. Old markets were gone, wages were cut, and prices for agricultural produce, forestry products, and fish fell to disastrously low levels. Into this situation came Dr. Coady—like Coaker, a spokesman for the common man. However, his prescription was the development of a co-operative movement. It is best told in his own words:

I can best illustrate the necessity [of the co-operative movement] . . . by portraying to you the difficulties that co-operative marketing will run into when it gets underway. Let us make it very simple. Take the farmers for example. They hear, we will suppose, for the first time about this new technique of co-operation. . . . They decide to form a marketing co-operative. When they begin to bring in their commodities—wheat, meat or anything else—they are stopped . . . [by a traffic cop with] . . a golden whistle. . . . Who is this man with the golden whistle? He is the first representative of the hierarchy of businessman. He is the merchant, the dealer, the wholesaler, the first in the hierarchy of private profit business. He promptly tells the farmers they cannot cross this golden line—they must stay back on their farms. . . . [This man] can smash the farmer's ranks. He can do this because his economic position gives him influence. He stands high in the political and social life of the community. . . . The reason for his power is to be found in that he owns economic institutions in the consumer field. He owns stores, wholesale or credit institutions. Were he and his kind out of the way, then the road would be easy. Thus, what so many people . . . consider the first step in co-operation is encountering an obstacle that can only be solved by the consumer [co-operative] approach.[7]

Strong language, but it worked, and the co-operative movement spread to all parts of Atlantic Canada and beyond. It would be false to suggest that co-operatives solved entirely the economic problems of the day. But there is no doubt that then, as now, they can be credited with performing a useful role in the economic life of the region. For this we are indebted, in large measure, to "the man from Margaree". Seek out reference books if you wish to understand the full significance of credit unions and co-operatives.

The preceding biographical sketches were presented in part to illustrate productive approaches in local history. They also serve to underline the diversity that may be found in such studies and the numerous opportunities for research. It is also of importance to investigate the careers of groups of individuals whose lives contain some bond of common interest. The timber trade and lumber industry of northern New Brunswick provide one example. Valuable stands of pine, spruce, and other timber placed the Miramichi valley in the forefront of the industry by the early years of the nineteenth century—so much so that by 1819 nearly one-quarter of all British vessels engaged in the North American timber trade were loaded at Miramichi anchorages. Several firms were involved; however, two led all the others and their story can be told through the careers of Alexander Rankin and Joseph Cunard.

On the northern bank of the river, Rankin, representative of the firm

Gilmour, Rankin and Co. with headquarters at Douglastown, held sway. The south bank was controlled by Cunard, brother of the famous Sir Samuel Cunard, founder of the steamship line that still bears the family name.* The commercial rivalry between the two men extended into all areas but was most evident in politics. Rankin, a Scot, was the first on the scene and brought with him a solid knowledge of the timber business gained through experience in the Baltic. One historian has written: "From the first Alexander Rankin was a force in the community and afterward became a force in the province. His personal bearing, his kindly manner and ability to direct men, attached to him all with whom he came in contact."[8] Rankin's early success gained him a seat in the Assembly in 1827, and nineteen years later he was named a member of the upper house, or Legislative Council. Eventually the fierce competition between the two firms broke into open warfare when Cunard managed to have the customs office moved from Douglastown to Chatham, the centre of his operations. So fierce was the animosity and such was the loyalty of opposing factions that for some time citizens dared not cross to the opposite side of the river. During a "fighting" election held during the summer of 1843 Rankin recruited 500 men to prevent "Cunarders" from voting, and two companies of the 30th Regiment were sent to restore order. Small wonder that the Miramichi has become noted for legends and folklore! Like his rival, Cunard also served as a member of the Assembly and the Council, yet today traces of both names have all but vanished from the Miramichi.

Later developments saw the replacement of many original firms by more specialized operations. By 1897 there were a dozen sawmills on the river between Loggieville, Chatham, and Nelson on the south shore and Douglastown, Newcastle, and Bridgetown on the north side. At this time pulp was becoming important, the spool-wood industry was consuming three million feet of birch each year, and the bark from several million feet of hemlock was annually being processed for tanning purposes. Again, as in the early period, a few key men stand out and the development of lumbering may be told through their careers. Hon. J. B. Snowball (later a senator and lieutenant-governor of New Brunswick) and John and Charles Sergeant are among those who achieved prominence at the turn of the century. The forest industry is significant in many parts of Atlantic Canada. Can you trace the career of the early promoters of lumbering and the timber trade in your area?†

*For a map of the early Miramichi shipyards see the *Atlantic Advocate*, November 1964, 38-9.

†An outstanding series of photographs depicting early lumbering operations may be found in Louise Manny and James R. Wilson: *Songs of Miramichi* (Fredericton: Brunswick Press, 1970).

The military field provides yet another focal point for biographical study and the nineteenth century in particular saw many outstanding military figures. These range from Captain William Parker and Major Augustus Frederick Welsford, natives of Halifax who distinguished themselves in the Crimean War, to Sir John Inglis (son of Bishop John Inglis) and William Hall of Hantsport, Nova Scotia (the first Nova Scotian winner of the Victoria Cross), both of whom won fame at the relief of Lucknow in the Indian Mutiny, and Willard and Harry Miller from Noel Shore, Nova Scotia, who were awarded the American Congressional Medal of Honour for bravery in the Spanish-American War. Perhaps the most unusual military figure of the century as far as Atlantic Canada is concerned was Sarah Emma Edmonds, a native of Magaguadavic Settlement, New Brunswick, whose exploits in the American Civil War became the subject of two books: her autobiography, *Nurse and Spy*, and *She Rode with the Generals* by Sylvia Dannett. As Miss Edmonds described it, her story "is a record of events which transpired in the experience of one who was on the field and participated in numerous battles serving in the capacity of a spy and as a field nurse for over two years."[9] By her own account she was able to penetrate the enemy (Southern) lines eleven times and provide valuable information to the Northern Command. Although exaggerated in places for dramatic effect, her account of the American Civil War provides fascinating reading.

Scientific achievement is another area that merits investigation. A roll call of the famous in this field would include such names as Abraham Gesner (1797-1864), Charles Fenerty (1821-92), and Simon Newcomb (1835-1909). What was the particular "claim to fame" of each of the above? What other names might be added to the list? An additional area for investigation might well be politics. Here one is faced with a wide choice of possibilities for research. Aside from obvious examples such as Tupper, Thompson, Borden, and Bennett (the four Maritimers, as of 1973, to hold office as prime minister of Canada), you may be interested in delving into the careers of lesser-known politicians. Consider Andrew Bonar Law (1858-1923) of Rexton, New Brunswick, the only prime minister of Britain born outside the British Isles, or William John Bowser (1867-1933), also a native of Rexton, who became premier of British Columbia. Nearby Richibucto was the birthplace of Peter J. Venoit (1863-1936), first Acadian premier of New Brunswick and later postmaster general in the federal cabinet. To move farther afield, Sir Simon Fraser (1834-1919), born in Lorne, Nova Scotia, emigrated to Australia as a young man and crowned his forty-year political career with a knighthood. A tablet of Australian granite was placed in St. Columba's Church in Hopewell, Nova Scotia, to mark his contribution to public life. Look carefully into the biographical records of people who once lived in your community and see if any achieved fame in politics—either at home or abroad. From the examples mentioned, ranging all the way from the timber barons of the Miramichi to world famous politicians, we can appreciate further the scope and diversity of this aspect of local history.

In this chapter we have discussed the careers of numerous individuals who have in different ways helped to make Atlantic Canada what it is today. What about your own family? Have you ever tried to trace your family tree? What do you know about the people who make up your own past? About your grandparents and great-grandparents? A good place to start is with your family name. Even if it proves to be impossible to research your family background, you can trace the origin of the name. Alice, in *Alice in Wonderland*, asked, "Must a name mean something?" and the answer came back that every surname in existence has a story behind it. A common family name, especially in New Brunswick, is Steeves. The original spelling was Stief and it is of Dutch-Baltic origin. In the early 1760s Heinrich and Rachael Stief left their homeland because of religious persecution. They emigrated first to Philadelphia, later moving with their seven sons to Hillsborough on the Petitcodiac River. About this time the spelling was changed to its modern form.*

Most surnames have changed in spelling over the years and a little investigation will show that they are derived from a wide variety of sources. Occupations, nicknames, place names, and words from other languages illustrate the wide variety of sources for the derivation of family names. As a class project, using your local telephone directory or voters' list as a guide, select the twelve most common surnames in your community. Establish the origin of each.† What does this tell you about the racial composition of the population? While such a survey can never be totally accurate, inasmuch as some people have had their last names changed by court order (for example, "White" today may have been originally "Le Blanc"), it will provide an indication of the major trends. If your research encompasses Lunenburg County in Nova Scotia, note that many German family names have been anglicized over the years. A few changes will illustrate the process: Bubickhofer—Publicover, Gorckum—Corkum,

---

*The history of this remarkable family may be found in *Samphire Greens* by Esther Clark Wright. See also *Loyalists of New Brunswick* (Moncton: Moncton Publishing Co., 1972) by the same author, for genealogical information on the Loyalist families of New Brunswick.

†Some useful books to consult: George F. Black: *The Surnames of Scotland: The Origin, Meaning and History* (New York: New York Public Library, 1962); W. O. Hassall: *History Through Surnames* (Toronto: Pergamon Press, 1967); Edward Machisaght: *The Surnames of Ireland* (Shannon: Irish University Press, 1969); P. H. Reaney: *A Dictionary of Surnames* (London: Routledge and Kegan Paul, 1958). See also W. G. Hoskins: "The Homes of Family Names", *History Today*, XXII, 3 (March 1972): 189-94.

Eisenhauer—Isner and Eisner, Schlagentweit—Slauenwhite, Weih-nacht—Whynot. There have been other name changes among those who came from Switzerland and Montbeliard to settle the same area in the 1750s. Can you list additional examples?

Ancestor-hunting, or genealogy, can be equally interesting and in your research you are bound to uncover many aspects of local history. How long has your family lived in your community? Did they come directly from the Old World? Did they migrate from some other part of your province to your present location? One investigator has explained the fascination of genealogy:

> For a whole year I was as engrossed as a detective on a murder case, or a spy in a wartime ring. Clues chased around my head; dates danced before my eyes; history practically came out my ears. ... I struggled to interpret curiously tantalizing evidence. Never have I had such fun, nor entertainment so richly escapist: I was writing a history of my father's family.[10]

Few will take up genealogy as a hobby and fewer still will make it their career; it can, none the less, provide one with an absorbing glimpse of one's own past. How far back can you trace your family?

A family study will begin with one's own parents and grandparents, and the basic information may well be available from personal records or a family Bible. You will quickly realize as you probe backward that numbers can be a problem. Allowing one child the essential quota of two parents and each parent his or her quota, we have only to go back two generations to tally 32 ancestors and ten generations to arrive at 1,024! While it is easiest to follow the male side when composing a family tree, you should attempt to trace as many lines as possible. Once you have obtained the basic data for your immediate family, you are ready to start on more serious research. Locate the oldest person in your family and through interview or letter obtain all possible information about family movements from place to place. Inquire about full names (this is especially important in families with common surnames), birthplaces, dates, and places of baptisms, marriages, deaths, education, and occupations. Every last item should be traced down because often a single fact—for example, that someone was a graduate of a certain school or college—may be the clue that will lead you to an elusive birth date. Distance may prevent a personal interview; however, this method is much to be preferred over contact by mail. A portable tape recorder can be of assistance and if you find a helpful source of information you may want to share it with your classmates. Private papers, diaries, letters, and clippings should be sought. Church records and old school registers can be of considerable aid. These are usually retained in the local community. Sometimes church records have been deposited in denominational archives, in a nearby university library, or in a diocesan office. Local clergymen will be able to give you information as to location. All four provincial archives possess genealogical material and much of this is on microfilm. One word of caution. Do not expect busy librarians or archivists to do your research. Inquiries to such sources should only be made if you have a question based on concrete evidence. In any event, consult your teacher before making such requests.

Useful information can often be found in printed genealogical studies. An outstanding example, Thomas Miller's *History and Genealogical Record of Colchester County*, first published in 1873, was reissued in 1972. This book contains detailed information on fifty-three Nova Scotian families and covers the period 1759-1873. Attached to county and local histories you will often find family records. Those of Acadian origin are particularly well served by two publications—Placide Gaudet: *Acadian Genealogies and Notes*, in Volume II of the Report of the Canadian Archives for 1905, and Bona Arsenault: *Histoire et Généalogie des Acadiens*. A check list of major sources for Acadian genealogical research may be found in: *Bulletin—Société Historique Acadienne*, III, 9 (octobre-novembre-décembre 1970): 373-84. For a model genealogy see J. E. Belliveau: "My ancestor Piau", *Atlantic Advocate*, August 1971, 58-68. Old directories, census records, historical atlases (see Chapter 5), and newspaper files—especially obituaries, deeds, and wills—are further sources of genealogical information.

Perhaps some of the most available clues will be found on tombstones in local cemeteries. Inscriptions, particularly older ones, will yield much that is of interest. You may find some unusual epitaphs, as did the writer in an abandoned cemetery near Sackville, New Brunswick:

> IN MEMORY OF WILLIAM FAWCETT, WHO WAS A PLAIN,
> INDUSTRIOUS, HOSPITABLE AND DEEPLY PIOUS MAN,
> WHOSE UNIFORM AND CHRISTIAN CONDUCT GAINED HIM
> THE RESPECT OF ALL WHO BECAME ACQUAINTED WITH
> HIM. WHILE READING ONE OF MR. WESLEY'S SERMONS
> HIS IMMORTAL SPIRIT WAS INSTANTLY PRECIPITATED
> INTO THE ETERNAL WORLD TO TAKE POSSESSION OF ITS
> FINAL REST BY SOME MONSTER OF INIQUITY THAT WILL
> BE DISCOVERED AT THE LAST DAY WHO INTENTIONALLY
> SHOT HIM DEAD THROUGH THE KITCHEN WINDOW ON THE
> EVENING OF JUNE 19, 1832 IN THE 63RD YEAR OF
> HIS AGE.
>
> READER BE THOU ALSO READY

If there are some nineteenth-century (or earlier) cemeteries in your communiy you may wish to undertake a project in "tombstone tracery". The first step is to obtain permission from the officials or others responsible for the cemetery. If the project is explained, such permission is usually given, provided that proper respect is shown for what is after all consecrated ground. Many of the older stones will have to be cleaned with a stiff brush to remove moss, other vegetation, or accumulated dirt. Next a sheet of paper should be fixed with masking tape to the stone. A satisfactory rubbing, or impression, can be made with ordinary crayons used broadside, or with heelball, a hard black shoemaker's wax used in making brass rubbings. Rubbing is a simple and accurate method of copying the inscriptions and motifs on old gravestones. While it is possible to record these in writing, rubbings even more than photographs preserve the character of a stone as well as its information. Furthermore, the information may be put to a variety of uses. You may want to do rubbings of only the more interesting stones; the statistical information for the others may be recorded or cards for later filing. Since age at death is usually recorded, statistical tables can be constructed and through them useful information derived. These records can also be utilized in developing genealogies. In your research, do not neglect decorative elements—stones with motfs that reflect the sentimentality of the Victorian period are of special interest. Not to be overlooked, as well, are memorial plaques usually found on church walls or sometimes attached to articles dedicated to the memory of a particular person. In the northeast corner of the Kirk of St. James in Charlottetown there is a white marble tablet bearing the following inscription:

IN MEMORY OF COLIN MACKENZIE M.D. ARMY MEDICAL STAFF,

A NATIVE OF ROSSHIRE SCOTLAND

WHO PERISHED IN THE WRECK OF THE STEAMER FAIRY QUEEN NEAR

PICTOU ISLAND

OCTOBER 1, 1853;

LANDING ON THIS ISLAND AN ENTIRE STRANGER

HE BECAME DURING HIS OFFICIAL STAY OF TWO YEARS

THE INTIMATE FRIEND OF MANY AND GAINED THE ESTEEM

OF ALL.

THIS TABLET RECORDS THE SORROW OCCASIONED BY HIS DEATH

AND ESPECIALLY THE LOSS SUSTAINED BY THE POOR TO WHOSE

SUFFERING HE EVER ATTENDED WITH PROMPTITUDE AND

BENEFICENCE

One does not have to be engaged in researching the MacKenzie family to be gripped by the sparse details* given here. Another fascinating sideline of genealogy!

*Further information on the loss of the *Fairy Queen* and the mystery that still surrounds it may be found in L. C. Callbeck: "Eight Bells for the *Fairy Queen*", *Atlantic Advocate*, April 1963, 43-6.

Once you have had some experience in compiling genealogical data, it is an easy step to move on to more complex studies. Often a single family will have produced in successive generations many individuals of importance in local history. Consider the Nova Scotian Archibalds. In 1762 four brothers of Ulster-Scottish stock with their families and household effects sailed into Cobequid Bay. Part of the pre-Loyalist New England migration to Nova Scotia, the Archibalds moved from New Hampshire to settle at Bible Hill near Truro. From this family there sprang S. G. W. Archibald, longtime M.L.A., attorney-general, and judge; Sir Adams Archibald, a Father of Confederation, member of the first federal cabinet, and lieutenant-governor of Manitoba and Nova Scotia; Sir Thomas Dickson Archibald, who rose to be judge of the Court of Queen's Bench in England; Charles Dickson Archibald, who also emigrated to England and amassed a fortune in industrial enterprises; Sir Edward Mortimer Archibald, attorney-general of Newfoundland and later British consul-general in New York; and Peter S. Archibald, president of the Bank of Nova Scotia. In addition to the above-mentioned, no less than five other members of the family were elected to the Nova Scotia House of Assembly and one was named a senator. Similar studies of many of the Loyalist families of New Brunswick (Ludlow, Robinson, Chipman, Wilmot, etc.) will also reveal impressive records. Finally, one point requires special emphasis. Every item in genealogical study must be supported by evidence. Thus, lessons learned in the quest for missing pages in a family history have great meaning in the broader study of the subject.

You will have seen, from this chapter, that biographical studies can play a significant role in local history. Our basic curiosity in the subject lies principally in what can be described as human interest—the desire to know more about our predecessors, to keep certain episodes alive in the memory, and to recapture, as best as we can, a fleeting glimpse of the past. This interest can most satisfactorily be kindled when source materials are close at hand and we become personally involved in the research. The widespread appeal of biographical studies is, then, no mere coincidence. Furthermore, a survey of the lives of the prominent and the not-so-prominent affords an opportunity to become better acquainted with the communities that claim them as native or adopted sons or daughters. For anyone interested in local history, biographical study is a quarry of useful information.

FOR READING AND REFERENCE

A. Biographies of Some Representative Atlantic Canadians

BEAVERBROOK, LORD: *Courage: The Story of Sir James Dunn.* Fredericton: Brunswick Press, 1961. One famous New Brunswicker traces the career of another.

CORBETT, E. A.: *Henry Marshall Tory: Beloved Canadian.* Toronto: Ryerson Press, 1961. The story of a native of Port Shoreham, Nova Scotia, who rose to become one of Canada's most outstanding educators.

EVANS, G. D. N.: *Uncommon Obdurate: The Several Careers of J. F. W. Des Barres.* Toronto: University of Toronto Press, 1969. See also a fictional account of Des Barres's life: Will R. Bird *An Earl Must Have a Wife* (Toronto: Clarke, Irwin, 1969).

GRANTMYRE, BARBARA: *Lunar Rogue.* Fredericton: Brunswick Press, 1963. Not science fiction, but a highly readable account of Henry Moon, *alias* Smith or Newman, who was in 1814 "the most famous man in New Brunswick".

GWYNN, RICHARD: *Smallwood: The Unlikely Revolutionary.* Toronto: McClelland and Stewart, 1968. We are too close in time to such a controversial figure for an objective assessment; however, this is a stimulating account of recent history. Compare with Smallwood's own account in *I Chose Canada* (Toronto: Macmillan of Canada, 1973).

RIDLEY, HILDA M.: *The Story of L. M. Montgomery.* Toronto: Ryerson Press, 1956. See also Wilfred Eggleston: *The Green Gables Letters* (Toronto: Ryerson Press, 1960).

WILD, RONALD: *Amor de Cosmos.* Toronto: Ryerson Press, 1958. The biography of a Nova Scotian (born William Alexander Smith) who emigrated to British Columbia and later served as premier of that province.

WORLEY, RONALD B.: *The Wonderful World of W. A. C. Bennett.* Toronto: McClelland and Stewart, 1971. A partisan picture of another Maritimer who, like de Cosmos and Bowser, became premier of British Columbia.

B. Basic Biographical Reference Works

Concise Dictionary of National Biography. London: Oxford University Press, 1961.

Dictionary of Canadian Biography. Toronto: University of Toronto Press. (Volumes are issued at regular intervals.)

The Macmillan Dictionary of Canadian Biography. Toronto: Macmillan of Canada, 1963.

The Oxford Companion to Canadian History and Literature. Toronto: Oxford University Press, 1967.

The Canadian Directory of Parliament. Ottawa: Public Archives of Canada, 1968. (This is an essential reference in tracing political careers.)

NICHOLSON, MARGARET E.: *People in Books*. New York: H. W. Wilson and Co., 1969. (A guide to biographical literature.)

C. Genealogical References

(In addition to books already mentioned in this chapter, you should check local and county histories—many of these contain valuable genealogical information. For New Brunswick families see *New Brunswick Check List*, Fredericton: Public Archives of New Brunswick, 1971, 112-42.)

Tracing Your Ancestors in Canada. Ottawa: Public Archives of Canada, 1972.

Check List of Parish Registers. Ottawa: Public Archives of Canada, 1969.

BLAKELEY, PHYLLIS R.: *Some Sources for Nova Scotian Genealogy*. Halifax: Public Archives of Nova Scotia, 1968. See also A. E. Marble: "Genealogy in Nova Scotia: How To Trace Your Ancestors", *Halifax Chronicle Herald*, May 12, 1973.

KENNEDY, PATRICIA: *How To Trace Your Loyalist Ancestors*. Ottawa: Ontario Genealogical Society, 1971.

SWIFT, MICHAEL: *Open Letter to Genealogists*. Fredericton: Provincial Archives of New Brunswick, n.d.

THE PRINCE EDWARD ISLAND CENTENNIAL COMMISSION, as part of the special celebrations in 1973, attempted to identify the "Farm Families of the Century". Genealogical information gathered during the course of the project is on file at the Provincial Archives, Charlottetown.

3. General

COLLINS, ROBERT: "Try Climbing Your Family Tree", *Reader's Digest*, January 1970, 47-51.

DAVIS, J. G.: "The Cemetery and History", *Social Studies Review*, III, 4 (April 1973): 9-15. Nova Scotia Teachers' Union.

SCHULTZ, NIKKI: "How To Trace Your Family Tree", *Family Circle*, November 1972, 94, 174-7.

STEEL, D. J., AND TAYLOR, L.: *Family History in Schools*. London: Sussex, Phillimore and Co., 1972.

SUGGESTIONS FOR FURTHER RESEARCH

1. Assume that your community has decided to mark the lives of its three most distinguished citizens (not now living) by erecting plaques that will summarize the highlights of their careers. As a class project, compile a list of those who might be included in a local "hall of fame". Do not limit yourself to obvious areas, i.e., politics or commerce, but seek out neglected fields such as education or sports. After the list has been drawn up, select the three most outstanding citizens and compose, in fifty words or less for each, the inscriptions to be placed on the commemorative plaques. It will be helpful to study inscriptions on plaques erected by the Historic Sites and Monuments Board of Canada. They are models of brevity and clarity.

2. Chapter 4 gives considerable detail on the "Legacy of the Sea" in Atlantic Canada. In every coastal community of the region there are "tales to be told" by those who once followed the sea. Interview such a person (preferably using a tape recorder) and obtain details of his career to share with the class. If you are extremely fortunate you may find someone who can sing an old sea shanty or ballad. Should you be unsuccessful in your search for a person with a sea-going background, or if you live inland, check the people in your community who saw service in the Royal Canadian Navy to see if you can obtain information on their wartime activities. A good example is the amazing story of the Newfoundland schooner, the *Helen Forsey* (see the *Canadian Legion Magazine*, July 1972, for details). Similar interviews may be conducted among those who served in the army or air force during the Second World War. Your local branch of the Royal Canadian Legion would be a good source of contacts in such a project.

3. We have become very conscious of the current women's liberation movement, so much so that we tend to forget the roles of women in days gone by. The career of Madame de la Tour is well known, and the story of Sarah Emma Edmonds is mentioned earlier in the chapter. Compile a list of other women who have played major roles in the history of Atlantic Canada. Some references: Mary Quayle Innis: *The Clear Spirit* (Toronto: University of Toronto Press, 1967); Thora McIlroy Mills: "Women's Lib in the 1890s: They Didn't Have To Fight for It", *Atlantic Advocate*, December 1972, 51-2; *A Century of Women*, compiled by the Zonta Club of Charlottetown, 1973.

Section III
APPLICATIONS OF LOCAL HISTORY

---

13. Researching History Where It Is

Atlantic Canada contains many reminders of the region's rugged, adventuresome, and turbulent past:

- haunting place names of Amerindian or European origin . . .
- remnants of faded dreams and past glories: l'Anse-aux-Meadows and Castle Hill Placentia, Port Royal and Louisbourg, Beauséjour and the Roma settlement . . .
- elegant mansions, dignified public buildings, and humble cottages weathered by wind and salt spray . . .
- folk songs, folklore, and literature that tell us much of what people were and are . . .
- art that interprets individuality and a sense of place and the triple legacy of the people, the land, and the sea . . .

In covering these topics the approach of the book has been, first, to sketch in broad strokes the history of the region and, second, to relate themes of general interest to the provincial or local level. You are now prepared to piece the jigsaw puzzle together and write a history of the part of Atlantic Canada that you know best—your own community. Some of you may be thinking: "We haven't the resources to undertake such a study. Our school lacks a good library and we are miles from a museum. Very few of the suggestions for reading or reference are available to us." If you have read the preceding chapters carefully and tackled some of the projects, you will already know the answers to these problems: you start where you are, utilizing nearby resources. If you have the spirit of inquiry, material on which to base your study will not be lacking. In quick review, let us look at some basic points that may lead you to the raw material of local history.

1. How did your community receive its name? What is its meaning?
2. What physical features have aided development or retarded expansion?
3. Who is the oldest resident of your district? (Arrange to interview as many senior citizens as possible; not only will they welcome the opportunity to reminisce but you will learn much local history.)
4. What evidence can you find of legends, folk songs, and folklore?
5. Compile a detailed record of inscriptions on tombstones in local cemeteries. What do these reveal about the people who once lived in your district?
6. Try to uncover old newspapers, letters, diaries, business records, accounts, deeds, wills, or other forms of documentary evidence.
7. Look closely at the architecture in the community. Review any inventories made of early buildings.
8. What industries now provide or once provided employment for the people? What significant industrial changes have taken place over the years?
9. What outstanding people have lived in your community? What can you learn about sons and daughters who have moved away to achieve fame elsewhere?
10. Is there any evidence that your community was once inhabited by Amerindians? Did your community figure in any prominent historical event—perhaps a battle, a visit by an early explorer, or a boundary dispute?

In the majority of cases the above questions may be answered without stirring more than a few miles from your school. Thus a lack of extensive resources need not be a deterrent for there will always be much of interest and significance close at hand. In compiling your local history you may find it helpful to review the diagrams, approaches, and techniques suggested earlier in the book. In addition to these general suggestions, a few specific hints on such matters as recording information, conducting interviews, planning field trips, and developing "historical scepticism" will be considered.

ON RECORDING INFORMATION

Bibliographic References
An organized system for recording the data obtained during the course of your research is essential, else you will waste valuable time and may mislay important information. The first step is to keep an accurate account of all your sources and references. By far the most convenient system is to use a series of 3″ x 5″ index cards to list separately all books, articles, interviews, etc. If you have a large number of cards you may find

it convenient to code them by colour. The call number of library books should always be noted, to simplify later rechecking. It is also useful to summarize in a sentence or two the gist of the book, as mere titles can sometimes be misleading. Questions such as "What is that book *Someone Before Us* all about?" will then be unnecessary. The following examples of bibliographic reference cards suggest a pattern that might be used.

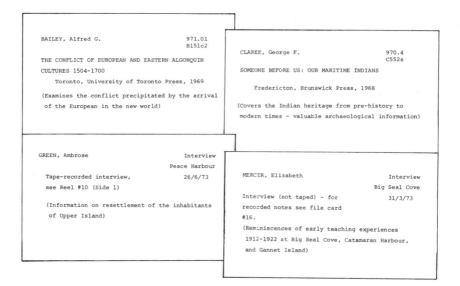

BAILEY, Alfred G.   971.01
                                               B151c2

THE CONFLICT OF EUROPEAN AND EASTERN ALGONQUIN

CULTURES 1504-1700

     Toronto, University of Toronto Press, 1969

(Examines the conflict precipitated by the arrival
of the European in the new world)

CLARKE, George F.   970.4
                                               C552s

SOMEONE BEFORE US: OUR MARITIME INDIANS

     Fredericton, Brunswick Press, 1968

(Covers the Indian heritage from pre-history to
modern times - valuable archaeological information)

GREEN, Ambrose   Interview
                                      Peace Harbour

Tape-recorded interview,   26/6/73
see Reel #10 (Side 1)

(Information on resettlement of the inhabitants
of Upper Island)

MERCER, Elizabeth   Interview
                                          Big Seal Cove

Interview (not taped) - for   31/3/73
recorded notes see file card
#16.

(Reminiscences of early teaching experiences
1912-1922 at Big Seal Cove, Catamaran Harbour,
and Gannet Island)

General References

It is essential to devise a convenient form for noting the actual information extracted from the various sources consulted. Again, cards, or pads of paper cut to 5″ x 8″ will be the most versatile. Additional cards or sheets may be stapled to the first as required. When consulting a book or article it is always wise to read or skim through the material before actually taking notes. Often, what seems at first glance to be useful may not be so. Be particularly careful to indicate occasions when you are quoting directly rather than summarizing information in your own words. All information quoted *verbatim* must be acknowledged. This is an especially important point when you are dealing with primary source materials that often have to be quoted in the original. (For the distinction between primary and secondary sources see page 116.) In some instances it may be simpler and speedier to photocopy certain references. If you accumulate a significant number of photocopies these may be stored in standard file folders. Two examples will illustrate the procedure for recording general information.

```
    NASKAPI                          SOURCE: Diamond Jenness

                                     THE INDIAN TRIBES OF CANADA

       (summary)
       page 272
       The Naskapi did not follow the traditional pattern of tribal organization -
       the various bands lacked organized government (exception - certain key
```

```
       MICMAC                          SOURCE: Nicolas Denys

       Fishing Practices               CONCERNING THE WAYS OF THE INDIANS

          (quotation)
          page 26
          "At the narrowest of the rivers, where there is the least water, they make
          a fence of wood clear across the river to hinder the passage of the fish.
          In the middle of it they leave an opening, in which they place a bag-like net..."
```

ON CONDUCTING INTERVIEWS

How often we have heard comments such as "If only Mr. X or Mrs. X had recorded what they knew about local history", or "If only Miss Y had compiled a genealogy of the family; she had all the first-hand information". These remarks are usually occasioned by the death of someone whose memory encompassed a long span of time. For the local historian they underline two points: (a) personal interviews can be a valuable source of information, and (b) the time to start is *now* before this knowledge is lost. While senior citizens are often the best resource people, do not neglect others who may be able to shed light on recent history—a mining disaster, a shipwreck, or some other item of local importance. Before embarking on an interview two points are essential. If the interview is to be tape-recorded, make certain that you are thoroughly familiar with the equipment and take along an extension cord—just in case it is needed. Read widely and research as thoroughly as possible the topics that are likely to be covered. Only then will you be able to frame meaningful questions. At all times be guided by the rules of tact and good sense. It is often wise to arrange an informal interview to test your subject. Explain your project carefully and preferably leave behind a list of key questions so that there will be time for reflection and review. This will pay dividends when you return later for a session of tape-recording. One who has conducted many interviews offers the following advice:

> The interviewer should recognize that it is human nature for people to be reluctant to admit that they do not know something and for them to avoid what is embarrassing or unpleasant. Individuals, also, are reluctant to talk about subjects they dislike or which may place them in an unsatisfactory position. Some will exaggerate their own importance to make their actions appear more significant or more commendable than they actually were. Still others have a natural inclination to shock or amuse while claiming to be truthful.[1]

Not only will interviewing yield information about local history, it can also provide valuable insights into human nature!

Sometimes the very presence of a microphone will cause your subject to "freeze". Rather than lose a valuable source of information, shut off the tape-recorder and take notes. If this cannot be done inconspicuously, summarize the main points immediately after the interview. Every interview should follow a prearranged plan. Have a few leading questions in mind before you begin. Remember that short, concise questions will elicit more information than a rambling monologue on your part. Probe, pin down dates, and cross-check information wherever possible. After the interview is over, what then? Most tapes, unless they are made by a professional, will require editing if they are to be preserved in permanent form. This should always be done, for after you have written your local history, others who follow may be interested in pursuing topics that were touched upon during your interviews but that were not followed up by you. Usually historical societies or regional libraries will be happy to accept tapes or cassettes that cover matters of community interest. In this way you will be making a permanent contribution to local history.

ON FIELD TRIPS AND TOURS

As with the personal interview, no historical field trip should be undertaken without prior research. If the purpose of the tour is to explore the physical features of the landscape and note their impact on historical development, make certain that you are thoroughly familiar with local topographical maps. If it is a visit to an old church, a building of architectural merit, or a famous historic site, read beforehand everything that is pertinent. Compile a check list of questions for which answers may be found on location. If guides are present they will be ready to handle your queries. In some instances you may find "interpretation centres" set up to explain features of historical interest. Make certain that you visit these. Sometimes a preliminary visit to get an overall impression can make a later and more extended visit meaningful. Always have notebook and pencil handy to record information, to jot down an inscription, or to list reminders for later research. A sketchbook and a camera can also help in the recording process. Field trips are like laboratory experiences in which you find out how history was made and how it should be written. There is no better way to gain an appreciation of local history.

ON DEVELOPING AN HISTORICAL SCEPTICISM

Frequently, throughout this book, you have been warned to be wary of the obvious, to check and recheck references—in short. to be genuinely sceptical about information obtained from any source, however reliable it may seem. A proud home-owner may tell you that his house dates from the early-nineteenth century, when it is actually of later origin. Someone else may assure you that his ancestors arrived on the *Hector*, when to believe all who relate this story would give that modest ship a passenger list rivalling that of a jumbo jet. Or perhaps you will encounter the well-worn legend that Captain Kidd's treasure is buried "out there". Pirate treasure there might be, but the likelihood of its being placed there by Captain Kidd is doubtful at best. Often historical misinformation may be presented in more innocent guise. Wilson's *Geography and History of Digby County* records the information that the St. Mary's Bay area, settled by the Acadians after the Expulsion, was granted township status and named Clare by Michael Franklin in honour of Daniel O'Connell's constituency in Ireland.[2] This was done, so the account goes, because Franklin was born in County Clare. A plausible story, especially when we remember that Clare elected one of the first Catholics to the Nova Scotia Assembly. (O'Connell was the first of his faith to be elected to the British House of Commons.) Investigation shows that the information is wrong on at least two counts. Clare was named in 1768, and O'Connell was not born until 1775, nor elected to the House of Commons until 1828. Franklin was a native of Devonshire, not County Clare. He died in 1782. Other similar examples might be cited; however, the point is clear. Never accept something as fact until you have been able to substantiate it.

ON WRITING YOUR LOCAL HISTORY

After your research is complete you are ready to put pen to paper and write the history of your home community. The first step is to develop a detailed outline. Not only will this help you organize your material, it will reveal any gaps that may be left in your research. Beyond this there is little advice to be given here. Your teacher is in the best position to advise you on matters of form and style. Perhaps the only historical axiom left to be underscored is that you must be prepared to back up every statement and conclusion with hard evidence. As a matter of general interest you should read widely in accounts written about other communities. These will often suggest leads that may be applied to your own locality.

Examples of Local Studies

A careful check of published bibliographies will reveal whether someone has already written about your community. William F. E. Morley: *The Atlantic Provinces: Canadian Local Histories to 1950* (Toronto: University of Toronto Press, 1967) lists all works published prior to 1950. Hugh A. Taylor (ed.): *New Brunswick History: A Check List of Secondary Sources*, published by the Provincial Archives of that province, gives comprehensive coverage for New Brunswick entries up to 1971. Do not limit your background reading to local histories alone—churches, business establishments, and the files of local newspapers will also yield valuable information. Listed below are a few random examples of local histories that may serve as models.

Newfoundland

Home of Wooden Boats and Iron Men, a local history of Dunville, Argentia, Fox Harbour, and Placentia. Published by the Dunville Branch, Women's Institute of Newfoundland and Labrador, 1970. Note that Women's Institutes in many areas of Atlantic Canada have undertaken similar projects.

Guy, R. M.: *Muddy Hole 1834-1866, Musgrave Harbour 1866*, a winning entry in the competition sponsored by the Newfoundland government for the encouragement of arts and letters. St. John's: Department of Education, 1971.

McCarthy, Michael: *History of St. Mary's Bay* (included in the above publication).

Read widely in back copies of the *Newfoundland Quarterly* for additional studies, e.g., Trinity, 1956; Harbour Grace, 1956-7; Catalina, 1956-7.

Prince Edward Island

Historic Highlights, Charlottetown, 1955 and 1964. Published by the Prince Edward Island Historical Society, these books contain useful information about a wide variety of Island communities.

Greenhill, Basil, and Giffard, Ann: *Westcountrymen in Prince Edward Isle*. Toronto: University of Toronto Press, 1967. More than a local history, this book is a detailed study of the ventures of Devon merchants in nineteenth-century Prince Edward Island; particularly helpful as a resource for Prince County.

Millman, Thomas R.: *A History of the Parish of New London P.E.I.*, privately published, 1959.

Moase, M. Louise, ed.: *The History of New Annan, P.E.I.*, New Annan

Women's Institute, 1971. N.B. A number of local histories were compiled during centennial year, 1973.

Nova Scotia

Coward, Elizabeth Ruggles: *Bridgetown: Its History to 1900*. Kentville: Kentville Publishing Co., 1955.

Duncanson, John V.: *Falmouth—A New England Township in Nova Scotia*. Windsor, Ontario: privately published, 1965.

Kaulback, Ruth E.: *Historic Saga of Leheve* (La Have). Halifax: Earl Whynot & Associates, 1970.

Patterson, F. H.: *Tatamagouche 1771-1824*. Truro: privately published, 1971. A 1972 reprint of this author's *History of Tatamagouche*, originally published in 1917, is available from Mike Publishers, Belleville, Ontario.

Powell, R. B.: *Scrapbook of Digby County and Municipality*. Digby: Digby Courier, 1968.

Smith, Perley W.: *History of Port Hood and Port Hood Island 1610-1967*, privately published, 1967.

New Brunswick

Collections of the New Brunswick Historical Society. These volumes, usually published annually, are an important source of information concerning local history in New Brunswick.

Aiton, Grace: *The Story of Sussex and Vicinity*. Sussex: Kings County Historical Association, 1967.

Ganong, W. F.: *History of Miscou and Shippegan*. Saint John: New Brunswick Museum, 1946.

Ganong, W. F.: *History of Caraquet and Pokemouche*. Saint John: New Brunswick Museum, 1948.

Webster, J. C.: *History of Shediac*. Saint John: New Brunswick Museum, 1953.

Wright, Esther Clark: *The St. John River and Its Tributaries*, privately published, 1966. Not strictly a local history; however, this book stands as a model for those wishing to enlarge their scope beyond a single community.

SOME ADDITIONAL PROJECTS

While the writing of the local history of your own community is the prime motivation for research, it is recognized that this project is not always possible. You may live in a town or city where such a study is too large, even for a group project. Or someone may have already written a detailed community history, leaving little for you to uncover. As an alternative, you may substitute the history of a particular school, church, or industry. Often a single street in some of the older towns and cities will provide interesting scope for investigation. Another suggestion is to devise an historical walking tour of your community. Saint John, Halifax, and St. John's have published brochures describing such tours, and the same idea may well be applied elsewhere. If there are sites of local historic interest in your community—the birthplace of a famous person, the location of a structure of bygone fame, or perhaps the first school or church—these could be marked for the benefit of visitors and residents alike. It should be possible for the Industrial Arts department in your school to design commemorative plaques to indicate locations such as these. If local history possesses a strong personal appeal for you, investigate the career possibilities in this field. Antiques and interior decoration, archaeology and historical restoration, teaching, and research are a few possibilities. Many others have been suggested or implied throughout this book. How many can you list? Finally, local history has much to offer as a hobby or avocation. A detailed knowledge of a given area can make an ordinary vacation come alive; investigating genealogy is an absorbing endeavour; and a knowledge of local history will add a new dimension to a study of the art, architecture, and literature of Atlantic Canada. Perhaps the most important thing to keep in mind is simply that local history is frequently "not found in books".

> "History?" said the woman at the door. "Who cares about history. If you want history, why don't you go into town—go to the library there. Lots of history in those books." "I mean history that isn't in books," I said.
> "There's no history that isn't in books," she said. "That's the only kind. No need to come asking questions. No need for that at all."[3]

Consider the writing of local history as a kind of exploration that has much in common with travel. When we visit some distant place we try to identify its special characteristics and catch its distinctive atmosphere. What appeals most are the things that are different—those qualities that set that place apart from all others. So with local history. Sometimes, like the traveller, you will have a map and carefully defined directions; on other occasions you will be entirely on your own. To a certain extent you may depend on information garnered from others, but in the end you must rely upon personal research and experience. Part of the joy of history, as with travel, lies in the individual discoveries that are made. Local history is not dull—it is both bright and colourful. It provides truth over conjecture, triumph and tragedy, wit as well as wisdom. Local history can capture, as no other subject, the very essence of your community, your province, or your region.

FOR READING AND REFERENCE

BAUM, WILLA K.: *Oral History*. Nashville: American Association for State and Local History, 1971.

CARR, E. H.: *What Is History?* Harmondsworth, Middlesex: Penguin Books, 1964.

CORFE, TOM (ed.): *History in the Field*. London: Blond (Educational) Ltd., 1970.

INGERSOLL, L. K.: *Techniques in Local History*. Saint John: New Brunswick Museum, 1969.

MUIR, LLOYD: *Is There a Place for Local History?* Saint John: New Brunswick Museum, n.d.

NEVINS, ALLAN: *The Gateway to History*. New York: Doubleday and Co., 1962.

PATTERSON, FRANK H.: "History Begins at Home", *Acadia Bulletin*, XLX, 5 (November 1964): 14-19.

ROGERS, ALAN *Approaches to Local History*. London: BBC Publications, 1972.

ROWSE, A. L.: *The Use of History*. London: English Universities Press, 1963.

STEVENSON, H. A., AND ARMSTRONG, F. H. (eds.): *Approaches to Teaching Local History*. Toronto: Oxford University Press, 1969.

TUCKER, L. L. (ed.): *The Challenge of Local History*. Albany, N.Y.: State Education Department, 1968.

WIGGINTON, ELIOT: *The Foxfire Book*. New York: Doubleday and Co., 1972, and *Foxfire 2*, 1973.

A Bibliographic Note

Throughout this book an effort has been made to list under the heading "For Reading and Reference" a selection of the most important books and articles that relate to each chapter. Out-of-print books (except in a few circumstances) have not been included, nor have non-print materials such as films, slides, tapes, etc., and other items that tend to become dated quickly.

Anyone who undertakes a serious study of this subject must begin with William Morley's *The Atlantic Provinces: Canadian Local History to 1950* (Toronto: University of Toronto Press, 1967). It contains a complete listing of all works in the field of local history up to 1950. For a guide to other bibliographies dealing with the region, see Douglas Lochhead: *Bibliography of Canadian Bibliographies* (Toronto: University of Toronto Press, 1972). Olga Bishop: *Publications of the Governments of N.S., N.B., and P.E.I.* (Ottawa: National Library, 1957) outlines the primary source material to be found in government publications of all kinds. William Matthews: *Canadian Diaries and Autobiographies* (Berkeley: University of California Press, 1950) contains references to items in the area of personal reminiscences. Check also the section on the Atlantic provinces in J. L. Granatstein and Paul Stevens: *Canada Since 1867: A Bibliographical Guide* (Toronto: Hakkert, 1974). It is to be hoped that you will have access to basic items such as inventories of the provincial and national archives, museum publications of every variety, and magazines and journals that feature articles on the history of Atlantic Canada. Files of key publications—*Acadiensis, Atlantic Advocate, Canadian Historical Review, Collections* of historical societies (both local and provincial), *Dalhousie Review, Newfoundland Quarterly, Nova Scotia Historical Quarterly*, the bulletins of the various heritage trust organizations, and publications relating to Project Atlantic Canada and The Canada Studies Foundation—are among those included in this category. Lastly, on the principle that local history must always be related to national history, basic Canadian history texts and references are also essential.

Footnotes

Abbreviations Used in the Notes

CHAR—Canadian Historical Association Report
CHR—Canadian Historical Review
CNBHS—Collections, New Brunswick Historical Society
CNSHS—Collections, Nova Scotia Historical Society
PAC—Public Archives of Canada
PANB—Public Archives of New Brunswick
PANFLD—Public Archives of Newfoundland and Labrador
PANS—Public Archives of Nova Scotia
PAPEI—Public Archives of Prince Edward Island

SECTION I   INTRODUCTION TO LOCAL HISTORY

1. Working Backwards into History

1. STEPHEN LEACOCK: "The Place of History in Canadian Education", *CHAR*, 1925, 34.
2. H. A. STEVENSON AND F. H. ARMSTRONG (eds.): *Approaches to Teaching Local History* (Toronto: Oxford University Press, 1969), 1-9.
3. ALVIN TOFFLER: *Future Shock* (New York: Random House, 1970), 346.
4. ALDEN NOWLAN: "A Poet's View of Canada", *Maclean's* Magazine, June 1971, 17.
5. CHARLES BRUCE: "Century 1867-1967: The Canadian Saga", *London Free Press*, February 13, 1967, 12-13.

2. Settlement and Political Development

1. "Circular letter from Governor Lawrence to the Governors on the continent", August 11, 1755, *Selections from the Public Documents of Nova Scotia* (Halifax: PANS, 1869), 278.
2. WILL R. BIRD: *Done at Grand Pré* (Toronto: Ryerson Press, 1955), 172.
3. T.C. HALIBURTON: *Sam Slick the Clockmaker* (Toronto: McClelland

and Stewart, 1941), 46.

4. WILLIAM CARSON: *Letter to the Members of Parliament of the United Kingdom . . .* (London: William Scott, 1812), 14-15.

5. A major appraisal of the "colonial retardation theory" is to be found in Keith Matthews: "Historical Fence Building: A Critique of Newfoundland Historiography" (unpublished manuscript in Centre for Newfoundland Studies, Memorial University of Newfoundland Library).

6. Ibid., p. 36.

7. SHANNON RYAN: "The Newfoundland Cod Fishery in the Nineteenth Century", paper presented to the Canadian Historical Association (Kingston, June 1973), 4.

8. EDWARD WIX: *Six Months of a Newfoundland Missionary's Journal* (London: Smith and Elder, 1836), 155-6.

9. Captain John Stanton to Governor Francis Legge, December 4, 1775 (PAC MG II Nova Scotia A 94).

10. See Gordon Stewart and George Rawlyk: *A People Highly Favoured of God* (Toronto: Macmillan of Canada, 1972).

11. ESTHER CLARK WRIGHT: *The Loyalists of New Brunswick* (Moncton: Moncton Publishing Co., 1972), 241.

12. PETER WAITE: *The Charlottetown Conference* (Ottawa: Canadian Historical Association, 1963), 3.

13. *Debates and Proceedings of the House of Assembly*, Nova Scotia, 1866, 469.

SECTION II   SOURCES OF LOCAL HISTORY

3. Place Names

1. W. F. GANONG: *Place-Nomenclature of the Province of New Brunswick* (Toronto: Canadian House, 1972), 176.

2. WINTHROP P. BELL: *The Foreign Protestants and the Settlement of Nova Scotia* (Toronto: University of Toronto Press, 1961), 405-7.

3. WATSON KIRKCONNELL: *Place Names of Kings County* (Wolfville; privately printed, 1971), 9.

4. GANONG: *Place-Nomenclature*, p. 176.

4. Legacy of the Sea

1. BRUCE: "Century 1867-1967", p. 12.

2. WIX: *Six Months . . .* , p. 168.

3. ROBERT OKE: *Plans of the Several Lighthouses in the Colony of Newfoundland* (PANFLD), 2.

4. Canada, *Sessional Papers*, X (1877), No. 4.

5. D. C. HARVEY (ed.): *Journeys to the Island of St. John* (Toronto: Macmillan of Canada, 1955), 24.

6. ARCHIBALD MACMECHAN: *Old Province Tales* (Toronto: McClelland and Stewart, 1924), 157.

7. Quoted in Beamish Murdoch: *A History of Nova Scotia*, 3 vols. (Halifax: John Barnes, Printer, 1867), vol. III, 371.

8. Ibid., p. 371.

9. Quoted in Foster Rhea Dulles: *Twentieth Century America* (New York: Houghton Mifflin, 1945), 277.

10. W. E. DE GARTHE: *Painting the Sea* (Kentville: Kentville Publishing Co., 1969), 9.

11. GEORGE DAVID CHASE: *Sea Terms Come Ashore* (Orono: University of Maine, 1942), 1.

12. LESLIE HARRIS: "St. Joseph's: Its History Remembered from Childhood", *Newfoundland Quarterly*, LXV, 4 (June 1967): 9.

5. Legacy of the Land and the People

1. HUGH MACLENNAN: "Confessions of a Wood-Chopping Man" in *Scotchman's Return and Other Essays* (Toronto: Macmillan of Canada, 1960), 91.

2. JOSEPH HOWE: Speech delivered at Bridgetown, N.S., June 8, 1859. *Speeches and Public Letters of Joseph Howe* (Halifax: Chronicle Publishing Co., 1909), vol. II, 359.

3. FREDERIC S. COZZENS: *Acadia, or A Month with the Bluenoses* (New York: Derby and Jackson, 1859), 13.

4. ESTHER CLARK WRIGHT: *The St. John River and Its Tributaries* (Fredericton: privately published, 1966), 6.

5. THOMAS RADDALL: *Tambour and Other Stories* (Toronto: McClelland and Stewart, 1945), 372.

6. NOEL IVERSON AND D. RALPH MATTHEWS: *Communities in Decline: An Examination of Household Resettlement in Newfoundland* (St. John's: Memorial University, 1968), 143.

7. BRUCE: "Century 1867-1967", pp. 12-13.

8. ROBIN W. WINKS: "Negroes in the Maritimes: An Introductory Survey", *Dalhousie Review*, 4 (Winter, 1968-9): 470-1.

9. Ibid., p. 457.

10. S. J. R. NOEL: *Politics in Newfoundland* (Toronto: University of Toronto Press, 1971), 3.

6. The Amerindian Heritage

1. S. E. MORISON (ed.): *The Parkman Reader* (Toronto: Little, Brown and Co., 1955), 64.

2. *The Indian Historian*, V, 3 (Fall 1972): 31.

3. *London Free Press*, December 4, 1972.

4. RALPH N. WINDSOR: *The Beothuck Indians*, research paper prepared for Education 418 (St. John's: Memorial University, 1972), 15.

5. VAINO TANNER: *Outlines of the Geography, Life and Customs of Newfoundland Labrador*, 2 vols. (Cambridge: At the University Press), vol. II, 241.

6. W. H. WHITELEY: "The Establishment of the Moravian Mission in Labrador and British Policy", *CHR*, XLV, 1 (March 1964): 29.

7. Ibid., p. 766.

8. DOUGLAS LEECHMAN: *Eskimo Summer* (Toronto: Ryerson Press, 1945), 245-6.

9. W. O. RAYMOND: *The River St. John* (Sackville: The Tribune Press, 1950), 25.

10. R. G. THWAITES: *Jesuit Relations and Other Documents* (Cleveland: Burrows Bros., 1895), I, 311.

11. Ibid., III, p. 77.

12. RAYMOND: *River St. John*, p. 29.

13. JAMES DEMILLE: "Sweet Maiden of Quoddy", *New Dominion and True Humorist* (Saint John, April 16, 1870), 171.

14. JAMES E. MILORD: "Genocide in Canada", *United Church Observer*, 2 (August 1970): 25.

15. SILAS T. RAND: *Legends of the Micmacs* (New York: Johnson Reprint Corp., 1971), 232-7.

16. CHRESTIEN LE CLERCQ: *New Relation of Gaspesia with the Customs and Religion of the Gaspesian Indians* (Toronto: The Champlain Society, 1910), vol. II, 122.

17. Ibid., pp. 296-7.

18. JULIA M. SETON: *American Indian Arts: A Way of Life* (New York: Ronald Press Co., 1962), 6-7.

19. W. W. ALWARD: "Architecture in New Brunswick", *Arts in New Brunswick* (Fredericton: Brunswick Press, 1967), 205.

20. *Dictionary of Canadian Biography* (Toronto: University of Toronto Press, 1966), vol. I, 12.

7. Archaeological Evidence

1. V. H. GALBRAITH: *An Introduction to the Study of History* (London: C. A. Watts and Co. Ltd., 1964), 30.

2. PHILIP VENNING: "Not Just a Treasure Hunt", *Times Educational Supplement*, September 1, 1972.

3. *Young Rescue*, 2 (October 1972), preamble on aims and objectives.

4. GEORGE FREDERIC CLARK: *Someone Before Us* (Fredericton: Brunswick Press, 1968), 23.

5. WALTER ZACHARCHUK: Unpublished manuscript on Restigouche operation. See also Walter Zacharchuk: "The Restigouche Excavation: An Interim Report", *Nautical Archaeology*, I (1972): 157-63.

6. H. L. CAMERON: "History from the Air", *Photogrammetric Engineering*, June 1958, 375.

7. JANE NUGENT: "The Name of the Game is Dig", *New Dimensions*, VI, 2 (October 1971): 11.

8. The reader interested in the details of this early culture is referred to the following: George MacDonald: *Debert: A Paleoindian Site in Central Nova Scotia* (Ottawa: National Museum of Canada, 1968); and to the series of five major articles on "Early Cultures of Nova Scotia" by J. S. Erskine in the Nova Scotia *Journal of Education*, May-June 1969 to June 1970 inclusive. Also, David Sanger: "The Discovery of the Red Paint People", *Atlantic Advocate*, 2 (October 1971): 32-8.

9. JAMES A. TUCK: "Aboriginal Inhabitants of Newfoundland and Labrador", *Historic Newfoundland* (St. John's: Dept. of Economic Development, 1972), 66.

10. HAROLD HORWOOD: *Newfoundland* (Toronto: Macmillan of Canada, 1969), 43.

11. ABRAHAM GESNER: *Geological Survey of Prince Edward Island*, an appendix to *Journals of the House of Assembly*, 1854.

12. CLARIBEL GESNER: "A Town Out of Time", *Atlantic Advocate*, 12 (August 1970): 39.

13. For illustrations see *Founded Upon a Rock* (Halifax: Petheric Press, 1970), 37, 39.

14. *Times Literary Supplement*, September 1, 1961.

8. Documentary Evidence and Literature

1. ARTHUR DOUGHTY: *The Canadian Archives and Its Activities* (Ottawa: King's Printer, 1924), 5.

2. WILLIAM B. HAMILTON: "Reminiscences of a Pioneer Teacher", *The Nova Scotia Teacher*, XL, 4 (April 1964): 48-9.

3. PETER B. WAITE: *The Life and Times of Confederation* (Toronto: University of Toronto Press, 1962), 4. See Chapter I, "Newspapers and Political Life", for an analysis of the impact of the press on the politics of British North America in the 1860s.

4. *Public Ledger*, June 9, 1835. (Five years later Winton's plant foreman, Herman Lott, was accosted on Saddle Hill and brutally beaten.)

5. *Archives and Education* (London: HMSO, 1968), 2.

6. KENT THOMPSON: *Stories from Atlantic Canada* (Toronto: Macmillan of Canada, 1973), xii.

7. HERBERT BUTTERFIELD: *The Historical Novel* (Cambridge: At the University Press, 1924), 16.

8. THOMAS RADDALL: *His Majesty's Yankees* (New York: Doubleday and Co., 1943), 402.

9. KENNETH ROBERTS: *I Wanted To Write* (New York: Doubleday and Co., 1949), 354.

10. DONALD CAMERON: "Letter from Halifax", *Canadian Literature*, XL (Spring 1969): 59.

11. WILL R. BIRD: *An Earl Must Have a Wife* (Toronto: Clarke, Irwin, 1972). See Author's Note.

12. DONALD CAMERON: "The Art of Historical Fiction", *Dalhousie Review*, XLIX, 4 (Winter 1969-70): 547.

13. DONALD GUTTERIDGE: "Riel: Historical Man or Literary Symbol?", *Bulletin Canadian Humanities Association* (Autumn 1970): 4.

14. E. J. PRATT: "Newfoundland" in *Collected Poems of E. J. Pratt* (Toronto: Macmillan of Canada, 1962), 3-4.

15. Ibid., "The Roosevelt and the Antinoe", p. 188.

16. Ibid., "The Shark", p. 5.

17. C. V. WEDGEWOOD: "Literature as Background Evidence", *Mosaic*, I, 1 (October 1967): 1.

18. MARC LESCARBOT: *The History of New France* (Toronto: The Champlain Society, 1907), vol. II, 321.

19. LISTER SINCLAIR: *The Blood Is Strong* (Toronto: The Book Society of Canada, 1956), 78-9.

20. Ibid., p. 7.

21. CHARLES BRUCE: "People From Away", *Atlantic Advocate*, 5 (January 1957): 59.

22. ANTONINE MAILLET: *La Sagouine* (Quebec: Leméac, Inc., 1971), 88.

23. MELVIN GALLANT: "New Brunswick Acadians Seek Control of Own Future", *Truro Daily News*, April 13, 1973.

24. HAROLD PADDOCK: "Black English in Newfoundland", *Memorial University Gazette*, 3 (June 1971): 3.

25. CHARLES F. MULLETT: "Language as a Social Study", *The History Teacher*, 1 (November 1972): 95-6.

26. BUTTERFIELD: *Historical Novel*, p. 14.

9. Folk Songs and Folklore

1. ANDREW FLETCHER: *Conversation Concerning a Right Regulation of Government for the Common Good of Mankind* (London: n.p., 1704), 12.

2. MACEDWARD LEACH in Elisabeth Greenleaf and Grace Mansfield: *Ballads and Sea Songs of Newfoundland* (Hatsboro, Pa.: Folklore Associates Inc., 1968), i.

3. J. D. ROGERS: *A History of the British Colonies* (Oxford: Oxford University Press, 1911), vol. V, 236-7.

4. GREENLEAF: *Ballads*, p. 237.

5. PAUL WEST: "The Unwitting Elegiac—Newfoundland Folksong", *Canadian Literature*, Winter 1961, 35.

6. HELEN CREIGHTON AND CALUM MACLEOD: *Gaelic Songs in Nova Scotia* (Ottawa: National Museum, 1964), 26.

7. Ibid., pp. 58-60.

8. RADDALL: *Tambour*, p. 371.

9. LESCARBOT: *History of New France*, vol. II, p. 346.

10. *The Complete Plays of Gilbert and Sullivan* (New York: Modern Library, 1949), 266.

11. GEORGE M. STORY: "The St. John's Balladeers", prepared and delivered as a dinner address to the Association of Canadian University Teachers of English (St. John's, May 30, 1971). 3. This article contains valuable information on the native poets of Newfoundland.

12. EDWARD D. IVES AND LAWRENCE DOYLE: *A Study in Local Songmaking* (Orono: University of Maine, 1971), 252.

13. Quoted in D. A. MUISE: "Some Nova Scotia Poets of Confederation", *Dalhousie Review*, L, 1 (Spring 1970): 73. This article analyses the theme of alienation in the anti-Confederation lyrics.

14. LOUISE MANNY AND J. R. WILSON: *Songs of Miramichi* (Fredericton: Brunswick Press, 1970), 145.

15. J. F. SPRAGUE: *North-Eastern Boundary Question* (Dover, Maine: privately published, 1910), 110-11.

16. *Woodstock Times*, March 9, 1839.

17. KENNETH AND MARY CLARK: *Introducing Folklore* (Toronto: Holt Rinehart and Co., 1961), 123.

18. RICHARD M. DORSON: *American Folklore and the Historian* (Chicago: University of Chicago Press, 1971), 148.

19. MANNY AND WILSON: *Songs of Miramichi*. p. 81.

20. HERBERT HALPERT AND G. M. STORY (eds.): *Christmas Mumming in Newfoundland* (Toronto: University of Toronto Press, 1969), 218.

21. Ibid., p. 65.

22. RUTH TOOZE AND BEATRICE KRONE: *Literature and Music as Resources for Social Studies* (Englewood Cliffs, N.J.: Prentice-Hall, 1969), 3.

10. Art and Architecture

1. J. M. S. CARELESS: *The Pioneers: The Picture Study of Canadian History* (Toronto: McClelland and Stewart, 1968), 32.

2. JOHN DEWEY: *Art as Experience* (New York: Minton, Balch and Co., 1934), 74.

3. DONALD ANDRUS: *Artists of Atlantic Canada* (Ottawa: National Museum of Canada, n.d.), catalogue of exhibition.
4. DOUGLAS SCOTT RICHARDSON: *A Tom Forrestall Exhibition* (Fredericton: Beaverbrook Art Gallery, n.d.), 15.
5. Ibid., p. 12.
6. ALAN GOWANS: *Looking at Architecture in Canada* (Toronto: Oxford University Press, 1958), 63.
7. A. G. HUNTER: *Guidebook to the Newfoundland Cathedral* (n.p., n.d.).
8. GOWANS: *Looking at Architecture*, pp. 123-4.
9. Nova Scotia Heritage Trust Information Sheet.
10. MARIAN MACRAE: *The Ancestral Roof: Domestic Architecture in Upper Canada* (Toronto: Clarke, Irwin, 1963), 3.
11. KENNETH HOMER: "Old Court House Restoration", *The Bugle and Gazette*, Woodstock, N.B., July 25, 1968.
12. Ibid.

11. Economic Development

1. *Debates of the House of Commons*, March 12, 1969 (Return tabled).
2. MURRAY BECK: *The Government of Nova Scotia* (Toronto: University of Toronto Press, 1957), 327.
3. ANDREW HILL CLARK: *Three Centuries and the Island* (Toronto: University of Toronto Press, 1959), 41.
4. Quoted in PAUL MACEWAN: "Davis Murder", *Cape Breton Highlander*, January 31, 1968.
5. Quoted in GEORGE MACLAREN: *The Pictou Book* (New Glasgow: Hector Publishing Co., 1954), 247.
6. T. C. HALIBURTON: *Sam Slick the Clockmaker: His Sayings and Doings* (London: George Routledge and Son, 1907), 43.
7. *Montreal Gazette*, December 16, 1901 (report of its St. John's correspondent).
8. A. F. LAIDLAW (ed.): *The Man from Margaree* (Toronto: McClelland and Stewart, 1971), 93.

12. Biographical Studies

1. J. P. MACPHIE: *Pictonians at Home and Abroad* (Boston: Pinkham Press 1914), iv.
2. HERBERT BUTTERFIELD: "The Role of the Individual in History", *History*, February and June 1955, 1.
3. M. H. ARBUTHNOT AND D. M. BRODERICK: *Time for Biography* (Glenview, Ill.: Scott, Foresman Co., 1969), 228.
4. *Dictionary of Canadian Biography*, vol. I, p. xvii.
5. Quoted in RON CROCKER: "Men Who Knew Coaker: The Memories Are Bittersweet", *Evening Telegram*, July 29, 1972.

6. HORWOOD: *Newfoundland*, p. 90.

7. LAIDLAW: *Man from Margaree*, p. 109.

8. LOUISE MANNY: Unpublished manuscript on Alexander Rankin (PANS).

9. S. EMMA EDMONDS: *Nurse and Spy in the Union Army* (Hartford: W. S. Williams and Co., 1867), 2.

10. EULA CARSCALLEN LAPP: "Beware Horse Thieves, Pirates and Witches", *Ontario Historical Society Papers and Records*, 3 (Summer 1958): 155.

SECTION III   APPLICATIONS OF LOCAL HISTORY

13. Researching History Where It Is

1. WILLIAM G. TYRRELL: American Association for State and Local History, Technical Leaflet #35, *History News*, XXI, 5 (May 1966): n.p.

2. ISAIAH WILSON: *A Geography and History of Digby County* (Halifax: Holloway Bros., 1900), 173.

3. A. KEEWATIN DEWDNEY: *A Book of Gables* (London: privately printed, 1964), 1.

47 57 67 77 87 97 08 HR 9 8 7 6 5 4 3 2 1